THE MENU

SAN DIEGO COUNTY

A Menu Guide to the Top 200
Restaurants in
San Diego County

DAVID NELSON

**David Thomas
Publishing**

For all those that toil
that we might dine well.

ISBN 0-9628274-7-9

PRINTED IN THE UNITED STATES OF AMERICA

Printed on Recycled Paper with Soy Based Inks

Cover Design by Heather Kier
Illustrations by Alex Epp

David Thomas Publishing

733 NW Everett St., Box 12, Studio 5E
Portland, Oregon 97209
(503) 226-6233

T H E
MENU

is the perfect business gift—useful, tasteful, and appreciated. **Special editions, including customized covers and full-color pages showcasing your product or service, are available for your clients, prospects, or employees.** Find out how simple and affordable this unique marketing program can be for your company.

Please call today:
1-800-755-MENU (6368)
during regular business hours
(Pacific Standard Time), or write:

Corporate Sales Department
David Thomas Publishing/Menubooks, Inc.
733 NW Everett Street, Box 12
Portland, Oregon 97209

Table of Contents

Restaurants by Cuisine

Introduction

I began reviewing San Diego County restaurants on July 3, 1980, and could have retired from the work long, long ago had I been wise enough to collect $10 every time someone demanded that I immediately name "the five best restaurants in San Diego."

Occasionally, the request simply would be for the name of the area's top eatery, and I always liked these questions best. But I will say right now that my consistent response has been, "San Diego does not have a best restaurant," and I stick by that assessment today.

We may have many good eateries, supplemented by a smaller number of truly fine establishments, but not one restaurant clearly leads the pack – at least in my opinion, which happens to be the opinion I value most. And while this proposition might cause civic boosters to shake their heads in sorrowful disbelief (after all, doesn't every major city need a best everything?), it can be taken as an affirmation of the sophistication that San Diego's restaurant row has acquired in the last dozen or so years.

I remember, in the embarrassingly recent past, when San Diegans tended to regard surf 'n' turf as the city's leading culinary statement, when fettuccine Alfredo was considered an exotic specialty and when there wasn't a single Thai restaurant to be found in San Diego County. At present, there are still those who treasure surf 'n' turf—and I am one who devoutly believes that we should eat what we like—but otherwise, the regional menu has expanded exponentially, to the point that we now have restaurants that specialize in the soignée cooking of Hong Kong or in the distinctively different cuisine of the French West Indies. As a city and region, we have become truly cosmopolitan in our tastes, and our collective table is much more bountifully spread as a result.

It is precisely for this reason that the suggestion that I in effect narrate a menu book so appealed to me. Back when leading San Diego restaurants served pretty much the same menu of steaks, prime rib and seafood, a book that printed their lists would have offered little in the way of variety. But now that San Diego offers dining options ranging from Afghan to Pacific Rim, it seems highly useful to be able to answer the question, "What would I like to eat tonight?" by picking up a book that enables you to browse through an international bazaar of cuisines. This book performs exactly that function.

Although I still would decline any invitation to designate an individual restaurant as the best in town, I by no means found it difficult to write a list that includes 200 solid, serious eateries. We have at least that number in the county at present, out of a congregation of food service establishments that now numbers in the thousands, and despite the slow economic times, more quality restaurants continue to open at a surprisingly healthy rate. The list is selective, of course, and defined by the considerations an individual critic brings to the debate. In my case, I always consider the food first and foremost, and assign lesser importance to decor and service, although neither is by any means inconsequential. In my opinion, certain basic amenities, such as table service and a beer and wine license, are essential to the definition of a restaurant. San Diego may be possessed of a few good sandwich shops, taco stands and the like, but you won't find them listed here.

If anyone in San Diego actually witnessed my mercifully brief career as a restaurant critic for a local television news program, no one was so unkind as to mention it. The low point of the experience was the segment in which I was required to take live telephone calls from viewers who in some cases seemed unlikely to know whether they should eat the can opener or the contents of the can. I remember one viewer who called to say that he lived on the La Mesa-El Cajon border, near the intersection of such-and-such, and wanted to know what might be the best Chinese lunch buffet in his immediate neighborhood that did not use MSG. My response? I don't approve of Chinese lunch buffets, period, with MSG or without, and neither in his neighborhood nor in Shangri-La, for that matter. So some readers' favorite restaurants may not be mentioned, and if this causes immense dissatisfaction or even merely hurt feelings, I say tough luck—they already know about these places and don't need to see them here. I am interested in quality, and I think that quality pervades these pages.

At the end of a professional visit to a restaurant, I frequently ask my guest this question: "Would you come back here for dinner tomorrow night if you were spending your own money?" And thus the list of restaurants in this book is largely self-selective, because I would pay to eat at any of them—quite frequently, in some cases, were I able to afford it. In the same way, the geographical distribution of the restaurants is self-selected; I let the chips fall where they may, as it were, and if more quality establishments are clustered in such neighborhoods as downtown San Diego and La Jolla, so be it. But this book does include listings from the South Bay to Oceanside, as well as many of the delightful but not so well known neighborhood restaurants that give the San Diego dining scene such a varied aspect.

A few practical notes:

Not so terribly long ago, there was virtually universal agreement about cuisine designations. A place that served onion soup automatically could be assumed to be French, while the presence of chop suey on the menu defined an establishment as Chinese, ravioli designated Italian, and so forth. Things are a tad more complicated now.

For example, several of San Diego's most exciting restaurants specialize in "Pacific Rim" cuisine, a term that didn't even exist a decade ago. Basically, it combines ingredients and styles from both sides of the Pacific, but when you consider the number of national cuisines from which elements can be borrowed, one can do little more than classify the style as (often) delicious. Add the consideration that French techniques frequently rule the manner in which Pacific Rim dishes are composed and the issue grows even murkier.

And then there's Italian cuisine, which formerly was fairly predictable in these parts but now includes many regional styles, and if you eat in seven of San Diego's top Italian houses on successive nights, you will notice that not one has much in common with the others beyond the accent of the proprietor.

So for my cuisine categories, I have sometimes used the obvious—whether a Chinese house tends to the Cantonese or the Szechuan, for example, it is designated Chinese. This is true of Italian, Mexican, Japanese and other distinctive cuisines as well. American-style places suddenly are a more difficult issue, however, and those that are contemporary in style are so designated, while those specializing in steaks and seafood receive their own listings. Of course, many of these have strong ethnic allegiances as well.

The geographical designations used should confuse no one. Within the city of San Diego, neighborhoods are well defined and well understood; suburban restaurants are listed under the names of their home towns.

David Nelson

Everyone's a critic. No experience more perfectly echoes that sentiment than dining out. It never fails — whenever someone finds out that I publish restaurant guides, they immediately proceed to tell me about their favorite places to eat. My mouth waters as they describe, in vivid detail, the dish they ordered, as well as what everyone else in their party ordered. In other words, they describe the restaurant's menu.

It follows that a great way to choose a restaurant would be to read its menu, provided the place is well recommended. In the last few years, it has been my pleasure to discover that literally thousands of readers like yourself share this same conclusion. As you enjoy using this book, please keep these points in mind:

1. MENUS AND PRICES CHANGE.

Most all of the restaurants in this book change their menu and/or prices frequently, many even daily. We have tried to feature menus that accurately reflect the style and approach of the chef.

2. YOU CAN'T PLEASE EVERYONE.

Even with no strings attached, we do (on rare occasion) encounter a restaurant that is either unwilling or unable to provide us with information, and thus, reluctantly, cannot be included.

Putting this book together was no small task. My heartfelt thanks go out to Deanna Demaree, Cordy Jensen, Susan Fishback, Lynn Burgess, Cynthia Ross, David Fisher, Frank Alvey, Topher Edwards, Alex Epp, Martha Wagner, Heather Kier and especially David Nelson.

Here's hoping that, as a fellow food-lover, you not only find *THE MENU* to be a useful handbook of your favorite places, but also a tempting map to new gastronomical discoveries.

Tom Demaree
Publisher

At the bottom of each restaurant listing you will notice a row of symbols or "icons" that represent certain features and services a particular restaurant may offer. These icons are designed to give you a quick reference to the features you may be looking for in a restaurant—at a glance.

Below is a list of the icons and what they represent:

— Wheelchair Access

— 100% Non-Smoking

— Major Credit Cards (For specific cards, see Features Guide)

— Full Bar

— Breakfast

— Lunch

— Dinner

— Sunday Brunch

— Jacket/Tie (May be required - call to be safe)

— Live Entertainment

The following table will answer the most often asked questions about the services offered by a particular restaurant. Please keep in mind that just as menus and prices change, so do amenities. It is always best to confirm those features important to you when making your reservation.

A few explanatory notes:

Types of Cuisine — The restaurants are grouped alphabetically by type of cuisine, starting with *Afghan*, all the way through *Vietnamese*. The cuisine category is referenced at the top of each restaurant listing and at the top right of each two-page menu spread. Index by Cuisine can be found on page 308.

Geographic Location — The address of the restaurant is located at the bottom of the left page on each menu. When there are additional locations, the best known or original location address is given, followed by the statement: call for additional locations. Restaurants located in San Diego are listed by their district or neighborhood, all others by their city name. Geographical index begins on page 311.

Hours — Dinner hours are included in each restaurant's listing. Quick reference icons at the bottom of each listing show which meals a restaurant serves. See icons on page 15.

100% Non-Smoking — Restaurants that do accommodate smoking guests generally offer non-smoking areas as well.

Wheelchair access — Most all of the restaurants without full wheelchair access are still able and happy to accommodate the special needs of any of their guests.

Dress — The three categories of dress referred to are only an indication of how *most* people dress for dinner. If you have a question, call ahead.

Personal Checks — Restaurants which accept personal checks require proper I.D.

Features Guide

Restaurant	PG	Wheelchair Access	100% Non-Smoking	Visa/MasterCard	American Express	Discover	Diners Club	Checks Accepted	Beer & Wine	Full Bar	Sunday Brunch	Breakfast	Lunch	Dinner	High Chairs	Take Out	Valet Parking	Private Parties	Live Entertainment	Casual / Jeans	Informal Dress	Jacket/Tie	Reserv Not Taken	Reserv Recom	Reserv Required
94th Aero Squadron	24, 124	♦		♦	♦	♦			♦	♦	♦		♦	♦	♦		♦			♦					♦
A Dong Restaurant	122			♦	♦				♦				♦	♦	♦	♦					♦				♦
Aesop's Tables	75, 126	♦	♦	♦	♦	♦	♦		♦	♦			♦	♦	♦	♦					♦			♦	
Albert's Restaurant	79	♦		♦	♦	♦			♦	♦			♦	♦	♦			♦			♦				♦
Alfonso's	101			♦	♦	♦			♦	♦			♦	♦	♦	♦	♦	♦	♦		♦				♦
Alizé	42, 128	♦		♦	♦	♦	♦			♦	♦		♦	♦	♦	♦	♦	♦	♦		♦				♦
Anthony's Star of the Sea	114	♦		♦	♦	♦	♦	♦		♦				♦			♦	♦					♦		♦
Athens Market	75	♦	♦	♦	♦	♦	♦		♦	♦		♦	♦	♦	♦	♦		♦			♦				♦
Atoll Restaurant, The	25, 130	♦		♦	♦	♦	♦	♦	♦	♦	♦	♦	♦	♦	♦			♦			♦				♦
Avalon	50, 132	♦		♦	♦	♦	♦			♦			♦	♦	♦			♦			♦				♦
Avanti Ristorante	79, 134	♦		♦	♦	♦	♦		♦	♦				♦	♦	♦		♦	♦	♦	♦				♦
Azzura Point	60	♦		♦	♦	♦	♦		♦	♦				♦	♦		♦	♦			♦				♦
Baci Ristorante	80, 136	♦		♦	♦	♦	♦		♦	♦			♦	♦	♦	♦		♦						♦	♦
Baja Beach Buffet & Cantina	102	♦		♦						♦	♦		♦	♦	♦	♦		♦			♦				♦
Banzai Cantina	60	♦		♦	♦	♦	♦			♦			♦	♦	♦	♦		♦			♦				♦
Bayou Bar & Grill	41	♦		♦	♦	♦	♦		♦	♦				♦				♦			♦				♦
Belgian Lion, The	59	♦	♦	♦	♦	♦	♦		♦					♦				♦			♦				♦
Bella Luna	80	♦		♦	♦			♦	♦				♦	♦				♦			♦				♦
Benihana of Tokyo	98	♦		♦	♦	♦	♦		♦	♦			♦	♦	♦		♦	♦			♦				♦
Bernard'O Restaurant	67	♦	♦	♦	♦	♦	♦	♦	♦				♦	♦	♦	♦		♦			♦				♦
Berta's Latin Am. Rest.	100, 138	♦		♦	♦				♦				♦	♦	♦		♦	♦	♦	♦	♦				♦
Beyond Chinese Cuisine	43	♦		♦	♦	♦	♦			♦			♦	♦	♦	♦	♦	♦			♦			♦	♦
Brendory's By The Sea	42	♦		♦	♦			♦	♦	♦			♦	♦	♦	♦					♦				
Brewski's Gaslamp Pub, Bistro	25	♦		♦	♦	♦	♦	♦	♦				♦	♦	♦	♦	♦	♦	♦	♦	♦				♦
Buffalo Joe's	26	♦		♦	♦	♦			♦	♦			♦	♦	♦	♦	♦		♦	♦	♦				♦
Bully's	37, 140			♦	♦		♦	♦	♦	♦	♦	♦	♦	♦	♦	♦	♦				♦			♦	
Busalacchi's	81	♦		♦	♦	♦	♦		♦	♦			♦	♦	♦	♦	♦	♦	♦	♦	♦				♦
Cafe Champagne	50	♦	♦	♦	♦				♦		♦		♦	♦	♦	♦		♦			♦				♦
Cafe Eleven	62, 142	♦		♦	♦	♦	♦			♦				♦		♦		♦			♦				♦
Cafe Japengo	61, 144	♦		♦	♦	♦	♦	♦	♦	♦			♦	♦	♦	♦	♦	♦	♦	♦	♦				♦
Cafe Luna	81, 146	♦		♦		♦			♦					♦	♦			♦			♦				♦
Cafe Pacifica	51	♦	♦	♦	♦	♦	♦		♦	♦			♦	♦	♦	♦	♦	♦			♦				♦
Cajun Connection	41	♦		♦	♦	♦			♦				♦	♦	♦	♦					♦			♦	♦
Caldo Pomodoro	82, 148	♦		♦	♦	♦	♦			♦				♦	♦	♦	♦		♦	♦		♦			♦
California Cuisine	51, 150	♦		♦	♦	♦	♦			♦				♦	♦			♦		♦	♦				♦
California Pizza Kitchen	110		♦	♦	♦	♦	♦		♦	♦			♦	♦	♦	♦	♦				♦			♦	
Calliópe's Greek Cafe	76	♦	♦	♦	♦	♦	♦		♦				♦	♦	♦	♦	♦				♦		♦		♦
Canes California Bistro	52	♦		♦	♦	♦	♦		♦	♦	♦		♦	♦	♦	♦		♦			♦		♦		♦
Carlos Murphy's	102, 152	♦		♦	♦	♦			♦	♦	♦	♦	♦	♦	♦	♦		♦	♦	♦					♦
Casa de Bandini	103	♦	♦	♦	♦	♦	♦	♦	♦	♦			♦	♦	♦			♦	♦	♦			♦		
Casa de Pico	103			♦	♦	♦	♦	♦	♦	♦			♦	♦	♦			♦	♦	♦			♦		
Chang-Cuisine of China	43, 154	♦		♦	♦	♦				♦			♦	♦		♦		♦			♦				♦
Charcoal House, The	37	♦		♦	♦	♦				♦			♦	♦	♦	♦		♦			♦			♦	♦
Chart House	38	♦		♦	♦	♦	♦	♦	♦	♦				♦	♦	♦	♦	♦				♦			♦
Chez Henri	68, 156	♦	♦	♦	♦				♦				♦	♦		♦	♦	♦			♦				♦

Features Guide

Restaurant	Pg	Wheelchair Access	100% Non-Smoking	Visa/Master Card	American Express	Discover	Diners Club	Checks Accepted	Beer & Wine	Full Bar	Sunday Brunch	Breakfast	Lunch	Dinner	High Chairs	Take Out	Valet Parking	Private Parties	Live Entertainment	Casual / Jeans	Informal Dress	Jacket/Tie	Reserv Not Taken	Reserv Recom	Reserv Required
Chez Loma	63, 158			♦	♦		♦		♦					♦	♦			♦	♦					♦	
ChickeNest Restaurant, The	66	♦	♦	♦	♦			♦	♦	♦		♦	♦	♦	♦	♦		♦		♦					♦
China Camp	44	♦		♦	♦	♦				♦			♦	♦	♦	♦		♦	♦	♦					♦
Christefano's Italian Rest.	82	♦		♦	♦		♦		♦				♦	♦		♦		♦		♦					♦
Cilantros	116	♦		♦	♦				♦	♦	♦		♦	♦	♦	♦	♦	♦		♦					♦
Cindy Black's	68, 160	♦		♦	♦	♦	♦		♦	♦			♦	♦	♦	♦	♦	♦		♦					♦
City Delicatessen	66	♦		♦					♦		♦	♦	♦	♦	♦	♦					♦		♦		
Coast Cafe	26, 162	♦	♦	♦	♦	♦	♦			♦		♦	♦	♦	♦	♦		♦	♦	♦					♦
Corvette Diner, The	27	♦		♦					♦			♦	♦	♦	♦	♦	♦	♦	♦	♦			♦		
Crab Catcher	114, 164	♦		♦	♦		♦		♦	♦	♦		♦	♦	♦	♦		♦		♦					♦
Croce's	52, 166	♦	♦	♦	♦	♦	♦		♦	♦	♦	♦	♦	♦	♦	♦	♦	♦	♦	♦		♦			♦
D.Z. Akin's	67, 168	♦	♦						♦			♦	♦	♦	♦	♦					♦		♦		
Daily's Fit & Fresh Restaurant	78	♦	♦										♦	♦		♦					♦		♦		
Dakota Grill & Spirits	53, 170	♦	♦	♦	♦	♦	♦		♦	♦			♦	♦	♦	♦	♦	♦	♦	♦		♦			♦
Dansk Restaurant	113	♦		♦	♦	♦	♦	♦	♦			♦	♦	♦	♦		♦		♦		♦				♦
Delicias	53	♦		♦	♦	♦	♦		♦	♦			♦	♦	♦		♦			♦				♦	♦
Dobson's	54, 172	♦		♦	♦		♦		♦	♦			♦	♦	♦		♦			♦				♦	♦
Dominic's Italian Rest.	83, 174	♦		♦	♦	♦			♦				♦	♦	♦	♦		♦		♦	♦				♦
El Bizcocho	69			♦	♦	♦	♦			♦	♦			♦	♦		♦	♦	♦			♦		♦	
El Tecolote	104	♦	♦	♦	♦	♦			♦				♦	♦	♦	♦					♦		♦	♦	
Elario's Restaurant	54, 176	♦	♦	♦	♦	♦	♦	♦	♦	♦	♦	♦	♦	♦	♦			♦	♦	♦	♦				♦
Elephant Bar Restaurant	27	♦		♦	♦				♦	♦	♦		♦	♦	♦	♦			♦	♦	♦				♦
Embers Wood-Fired Pizza	110	♦	♦	♦		♦			♦				♦	♦	♦	♦				♦					♦
Emerald Chinese Seafood	44, 178	♦		♦	♦		♦		♦				♦	♦	♦	♦				♦					♦
Epazote	116	♦							♦	♦	♦		♦	♦	♦	♦	♦	♦	♦	♦					♦
Fifth & Hawthorn	55, 180			♦	♦	♦	♦		♦	♦			♦	♦						♦					♦
Fio's Cucina Italiana	83, 182	♦		♦	♦	♦	♦		♦	♦			♦	♦	♦		♦	♦		♦					♦
Fish Market, The	115, 184	♦		♦	♦	♦	♦		♦	♦	♦		♦	♦	♦	♦	♦	♦		♦					♦
Five Star Thai Cuisine	119	♦	♦	♦	♦	♦	♦		♦				♦	♦	♦	♦				♦					♦
Fortune Cookie Restaurant	45	♦		♦	♦	♦	♦		♦	♦			♦	♦	♦	♦				♦					♦
French Gourmet, The	69	♦		♦	♦	♦	♦	♦	♦	♦			♦	♦	♦	♦				♦					♦
George's at the Cove	55		♦	♦	♦	♦	♦		♦	♦			♦	♦	♦	♦	♦	♦					♦	♦	
Giuseppe's Italian Restaurant	84	♦	♦	♦					♦				♦	♦	♦	♦				♦				♦	
Golden Garden Rest.	45, 186	♦		♦	♦	♦	♦		♦				♦	♦	♦	♦			♦	♦					♦
Golden State Seafood Rest.	46	♦		♦					♦		♦	♦	♦	♦	♦	♦		♦			♦				♦
Grant Grill	70	♦		♦	♦	♦			♦	♦	♦	♦	♦	♦	♦		♦	♦	♦	♦					♦
Great Wall Cafe	46	♦		♦	♦	♦	♦		♦				♦	♦	♦	♦				♦					♦
Grecian Gardens	76	♦		♦	♦				♦	♦			♦	♦	♦	♦			♦	♦	♦				♦
Greek Tycoon, The	77, 188		♦	♦		♦	♦	♦					♦	♦	♦	♦			♦	♦	♦				♦
Grill, The	61	♦		♦	♦	♦	♦	♦	♦	♦		♦	♦	♦	♦	♦	♦	♦	♦	♦					♦
Guadalajara Grill	104, 190	♦		♦	♦				♦	♦	♦		♦	♦	♦	♦		♦	♦	♦		♦			♦
Guava Beach Bar & Grill	28			♦	♦				♦	♦			♦	♦	♦	♦	♦		♦	♦				♦	
Harbor's Edge	56, 192	♦		♦	♦		♦	♦		♦	♦	♦	♦	♦	♦		♦	♦	♦	♦	♦				♦
Harry's Coffee Shop	28, 194			♦	♦	♦	♦	♦	♦			♦	♦		♦	♦					♦		♦		
Hell's Kitchen	29	♦		♦					♦				♦	♦		♦					♦		♦		

18

RESTAURANT	PG	Wheelchair Access	100% Non-Smoking	Visa/Master Card	American Express	Discover	Diners Club	Checks Accepted	Beer & Wine	Full Bar	Sunday Brunch	Breakfast	Lunch	Dinner	High Chairs	Take Out	Valet Parking	Private Parties	Live Entertainment	Casual / Jeans	Informal Dress	Jacket/Tie	Reserv Not Taken	Reserv Recom	Reserv Required
Hob Nob Hill	29, 196	♦		♦	♦	♦			♦			♦	♦	♦	♦					♦				♦	
Hops! Bistro and Brewery	30	♦		♦	♦	♦	♦		♦					♦	♦	♦	♦				♦				♦	
Il Fornaio	84	♦		♦	♦	♦	♦			♦	♦			♦	♦		♦	♦	♦		♦				♦	
Islands	30	♦	♦	♦	♦				♦	♦				♦	♦	♦	♦				♦			♦		
Italia Mia	85	♦		♦	♦	♦	♦		♦	♦	♦			♦	♦	♦	♦		♦		♦				♦	
Jack & Giulio's	85, 198	♦	♦	♦	♦				♦					♦	♦	♦	♦				♦				♦	
Jake's Del Mar	31	♦	♦	♦	♦					♦	♦			♦	♦	♦	♦	♦	♦		♦				♦	
Kabuki Japanese Restaurant	99	♦		♦	♦		♦		♦					♦	♦	♦	♦				♦				♦	
Kaiserhof Restaurant	74, 200	♦		♦	♦	♦	♦		♦	♦	♦			♦	♦	♦	♦				♦				♦	
Kansas City Barbeque	31, 202	♦		♦		♦			♦					♦	♦		♦		♦		♦			♦		
Karinya Thai Cuisine	119, 204	♦		♦					♦					♦	♦	♦	♦		♦		♦				♦	
Karl Strauss' Old Columbia	32	♦		♦					♦					♦	♦	♦	♦		♦		♦				♦	
Kenny's Steak House	38, 206	♦		♦	♦		♦	♦	♦	♦				♦	♦	♦	♦	♦	♦	♦	♦				♦	
Khayyam Cuisine	109	♦	♦	♦			♦		♦					♦	♦	♦	♦		♦		♦				♦	
Khyber Pass	24, 208	♦		♦	♦	♦			♦					♦	♦	♦	♦		♦		♦				♦	
Kiva Grill	117, 210	♦		♦	♦	♦	♦		♦	♦	♦			♦	♦	♦	♦	♦	♦		♦				♦	
La Bonne Bouffe	71, 212	♦		♦	♦		♦	♦	♦						♦			♦			♦				♦	
La Fonda Roberto's	105, 214	♦		♦	♦	♦				♦	♦			♦	♦	♦			♦		♦				♦	
La Gran Tapa	117, 216			♦	♦			♦	♦	♦	♦			♦	♦	♦	♦		♦	♦	♦				♦	
Lader's	86		♦	♦					♦					♦	♦	♦	♦					♦			♦	
L'affaire	63	♦		♦					♦		♦			♦	♦	♦	♦		♦		♦				♦	
Lamont Street Grill	32	♦		♦	♦	♦			♦	♦					♦				♦		♦				♦	
Le Bambou	122	♦	♦						♦					♦	♦	♦	♦				♦				♦	
Le Fontainebleau	64	♦		♦	♦	♦	♦	♦	♦	♦	♦	♦	♦	♦	♦			♦	♦	♦			♦		♦	
Le Peep	33, 218	♦		♦	♦			♦			♦	♦	♦		♦	♦		♦		♦				♦		
L'Escale	70	♦						♦	♦	♦	♦	♦	♦	♦	♦			♦	♦	♦	♦				♦	
Liaison	71, 220	♦		♦	♦	♦	♦	♦	♦						♦		♦		♦		♦				♦	
Lorna's Italian Kitchen	86		♦	♦		♦			♦					♦	♦	♦	♦				♦			♦		
Machupicchu Restaurant	109	♦		♦					♦					♦	♦	♦	♦		♦		♦				♦	
Manhattan	87, 222			♦	♦		♦	♦	♦	♦				♦	♦	♦		♦	♦		♦				♦	
Marine Room, The	72	♦	♦	♦	♦	♦	♦		♦	♦				♦	♦	♦		♦		♦			♦		♦	
Marius	72, 224	♦		♦	♦		♦		♦	♦					♦		♦	♦				♦		♦		
Mexican Village Rest.	105, 226	♦		♦	♦	♦	♦			♦	♦			♦	♦	♦	♦		♦	♦	♦				♦	
Mille Fleurs	73		♦	♦	♦		♦			♦				♦	♦			♦	♦		♦					♦
Milligan's Bar & Grill	33, 228	♦						♦	♦	♦	♦			♦	♦	♦	♦	♦	♦	♦	♦				♦	
Ming Court	47, 230	♦		♦	♦	♦	♦			♦				♦	♦	♦	♦		♦	♦	♦				♦	
Mister A's	64, 232	♦		♦	♦	♦	♦		♦	♦				♦	♦	♦		♦	♦	♦			♦		♦	
Montanas American Grill	56, 234	♦		♦	♦				♦					♦	♦		♦		♦		♦				♦	
Mykonos	77, 236	♦		♦	♦		♦		♦	♦				♦	♦	♦	♦		♦	♦	♦				♦	
Nicolosi's Italian Restaurant	87	♦		♦	♦				♦	♦				♦	♦	♦	♦		♦			♦		♦		
Old Town Mexican Cafe	106, 238	♦		♦	♦	♦		♦	♦	♦	♦	♦	♦	♦	♦	♦	♦		♦		♦			♦		
Old Trieste	88			♦	♦		♦			♦				♦	♦			♦				♦			♦	
Old Venice Restaurante	88	♦		♦	♦	♦	♦	♦	♦	♦	♦	♦	♦	♦	♦	♦			♦	♦		♦		♦		
Olé Madrid Café	118, 240	♦		♦	♦				♦	♦				♦	♦	♦		♦	♦	♦	♦				♦	
Osteria Panevino	89	♦	♦	♦	♦	♦	♦	♦		♦				♦	♦		♦	♦			♦				♦	

Features Guide

Restaurant	PG	Wheelchair Access	100% Non-Smoking	Visa/Master Card	American Express	Discover	Diners Club	Checks Accepted	Beer & Wine	Full Bar	Sunday Brunch	Breakfast	Lunch	Dinner	High Chairs	Take Out	Valet Parking	Private Parties	Live Entertainment	Casual / Jeans	Informal Dress	Jacket/Tie	Reserv Not Taken	Reserv Recom	Reserv Required
Pachanga	106, 242	◆		◆	◆	◆	◆	◆	◆	◆			◆	◆	◆	◆	◆	◆			◆			◆
Pacifica Del Mar	62	◆	◆	◆	◆	◆	◆	◆		◆	◆			◆	◆			◆	◆		◆				◆
Palenque	107	◆		◆	◆	◆	◆	◆	◆	◆			◆	◆				◆			◆				◆
Panda Country Rest.	47, 244	◆		◆	◆				◆	◆			◆	◆	◆	◆		◆			◆				◆
Panda Inn	48	◆		◆	◆	◆	◆		◆	◆			◆	◆	◆	◆		◆			◆				◆
Peking Palace	48	◆		◆	◆	◆				◆			◆	◆	◆	◆		◆			◆				◆
Peohe's	34	◆		◆	◆	◆	◆		◆	◆	◆		◆	◆	◆	◆		◆		◆	◆	◆			◆
Pernicano's	89	◆	◆	◆					◆				◆	◆	◆	◆		◆			◆			◆	
Phuong Trang	123, 246	◆		◆			◆			◆			◆	◆	◆	◆					◆			◆	
Piatti	90	◆		◆	◆				◆	◆	◆		◆	◆	◆	◆		◆		◆	◆				◆
Pizza Nova	111	◆		◆	◆	◆	◆	◆	◆				◆	◆	◆	◆					◆		◆		
Pizzeria Uno	111, 248	◆		◆	◆	◆			◆				◆	◆	◆	◆	◆				◆		◆	◆	
Prego	90, 250			◆	◆		◆		◆	◆			◆	◆		◆	◆	◆	◆	◆	◆				◆
Putnam's	57	◆		◆	◆		◆		◆	◆	◆	◆	◆	◆	◆	◆	◆	◆	◆	◆	◆				◆
Qwiig's	34	◆		◆	◆	◆				◆	◆		◆	◆	◆						◆				◆
Rainwater's on Kettner	39, 252			◆	◆		◆		◆	◆			◆	◆		◆	◆	◆	◆		◆				◆
Rancho El Nopal	107	◆		◆	◆	◆	◆	◆	◆	◆			◆	◆	◆	◆		◆	◆		◆				◆
Rancho Valencia Rest.	73, 254	◆		◆	◆		◆	◆	◆	◆	◆	◆	◆	◆	◆	◆	◆	◆			◆				◆
Red Tracton's	39	◆		◆	◆	◆	◆		◆	◆			◆	◆		◆	◆	◆	◆	◆	◆				◆
Roxanne's Boondocks	40, 256	◆		◆	◆		◆	◆	◆	◆			◆	◆	◆	◆				◆	◆	◆			◆
Royal Thai Cuisine	120	◆		◆	◆	◆			◆	◆	◆		◆	◆	◆	◆	◆	◆			◆				◆
Saigon Restaurant	123, 258	◆	◆						◆		◆	◆	◆	◆	◆	◆					◆				◆
Sala Thai	120	◆	◆	◆	◆	◆	◆		◆				◆	◆	◆	◆		◆			◆				◆
Sally's	101, 260	◆		◆	◆	◆			◆	◆			◆	◆	◆	◆	◆	◆	◆		◆				◆
Salvatore's	91	◆		◆	◆		◆		◆	◆			◆	◆	◆			◆	◆				◆	◆	◆
Sammy's California Pizza	112, 262	◆	◆			◆			◆				◆	◆	◆	◆					◆			◆	
Santa Fe Cerveceria	108, 264	◆		◆	◆		◆		◆	◆	◆		◆	◆		◆		◆			◆			◆	
Sante	91	◆		◆	◆		◆		◆	◆			◆	◆				◆	◆	◆	◆				◆
Särö Restaurant	113, 266	◆		◆	◆		◆	◆		◆			◆	◆				◆			◆				◆
Saska's	40, 268			◆	◆		◆	◆	◆	◆	◆	◆	◆	◆	◆	◆	◆		◆		◆				◆
Scalini	92	◆		◆	◆	◆	◆		◆	◆				◆		◆	◆	◆	◆				◆		◆
Sfuzzi	92	◆		◆	◆		◆		◆	◆	◆		◆	◆	◆	◆	◆	◆			◆				◆
Shien of Osaka	99, 270	◆	◆	◆	◆		◆		◆				◆	◆	◆	◆					◆				◆
Shores at Sea Lodge, The	35	◆		◆	◆	◆	◆		◆	◆	◆	◆	◆	◆	◆	◆	◆		◆		◆				◆
Siam Restaurant	121	◆		◆	◆	◆	◆		◆				◆	◆	◆	◆	◆	◆			◆		◆		◆
Sirino's Restaurant	93	◆	◆	◆	◆	◆			◆	◆				◆	◆	◆		◆		◆	◆				◆
Sorrentino's Ristorante	93	◆	◆	◆	◆		◆		◆	◆				◆	◆	◆		◆			◆				◆
Spices Thai Cafe	121	◆	◆	◆	◆		◆		◆				◆	◆	◆	◆		◆			◆				◆
Star House Chinese Rest.	49	◆		◆	◆	◆	◆		◆				◆	◆	◆	◆		◆			◆			◆	
Star of India	78, 272	◆		◆	◆	◆	◆		◆		◆		◆	◆	◆	◆		◆			◆				◆
Stefano's	94, 274	◆		◆	◆	◆	◆		◆	◆				◆	◆	◆		◆	◆	◆	◆				◆
Stella's Hideaway	112, 276	◆		◆	◆	◆				◆				◆		◆			◆		◆				◆
Tengu Restaurant	100	◆		◆	◆		◆		◆	◆			◆	◆	◆	◆		◆			◆			◆	
Thee Bungalow	65	◆	◆	◆	◆	◆	◆			◆				◆							◆				◆
Tony's Jacal	108	◆		◆	◆			◆		◆		◆	◆	◆	◆	◆		◆			◆			◆	

20

Features Guide

Restaurant	PG	Wheelchair Access	100% Non-Smoking	Visa/MasterCard	American Express	Discover	Diners Club	Checks Accepted	Beer & Wine	Full Bar	Sunday Brunch	Breakfast	Lunch	Dinner	High Chairs	Take Out	Valet Parking	Private Parties	Live Entertainment	Casual / Jeans	Informal Dress	Jacket/Tie	Reserv Not Taken	Reserv Recom	Reserv Required
Top O' The Cove	74, 278	♦		♦	♦			♦		♦	♦	♦		♦	♦			♦	♦	♦				♦	
Top of the Market	115, 280	♦		♦	♦	♦	♦		♦	♦	♦		♦	♦	♦	♦	♦	♦			♦				♦
Torreyana Grille	57, 282	♦		♦	♦	♦	♦			♦	♦	♦	♦	♦	♦		♦	♦	♦		♦				♦
Tourlas	58, 284	♦	♦	♦	♦	♦	♦			♦	♦	♦	♦	♦	♦		♦	♦	♦	♦	♦				♦
Trattoria Acqua	94, 286	♦	♦	♦	♦					♦	♦		♦	♦	♦	♦	♦	♦	♦		♦				♦
Trattoria La Strada	95, 288	♦		♦	♦	♦	♦	♦		♦	♦		♦	♦	♦	♦	♦	♦			♦				♦
Trattoria Mannino	95, 290	♦	♦	♦	♦	♦	♦	♦	♦	♦	♦		♦	♦	♦	♦		♦	♦	♦	♦				♦
Triangles	58	♦	♦	♦	♦			♦		♦	♦		♦	♦	♦	♦		♦			♦				♦
Triple Crown Restaurant	65, 292	♦	♦	♦	♦	♦	♦						♦	♦			♦				♦		♦	♦	
Trophy's Sports Grill	35	♦		♦	♦				♦	♦			♦	♦	♦	♦	♦		♦		♦			♦	
Tuscany	96, 294	♦	♦	♦	♦				♦				♦	♦				♦			♦				♦
Tutto Mare	96, 296			♦	♦		♦		♦	♦			♦	♦		♦	♦	♦	♦	♦	♦				♦
Valentino's	97	♦	♦	♦	♦		♦		♦	♦			♦	♦	♦	♦		♦	♦	♦	♦				♦
Villani's	97	♦		♦	♦	♦	♦		♦	♦		♦	♦	♦	♦	♦	♦	♦	♦	♦	♦				♦
Whaling Bar, The	36, 298	♦		♦	♦		♦			♦			♦	♦	♦		♦	♦			♦				♦
When In Rome Restaurant	98	♦		♦	♦				♦	♦			♦	♦	♦		♦	♦			♦				♦
Wine Sellar & Brasserie, The	59, 300		♦	♦	♦	♦	♦	♦	♦	♦				♦				♦	♦		♦				♦
Yen Ching Restaurant	49	♦		♦		♦	♦		♦				♦	♦	♦	♦					♦				♦
Yo España	118, 302		♦	♦	♦		♦		♦	♦	♦		♦	♦	♦	♦		♦			♦				♦
Zodiac Restaurant	36, 304	♦			♦			♦	♦				♦		♦	♦		♦		♦					♦

21

The Restaurants

Afghan - Khyber Pass see pg. 208

San Diego has been slow at times to embrace cuisines it considers too exotic — this is, after all, a city in which surf 'n' turf reigns supreme. Even so, the intriguing, authentic Afghan cooking at the modest but atmospheric Khyber Pass was greeted with open arms, and this restaurant has settled in quite comfortably in a neighborhood dominated primarily by Asian restaurants that hail from rather further east. Rice plays so central a role in Afghan cooking that meats are more a garnish to it than a main point, and the wonderfully varied, highly unusual rice dishes here are all worth a try. Lamb, naturally, is done quite well, as are crisp pastries offered as appetizers and deeply flavored, richly savory soups.

Address: 4647 Convoy St • Kearny Mesa
Phone: (619) 571-3777
Dinner Hours: 7 Days a Week 5 – 10

American - 94th Aero Squadron see pg. 124

A long-running favorite in San Diego, this eatery proves the enduring popularity of theme restaurants, especially when the theme involves the romance of flight. Located near Montgomery Field, 94th Aero Squadron takes full advantage of the situation and delights its clients with an atmosphere that seems to lift them into the clouds. The menu is considerably more down-to-earth, and features the steaks, prime rib and all-American seafood preparations of which San Diegans are inordinately fond; the lively Sunday brunch enjoys immense popularity. Servers are relaxed and friendly, but notably efficient.

Address: 8885 Balboa Ave • Kearny Mesa
Phone: (619) 560-6771
Dinner Hours: Sun – Thurs 4:30 – 10, Fri – Sat 4:30 – 11

There are days when this restaurant is so packed that there seems no hope of getting in; lavish buffets, especially during Sunday brunch, are partly to blame for this situation. But the locale in the recently and extravagantly renovated Catamaran Hotel also plays a major part in the popularity; the restaurant looks out at the northern edge of Mission Bay, and the delightful outdoor tables are just a few moments' stroll from the sand. The kitchen prepares a menu that alternates between American standards and light, lively California cuisine creations; the seafood is notably fresh and tasty.

Address: Catamaran Resort Hotel • 3999 Mission Blvd • Mission Beach
Phone: (619) 539-8635
Dinner Hours: Sun – Thurs 5:30 – 10, Fri – Sat 5:30 – 11

Immensely popular with both the younger crowd and with the visitors who flock to the Gaslamp Quarter, Brewski's occupies a handsome space in one of the district's more imposing buildings. A good part of the square footage is occupied by the microbrewery that contributes so mightily to Brewski's popularity; the handcrafted brews and ales are widely considered as vastly superior to national, commercial brands. The mood normally is lively, and the atmosphere can be a touch noisy — which seems to suit just fine the crowd that assembles to munch on massive hamburgers, inventive sandwiches and over-sized, cleverly composed salads.

Address: 310 Fifth Ave • Gaslamp Quarter
Phone: (619) 231-7700
Dinner Hours: Mon – Sat until 12, Sun until 10

25

Buffalo Joe's

★ ★ ★ ★ ★ ★
Barbecue Grill & Saloon

It's hard to decide whether this lively establishment is better visited for the food or the fun, but plenty of both are available. As the downtown San Diego headquarters of the cowboy boot set, Buffalo Joe's shamelessly caters to the current Country Western mania by offering an outrageously down-home atmosphere along with huge portions of barbecued meats and other simple, old-fashioned American fare. Much of the cooking is in fact delicious, and the mood undeniably is most enjoyable — many patrons come to dance, and dance they do on a room-sized dance floor. Live music is the rule.

Address: 600 Fifth Ave • Gaslamp Quarter
Phone: (619) 236-1616
Dinner Hours: 7 Days a Week until 10

Coast
C A F E

Amid the glitz and glitter of trendy Golden Triangle eateries, the Coast Cafe quietly serves a quality menu of simple American fare in a soothingly restful environment. Although located in the Embassy Suites hotel, the Coast Cafe avoids the stuffy trappings of a hotel dining room; most guests seem to appreciate the option of the reasonably priced, all-you-can-eat pasta bar, at which a cook composes pastas to order with a wide selection of garnishes and sauces. On the more formal side, the menu offers hefty steaks, a light vegetarian platter and such downhome specialties as meatloaf and chicken pot pie.

Address: Embassy Suites • 4550 La Jolla Village Drive • Golden Triangle
Phone: (619) 453-1126
Dinner Hours: 7 Days a Week until 11

Perhaps the most popular spot in San Diego to take children, this 1950s themed eatery celebrates the Fonzie Decade to the limit. A gleaming corvette is the center-piece of the scene, and the walls are hung with enough memorabilia to stock a respectable museum. A disc jockey in a glass booth keeps the platters spinning and generally choreographs the mood, and waitresses chew gum, sing and dance on request and somehow manage to negotiate the hurly-burly and get the mashed potatoes and gravy to the table hot. In terms of the food, if it was eaten in the Fifties, Corvette serves it — especially good burgers, chili, sandwiches and meatloaf, along with the thickest, creamiest shakes in town.

Address: 3946 Fifth Ave • Hillcrest
Phone: (619) 542-1001
Dinner Hours: Sun – Thurs until 11, Fri – Sat until 12

If the Elephant Bar weren't an elephant bar it would be a fern bar, but no matter — the decorators of these fun establishments have packed about as much sub-Saharan kitsch and hokum under one roof as can reasonably be accommodated. The atmosphere, to put it mildly, takes guests on a long, relaxed safari through elephant country. Nourishment is provided by a menu crammed with contemporary favor-ites, with a heavy emphasis on salads and pastas. Plates tend to be substantial — who would expect otherwise in an elephant-themed setting — and among the hefty entrees are such things as a Cajun fried shrimp platter and St. Louis-style spareribs.

Address: 17051 West Bernardo Dr • Rancho Bernardo
Phone: (619) 487-7181
Dinner Hours: Sun – Thurs 5 – 10, Fri – Sat 5 – 11

Although a prime gathering spot for all types of San Diegans, Mission Beach offers relatively little in the way of fine dining. One of the few exceptions to the rule is Guava Beach Bar & Grill, which while laid-back and beachy in terms of mood, is attractively decorated and staffed with servers who give their patrons attentive service. The menu could be said to be a survey of Pacific Coast cuisine from mid-California south to Baja beaches and beyond; there are pastas, and fresh, crisp salads, as well as excellent lobster tacos and very well-flavored tortilla soup. The wine list is particularly well chosen for the neighborhood.

Address: 3714 Mission Blvd • Mission Beach
Phone: (619) 488-6688
Dinner Hours: Mon – Fri 4 – 12, Sat – Sun until 12

Every town deserves at least one Harry's. La Jolla is full of hang-outs, ranging from the ridiculous to the sublime, but Harry's seems a favorite with the whole town. It exists not just for breakfast and lunch, but for gossip and visiting, and more information passes here daily than could be accommodated by the pages of the village newspaper. The fame of the place is sufficiently far-flung that Harry's tee-shirts have been glimpsed on the Cote d'Azur; no-one feels obligated to dress for breakfast here, although the fluffy omelettes and other morning specialties do tend to be greeted with respectful nods. This most popular eatery also serves a full lunch menu of American standards.

Address: 7545 Girard Ave • La Jolla
Phone: (619) 454-7381
Breakfast, Lunch Hours: Mon – Sat until 2:30 pm, Sun until 2 pm

The decidedly unique intention of this casually hip Pacific Beach eatery is to present a style cuisine that is hotter than Hades. Chef Neil Stuart approaches the kitchen with the stated intention of banning the bland; the result is a list that alternately steams and sizzles. To be sure, not every dish is blazingly hot, or even particularly piquant; Stuart understands the need for balance and presents a thoughtful menu that ranges from a Jamaican "jerked" pork sandwich to guava-glazed baby pork ribs. Hot items include nachos spiked with chipotle chilies and chile-rubbed rotisserie chickens dressed with a choice of seven (some quite spicy) sauces.

Address: 825 Garnet Ave • Mission Beach
Phone: (619) 274-8084
Dinner Hours: 7 Days a Week until 11

It would be difficult to imagine San Diego without Hob Nob Hill. This mid-town eatery has gradually expanded since 1944, and retains the loyalty of a clientele that has grown up with it. Waitresses are of the old school, and somewhat motherly; needs are met immediately by whichever server is nearest. The menu reads like a catalogue of all-American favorites, and the restaurant is famed for its breakfast breads and pastries. Breakfast is a special treat here, and the place is busy from opening onwards — corned beef hash approaches perfection here, and even such simple items as buttermilk pancakes seem to taste better when enjoyed in one of Hob Nob's old-fashioned booths.

Address: 2271 First Ave • Downtown
Phone: (619) 239-8176
Dinner Hours: 7 Days a Week 4 – 9

American - Hops! Bistro and Brewery

Among the very few good shopping center restaurants to be found in the county, Hops! combines an extensive, imaginative menu with the flavorful offerings of the on-premises microbrewery. The beers and ales are very good, and as the nicest of gestures, Hops! offers a sampler that includes generous tastes of each. The wine list also is extremely well chosen. The broad menu encompasses such appetizers as roast duck quesadillas and a savory tortilla soup with smoked chicken; the selection of sandwiches and entree-sized salads also is extensive. Among entrees, the pastas, stir-fried scallops and pan-sauteed veal in mushroom sauce all are excellent.

Address: 4353 La Jolla Village Dr • Golden Triangle
Phone: (619) 587-6677
Dinner Hours: 7 Days a Week until 10

American - Islands

The Chart House chain, known for extravagant menus served in choice locations, went to the opposite end of the scale when it developed Islands, an immensely popular family eatery that combines an enjoyable Hawaiian atmosphere with menu items priced not too far above prices charged by fast food establishments. Hamburgers, chicken breast sandwiches and soft tacos form the backbone of the menu; in each case, the choices range from the fairly plain to the imaginative; the Hawaiian burger, for example, is garnished with pineapple and teriyaki sauce. Kids love the decor which seems to take them outdoors into a magical, tropical milieu.

Address: 7637 Balboa Ave • Clairemont • Call for Additional Locations
Phone: (619) 569-8866
Dinner Hours: Sun – Thurs until 10, Fri – Sat until 11

Jake's DEL MAR

The beachfront dining — which shouldn't be such a rarity in San Diego County, but is not all that easily found — has kept the crowds coming to this enormously popular Del Mar spot for more than a generation. The Sunday brunches are especially beloved by locals and visitors alike, and it's best to arrive either early, or rather late. The fare is Southern California Coastal, which is to say uncomplicated but hearty; the seafood and steaks both are quite reliable, and served in generous portions by a staff that seems to enjoy its work.

Address: 1660 Coast Blvd • Del Mar
Phone: (619) 755-2002
Dinner Hours: Mon – Thurs 5 – 9:30, Fri – Sat 5 – 10, Sun 4:30 – 9:30

American - Kansas City Barbeque   see pg. 202

This old-fashioned, down-home, charmingly grungy restaurant in an increasingly swanky corner of downtown San Diego (a new branch operates in Encinitas) will be forever known as the location in which several key scenes of the film "Top Gun" were shot. Guests looking for a restaurant with ambiance will find it here; those interested in richly flavored barbecued meats will find it pointless to look elsewhere, because Kansas City's offerings bear top honors. American down to its socks, Kansas City offers good crisp onion rings, creamy potato salad and sweetly rich baked beans as necessary accompaniments to a selection of slowly cooked meats that include spareribs, chicken and truly zesty hot link sausages. The sweet potato pie seems a natural conclusion here.

Address: 610 West Market St • Downtown • Call for Additional Locations
Phone: (619) 231-9680
Dinner Hours: 7 Days a Week 5 – 1

American - Karl Strauss' Old Columbia Brewery & Grill

Stop in around happy hour to find this place at its liveliest; it is at this time that workers from the surrounding forest of office towers drop in for a hand-crafted beer or ale, and perhaps an early dinner chosen from the restaurant's extensive menu of simple but robust fare. The vats in which the house lagers are brewed are on display through glass partitions, and all the beers can be said to be excellent. The menu also pleases — most dishes seem to have been designed as perfect accompaniments to beer — and among snack choices are such tasty offerings as beer-battered onion rings and roasted poblano peppers stuffed with cheese. Many entree-sized salads are available as alternatives to such truly hearty dishes as the Philly steak sandwich and the grilled sausage platter.

Address: 1157 Columbia Street • Downtown • Call for Additional Locations
Phone: (619) 234-2739
Dinner Hours: Sun – Wed 4:30 – 10, Thurs – Sat 4:30 – 12

American - Lamont Street Grill

This long-running, long-popular restaurant was designed as an upscale neighborhood establishment in the days when San Diego barely knew the meaning of the term. The concept — which specifies serving good, none-too-highly priced cuisine in comfortable but informal surroundings — caught on immediately, and Lamont Street Grill remains a leader among Pacific Beach eateries. The menu takes many cues from California cuisine, and emphasizes novel flavors and the freshest of ingredients; salads, naturally ,are done very well here, as are seafood and interesting meats and pasta. The desserts, like the restaurant, are quite satisfying.

Address: 4445 Lamont St • Pacific Beach
Phone: (619) 270-3060
Dinner Hours: Sun – Thurs 5:30 – 10, Fri – Sat 5:30 – 10:30

It may seem unreasonable to refer to a restaurant as a temple of breakfast, but no other term suits Le Peep quite so well. The Del Mar outpost of a highly regarded national chain, this restaurant rises above coffee shop standards in decor and service, and offers a menu laden with quite wonderful house creations. Among these are "gooey buns," or English muffins lavished with outrageously rich cargoes of cinnamon, brown sugar, almonds and cream cheese, and skillet dishes that blend all types of breakfast foods in a single hearty combination. If it can be done with eggs, Le Peep does it. Lunch also is served, and by no means as an afterthought; highly original house creations also dominate this very rewarding list.

Address: 3545 Del Mar Heights Rd • Del Mar
Phone: (619) 755-8008
Breakfast, Lunch Hours: 7 Days a Week 7 – 2:30

Proprietor Jim Milligan accomplished with this Bird Rock establishment exactly what every restaurateur would like: building the sort of place at which he himself would enjoy eating in every day for the rest of his life. The result, Milligan's, combines an elegant interior enhanced by somewhat racy paintings of women and more than a few mirrors, with a menu that draws on old-fashioned American bounty. Bread baskets brim with cornbread and biscuits (honey is served alongside, naturally), and for genuine, crisp-and-juicy fried chicken, there is no place better. Steaks and other meats are cooked with a sharp eye, and seafood also is given excellent attention. The lounge is quite popular with locals.

Address: 5786 La Jolla Blvd • La Jolla
Phone: (619) 459-7311
Dinner Hours: 7 days a Week 5-10

Peohe's

A one-of-a-kind outpost of the Chart House chain, this Hawaiian-themed restaurant offers brooks, waterfalls and lush greenery indoors, and a striking view of downtown San Diego across the bay. The place bustles and the staff hustles, but diners eat in some comfort at large tables strategically placed to take advantage of the view. And although the menu is extensive, this also is a good stop for a snack, since the raw bar is among the best-stocked in town. The dinner list veers from such beefy offerings as prime rib with garlic mashed potatoes to such islands' fantasies as coconut-crusted shrimp and grilled chicken breast with a chili-fired mango glaze.

Address: 1201 First St • Coronado
Phone: (619) 437-4474
Dinner Hours: Mon – Thurs 5:30 – 10:30, Fri – 5:30 – 11, Sat 5 – 11, Sun 3 – 10

Qwiig's

The name of this restaurant has puzzled guests for years, although the explanation is simple enough — the word is an acronym for the name of an athletic club founded at Point Loma High School during World War II. A retired member of the club operates the restaurant, which pays homage to its Ocean Beach location by being quintessentially beachy in mood — the servers, if efficient, are friendly and relaxed, and thus match the clientele perfectly. The view of the Pacific is good, but whatever is on the plate usually provides just as fine a view; Qwiig's does very well with seafood, and serves a number of good specialties from a well-stocked oyster bar. Prime rib and other hearty entrees also please.

Address: 5083 Santa Monica Ave • Ocean Beach
Phone: (619) 222-1101
Dinner Hours: 7 Days a Week 5:30 – 10

American - Shores at Sea Lodge, The

The Shores

As of this writing, noted chef Richard Savitch was just settling into his new role as head of the kitchen at this enchanting seaside hostelry. The views of the beach and of La Jolla Cove long served as the principal attraction of the handsome dining room, but now there are more enhancements to the cuisine supervised by Savitch. His approach ensures that fresh foods will be given careful but often novel treatments; he has a particularly fine hand with seafood. Breakfast in this room is a particular treat, and the buffet always includes a wealth of fresh berries, as well as such luxuries as smoked salmon with all the trimmings and an excellent selection of breakfast breads and pastries.

Address: 8110 Camino del Oro • La Jolla
Phone: (619) 456-0600
Dinner Hours: 7 Days a Week 5 – 10

American - Trophy's Sports Grill

TROPHY'S
— Sports Grill —

The ownership of this extremely popular spot includes several major figures from professional sports, and display cases near the entrance are loaded with big-time trophies and other memorabilia. The mood is lively but polite, and if watching sports is your game, there are more than a dozen monitors constantly tuned to various games and competitions. The menu is simple but pleasing, and generally very well prepared. The list of entree-sized salads is especially well composed, and such entrees as barbecued ribs and pasta in a creamy seafood sauce are quite pleasing.

Address: 7510 Hazard Center Dr, Ste 215 • Mission Valley • Call for Additional Locations
Phone: (619) 296-9600
Dinner Hours: Sun – Thurs until 10, Fri – Sat until 12

The
WHALING
BAR

This ground-floor cafe in La Jolla's venerable pink palace, the La Valencia Hotel, is gently lit and redolent of intimacy. Immensely popular with Old La Jolla types as well as visitors, this room has the feel of old money, enhanced by the relaxed but sophisticated atmosphere, the deferential service and the general feeling that if this weren't a hotel, it would be an exclusive private club. The Whaling Bar is the place to see and be seen, and the menu concentrates on traditional favorites, and steaks, seafood and salads are very good. Everyone seems to love the creme brulee.

Address: La Valencia Hotel • 1132 Prospect St • La Jolla
Phone: (619) 454-0771
Dinner Hours: 7 days a Week 6 – 10

THE
ZODIAC

A lonely hold-over from the days when department store tea rooms served truly fine fare, The Zodiac at Neiman Marcus continues to entice with a serious menu that makes it one of the more delightful spots to lunch in Mission Valley. The room itself is broken into a series of small alcoves, all of them lined in mirrors, so that your own image seems to echo back and forth through infinity. Since this is Neiman Marcus, various little extras are included throughout the meal, notably a cup of chicken broth offered as a bracing pick-me-up, and loaves of rich, flavorful monkey bread. The menu offers the ultimate in ladies' lunch, including souffléed omelettes, a wonderful curried chicken salad and ravishing desserts.

Address: 280 Fashion Valley Road • Fashion Valley Shopping Mall • Mission Valley
Phone: (619) 692-9100
Lunch Hours: Mon – Sat 11 – 4

Bully's

This long-running local chain enjoys fierce customer loyalty for three very simple reasons: Bully's gives guests what they want, serves them plenty of it and doesn't charge too much for the experience. The result of this philosophy is restaurants consistently packed with diners chowing down on massive steaks and hefty slabs of prime rib. The seafood selections are also quite good, and both early-bird specials and late-night dining options provide additional attractions. The mood at all three Bully's is lively, fun and informal, and the servers seem especially adept at their duties.

Address: 5755 La Jolla Blvd • La Jolla • Call for Additional Locations
Phone: (619) 459-2768
Dinner Hours: 7 Days a Week 4:30 -12

Lyn Anderson's
Charcoal House

Restaurants don't come much more American — or much more typically San Diego in style, for that matter — than this La Mesa institution, which makes a virtue of large portions of simple, high-quality fare. Prime Midwestern beef stars on the menu, which offers prime rib in cuts ranging from eight ounces to a full pound, and steaks that vary from a relatively petite top sirloin to a belly-bursting porterhouse. Lamb chops, pork chops, baby back pork ribs and a cognac-sauced filet mignon also are featured, along with numerous seafood items and a good selection of chicken dishes. The mood, especially on weekend evenings, is animated and enjoyable.

Address: 9566 Murray Dr • La Mesa
Phone: (619) 465-7050
Dinner Hours: 7 Days a Week 4:30 – 10

CHART HOUSE.
GREAT FOOD. GREAT SERVICE. OR IT'S ON US!

Among the flagships of the San Diego-based, nationwide Chart House chain, the Chart House at the San Diego Rowing Club offers guests the opportunity to dine over the water in perhaps the most historic structure on San Diego Bay. Large and frequently crowded, this restaurant offers a comprehensive menu of seafood and steaks prepared in the straightforward, simple manner that many locals and visitors prefer, preceded by a trip to a remarkably well-stocked salad bar. Specialties include fresh artichokes with garlicky aioli sauce, baseball-cut top sirloin steaks and a fine variety of fresh fish.

Address: 525 East Harbor Dr • Downtown • Call for Additional Locations
Phone: (619) 233-7391
Dinner Hours: Sun – Thurs 5 – 10, Fri – Sat 5 – 11

KENNY'S
STEAK HOUSE
OF NEW YORK

New York may not have invented the steak house — if anything, one would think that the honor would go to Chicago — but New York certainly has developed this type of eatery into an art form. The Gaslamp Quarter's Kenny's Steak House is the branch of a Manhattan establishment that also operates an outpost in Santa Monica, and everything here is done on the grand scale — the steaks are massive, the side dishes are oversized and the flavors are simple but big. Only the finest Iowa corn-fed beef is served, and meat of this quality needs nothing more than proper cooking to be perfect, as it is. The menu goes well beyond beef to order, to quality seafood and pastas, as well as such preparations as steak Diane. The setting has a solid, old-fashioned look, and servers perform with panache.

Address: 939 Fourth Ave • Gaslamp Quarter
Phone: (619) 231-8500
Dinner Hours: Mon – Thurs 5 – 9:30, Fri – Sat 5 – 11

Rainwater's
ON·KETTNER
An Eastern-Style Chophouse

This restaurant maintains the standard of East Coast, big city luxury dining that largely has been abandoned by other San Diego eateries. The emphasis in all cases is on the grand, from the banquettes of such depth that guests sometimes feel they have checked in for the night, to steaks of a size that recall the good old days at Chicago's once-pre-eminent Stockyard Inn. The emphasis is on simplicity and on the flavors of top-quality food that speaks for itself, as emphasized by such offerings as the selection of Russian caviars, the freshly shucked oysters on the half-shell and the immense New York sirloin for two. Black bean soup with Madeira and crisp cornsticks complete the impression of old-fashioned comfort and plenty.

Address: 1202 Kettner Blvd • Downtown
Phone: (619) 233-5757
Dinner Hours: Mon – Sat 5 – 12, Sun 5 – 11

Red Tracton's
RESTAURANT

The location across from the Del Mar racetrack may be a giveaway that this plush eatery has a special attraction for those who have had an exceptionally good day at the betting windows. It is necessary to come here with a fairly full pocketbook, since the prices are by no means modest; on the other hand, the quality is extremely high and portions are immense. Prime meats, cut in enormous slabs, star on this menu, followed by impeccably fresh seafood served in equally hefty portions. The side dishes are also delightful, and if you crave real hash browned potatoes, this is the place to find them.

Address: 550 Via De La Valle • Del Mar
Phone: (619) 755-6600
Dinner Hours: Sun – Thurs 4 – 10, Fri – Sat 4 – 11

Roxanne's
Boondocks

This small, cheerful restaurant hidden in the corner of a modest La Mesa shopping center once astonished the San Diego restaurant community by being selected the favorite eatery of local American Express card holders. The popularity of this small, dark hideaway is easily enough understood, however — the atmosphere and service are friendly and welcoming, and the menu specializes in the hearty steaks, prime rib and seafood dear to San Diego palates. But the menu is by no means plain Jane, since it includes a fine array of house specialties, including a zesty Kansas City-style pepper steak and miniature lobster tails served by the bucketful.

Address: 8320 Parkway Dr • La Mesa
Phone: (619) 465-3660
Dinner Hours: Mon – Thurs 4 – 9:30, Fri – Sat 4 – 10, Sun 4 – 9

Saska's

Now four decades old, Saska's is not only by far the oldest purveyor of good food in Mission Beach, but one of the longest-running restaurants in the city. A unique mood has kept this place popular through the years; in the eyes of many, you can't get any beachier than Saska's. A favorite playground after the sun sets beyond the furthest waves, Saska's is ultimately casual, but hip; the wood walls, photos of past beach scenes and shorts-wearing waiters all add to the scene. The cuisine meanwhile is hearty but simple, and is the foundation upon which Saska's has built its 40-year reputation. The steaks are prime, the seafood is fresh and both are cooked with considerable skill.

Address: 3768 Mission Blvd • Mission Beach
Phone: (619) 488-7311
Dinner Hours: Sun – Thurs 5:30 – 2, Fri – Sat 5:30 – 3 a.m.

40

Cajun - Cajun Connection

CAJUN CONNECTION This cheerfully informal San Marcos restaurant is the only North County outpost of Cajun and New Orleans-style cooking, which makes it the best by default — but measured by any standard, the cooking here is quite good. It helps to have a taste for alligator, since this is one of the favorite meats of the house, but there is a great deal else from which to choose. Fortunately, this restaurant understands that true Louisiana cooking is not built on hot sauce alone, and the flavors of the gumbo, the crawfish etouffee and other classics are distinguished and smooth.

Address: 740 Nordhal Rd • Suite 114 • San Marcos
Phone: (619) 741-5680
Dinner Hours: Tues – Sat until 9:30, Sun 4 – 9

Cajun/Southern - Bayou Bar & Grill

BAYOU BAR & GRILL The Cajun craze hit San Diego late, and fortunately arrived in the form of this charming Gaslamp Quarter establishment.   Proprietor Bud Deslatte serves the genuine cooking of New Orleans and the bayous, and not the phony, absurdly spiced stuff that passes for Creole and Cajun food at so many establishments.   The decor celebrates New Orleans, the recorded music celebrates New Orleans — if you can't afford a ticket to Louisiana at Mardi Gras time, a visit to Bayou Bar & Grill is not a bad substitute. The menu makes much of such Louisiana staples as red beans and rice, and a heady seafood gumbo; there are marvelous crayfish, duck and shrimp dishes as well.

Address: 329 Market St • Gaslamp Quarter
Phone: (619) 696-8747
Dinner Hours: Sun – Thurs 5 – 10, Fri – Sat 5 – 11

Brendory's By The Sea

Operated by retired police officer Dorance Aldridge and his wife, Brenda, this delightful eatery in the Bonita horse country pairs down-home Old South cuisine with the spicier confections of New Orleans and the Louisiana bayous. Both styles are presented with boldness, and with a nearly overwhelming generosity; it is best to arrive in the comfortable dining room with a fierce appetite whetted by the most Spartan of lunches. The Aldridges work wonders with their all-American menu, excelling equally well with traditional fried chicken and such Cajun offerings as catfish Creole and hot link sausage gumbo. The selection of side dishes has caused grown men to weep with nostalgia.

Address: 710 Sea Coast Dr, Ste F • Bonita
Phone: (619) 423-3991
Dinner Hours: Sun 2 – 8, Tues – Thurs 2 – 8:30, Fri – Sat 2 – 10

A L I Z É

This brand-new restaurant opened at the end of June (1994) atop downtown's haute chic Paladion center. Although it has Tiffany, Gucci, Cartier and Salvatore Ferragamo for neighbors, Alizé specializes in relatively straightforward, uncomplicated — and utterly charming — cuisine: the cooking of the French Caribbean islands. The third venture of restaurateur Philippe Beltran and chef Olivier Boiteau (the pair formerly operated the French Side of the West and Petit Louis), Alizé maintains the popular approach of offering fixed-price, multi-course dinners. All meals include a starter of the day, a choice of soup or salad, one of Boiteau's delicate desserts and an entree chosen from a list that encompasses herb-stuffed lobster, lightly curried shrimp and chicken, and rack of lamb seasoned with aged rum. It's all quite marvelous.

Address: The Paladion • 777 Front St, Ste 430 • Downtown
Phone: (619) 234-0411
Dinner Hours: Sun – Thurs 5:30 – 10, Fri – Sat 5:30 – 11

The exploding Gaslamp Quarter restaurant row now features cuisines that San Diego never has seen before, but until recently it lacked a quality Chinese restaurant. The slack has been taken up by Beyond, which not only presents a very good-looking face to the world — the decor is quite elegant — but offers an imaginative menu that goes beyond traditional Chinese fare to encompass such things as Chinese-style pizzas. These are called "chinniza" and consist of crusts topped with such unexpected items as yu-shiang eggplant with bean curd. The kitchen also gives careful treatment to more traditional offerings, and the house specialties page lists a number of excellent items.

Address: 618 Fifth Ave • Gaslamp Quarter
Phone: (619) 238-2328
Dinner Hours: 7 Days a Week until 12

CHANG

As one of the more upscale Chinese operations in the county, Chang offers carefully prepared cuisine at two comfortably furnished establishments. The smaller and folksier of the two is located inside Grossmont Center; the mini-chain's new and grander restaurant is located at the entrance to the Golden Triangle's imposing Costa Verde center. The cuisine at both takes a sophisticated tone that emphasizes Szechuan fire and Mandarin-style subtleties; such dishes as lemon scallops and crispy beef are immense favorites at Chang. The menus offer full surveys of popular Chinese dishes.

Address: 8670 Genesee Ave • Golden Triangle • Call for Additional Locations
Phone: (619) 558-2288
Dinner Hours: 7 Days a Week until 10

CHINA CAMP   New management has assumed the operation of this long-running downtown favorite, which is designed to look like one of the many Chinese camps that proliferated in the Sierras and other parts of California during the railroad building and gold mining days. At present, the menu puts less emphasis on the hybrid cuisine that developed in those camps than it did formerly, and mainstream Chinese fare is more the rule. The steamed dumplings, crispy Hunan chicken and crystal shrimp are all quite reliable. Visitors to San Diego especially enjoy the unusual, period decor.

Address: 2137 Pacific Hwy • Downtown
Phone: (619) 232-1367
Dinner Hours: Sun – Thurs 2:30 – 10, Fri – Sat 5 – 10:30

This sleek, chic, handsome establishment at the southern end of Convoy Street's booming Asian restaurant row can claim several firsts among San Diego restaurants, including first to have a proprietor (Susan Lew) named to the San Diego Port Commission, and first to present Chinese fare in a manner fairly close to the way it is served in China. Tanks in the main dining room present a vast selection of live, seasonal seafood that can be ordered cooked in myriad ways, but do not neglect such always-available sensations as the honey-walnut shrimp and the stuffed scallops. At lunch, Emerald serves a wonderfully impressive array of dim sum, dished from carts that circle the rooms constantly.

Address: 3709 Convoy St, Ste 101 • Kearny Mesa
Phone: (619) 565-6888
Dinner Hours: 7 Days a Week 5 – 12

FORTUNE COOKIE

RESTAURANT

Rancho Bernardo can lay claim to many pleasant amenities, among them the most elegant Chinese restaurant in San Diego County. The waiters wear black tie, and offer a decidedly superior level of service. The menu also is a cut above the norm, and is laden with such house specialties as tiny steamed buns filled with pork and cabbage, the wonderful "Mandarin Casserole" soup, which combines cabbage with ham, shrimp, chicken and vegetables in a notably rich broth, and the unusually named but quite tasty Cleopatra chicken. A more deluxe menu page headed "customized supplemental dishes" lists such treats as spicy tung-an shrimp, a Hong Kong-style pepper steak and the honey-sweetened sizzling red snapper.

Address: 16425 Bernardo Center Dr • Rancho Bernardo
Phone: (619) 451-8958
Dinner Hours: Sun – Thurs 3 – 10, Fri – Sat 3 – 11

North County can take pride in its selection of Asian eateries, most of which are simple, unpretentious neighborhood affairs. One that goes further, both in terms of decor and menu, is the Golden Garden, which combines a pleasantly decorated environment and swift, attentive service with a list that travels well beyond the usual. The chef's specialties page of the menu is designated "Grand Style," and it is here that much of interest can be found, including an unusual variation on minced chicken in lettuce that adds a shrimp mince to the picture, and the elaborate "snow hill" chicken. The pot stickers are particularly plump and juicy.

Address: 2216 El Camino Real, Ste 107-109 • Oceanside
Phone: (619) 722-8210
Dinner Hours: Mon – Fri until 9, Sat – Sun until 10

Chinese - Golden State Seafood Restaurant

Few restaurants lack style to quite the same degree as this homely but wonderful gem of a Chinese eatery. Located in one of Mira Mesa's ubiquitous shopping malls, Golden State takes an authentic approach to Chinese cookery, especially that very large branch devoted to seafood preparations. Mirroring the decor, the service is perfunctory at best, but the food is largely sublime. The seafood is exquisitely fresh, and tastes it, and preparations are done with sure, knowing hands. The platter of cured meats and jellyfish is a joy, as are the braised scallops with black pepper sauce and many other dishes.

Address: 9460 E8 Mira Mesa Blvd • Mira Mesa
Phone: (619) 578-8818
Dinner Hours: 7 Days a Week 3 – 10:30

Chinese - Great Wall Cafe

The dominant mood of Old Town dining always has been Mexican, but Great Wall changed that in a hurry by presenting good-quality Chinese fare on a broad, sheltered terrace that surrounds a tiny indoor dining room. Outdoors is where you want to be, enjoying such treats as minced chicken in lettuce leaves and spicy Szechuan dumplings. The menu veers off the beaten Chinese track to suggest such hard-to-find specialties as "Buddha's Jump Over the Wall," a hot pot presentation of meat, seafood and vegetables; the Peking duck also is quite good.

Address: 2543 Congress St • Old Town
Phone: (619) 291-9478
Dinner Hours: Sun – Thurs until 9:30, Fri – Sat until 10:30

MING COURT

Few Chinese restaurants offer the elegance of setting or sophisticated mood (live piano music is a regular feature) taken for granted by guests of this top-quality Del Mar restaurant. Mood apart, there is much to be enjoyed on this menu, which goes well beyond standard offerings to include such treats as the robust five-spice pork chops and the interesting cilantro chicken, which employs a favorite local herb in a distinctly Chinese manner. The cooking is reliably top-grade, and flavors generally are quite pronounced; other notably enjoyable offerings include the tongue-tingling sar-char beef and a dish of crabmeat gently folded with mushrooms.

Address: 12750 Carmel Country Rd #107 • Del Mar
Phone: (619) 793-2933
Dinner Hours: Sun – Thurs until 10, Fri – Sat until 11

The level of cooking at this chic La Jolla – Golden Triangle restaurant is high, and Panda Country remains a consistent purveyor of top-notch, carefully prepared Chinese cuisine. Stuffed dumplings are a particular highlight here, but for entrees, pay close attention to the specialties page, which offers such sublime winners as the delicately subtle double mushroom chicken and, at the opposite pole, the bold, hotly flavored house special shrimp in a sizzlingly pungent sauce. The service is prompt and pleasant.

Address: 4150 Regents Park Row #190 • Golden Triangle • Call for Additional Locations
Phone: (619) 552-1345
Dinner Hours: 7 Days a Week until 10

Chinese - Panda Inn

Long recognized as one of the top purveyors of Chinese cuisine in downtown San Diego, Panda Inn continues to serve a notable menu that brims with house specialties. The decor and service, like the menu, are notably elegant and refined; indeed, the service sets a tone that other eateries emulate. The location atop Horton Plaza makes it a natural for a break in a day of shopping or after the movies. The cooking generally is excellent, but truly outstanding dishes include the spicy-savory seafood pasta salad, the plump steamed dumplings, the crisp-tender Szechuan string beans and the "burnt" pork.

Address: 506 Horton Plaza • Downtown • Call for Additional Locations
Phone: (619) 233-7800
Dinner Hours: Sun – Thurs 4:30 – 10, Fri – Sat 4:30 – 11

Chinese - Peking Palace

This particularly well-decorated establishment offers a good, well-balanced menu of Chinese standards, enriched with such chef's specialties as the "seafood festival," which combines all manner of shellfish in a delicate wine sauce, and the "subgum crackling," in which a choice of meats is cooked in tomato sauce and served over oil-crisped rice. The Peking orientation of the restaurant also indicates such dishes as a very well-done Peking duck, but the menu by no means ignores other regional cuisines. Szechuan cooking is given special attention, and numerous spicy dishes from this school of cooking are given careful treatment.

Address: 11968 Bernardo Plaza Dr • Rancho Bernardo
Phone: (619) 487-9282
Dinner Hours: Sun – Thurs until 9, Fri-Sat until 10

STAR HOUSE

This small, unassuming but pleasant restaurant in San Marcos serves one of the more original and better prepared Chinese menus in North County. Operated by a family from Hong Kong, Star House is nearly alone among local Chinese houses in offering daily specials, and these usually are well worth trying. Pot stickers are consistently well-stuffed and juicy; other notable items on this consistently reliable menu include shrimp with aromatic garlic sauce and the smoothly spicy Chan Pi beef.

Address: 740 Nordahl Rd, #124 • San Marcos
Phone: (619) 489-6223
Dinner Hours: Mon – Thurs 3 – 9, Fri – Sat 3 – 10

Tucked away in a quiet neighborhood shopping center, this restaurant long has been popular for reliably cooked, expertly seasoned Chinese fare. Dishes named for the restaurant seem especially good, and often unique to this establishment; tasty examples would be the notably pungent Yen Ching chicken and the delicately savory Yen Ching pork, a stir-fry of shredded meat and black bean sauce that guests fold inside fragile pancakes. Among soups, both the seaweed and the winter melon options are quite tasty. Other interesting dishes include the subtly flavored "beef over snow" and the simple but surprisingly flavorful sauteed spinach.

Address: 4722 Clairemont Mesa Blvd • Clairemont
Phone: (619) 272-9470
Dinner Hours: Sun – Thurs until 9:30, Fri – Sat until 10

This innovative restaurant, not far from one of La Jolla's principal beaches, is the creation of chef-proprietor Tom Smith, who realized that pricing means as much in La Jolla as anywhere and consequently composed an affordable menu that offers both value and high quality. The cooking is fairly simple and straightforward, but does benefit from nouvelle and California cuisine touches, particularly in the pasta department. Grilled steaks and seafood consistently please the loyal and enthusiastic clientele. The decor and atmosphere are informal but attractive, and servers seem very well trained.

Address: 6941 La Jolla Blvd • La Jolla
Phone: (619) 456-2535
Dinner Hours: 7 Days a Week 5 – 10

The name of this restaurant says it all. Set in the rolling hills of the Temecula Valley wine country just north of the San Diego County border, Cafe Champagne presents the wines — sparkling and still — of the Thornton Winery in a lovely pairing of grape and food. The trellis-covered outdoor tables, given the views and the breezes that sometimes course through the valley, are favorites, especially for meals taken during the middle of the day. The menu incorporates the winery's vintages and allows a rare local opportunity to enjoy a bottle of the same wine, often a methode champenoise sparkler, that contributed to the confection of the dish.

Address: Thornton Winery/32587 Rancho Calif. Rd • Temecula • Call for Addit. Locations
Phone: (909) 699-0088
Dinner Hours: 7 Days a Week 4:30 – 9

Contemporary American - Cafe Pacifica

The original venture undertaken by the Kipp Downing-Deacon Brown partnership, Cafe Pacifica remains an outpost of light, imaginative California cuisine in tourist-populated Old Town, and draws a steady local clientele as a result. The dining rooms are small and crowded, a combination that somehow gives them considerable charm, and whimsically decorated as well. Seafood is the focus of the menu, and the kitchen prepares the top-quality raw ingredients with considerable thoughtfulness and care, as well as a good bit of imagination. This restaurant popularized creme brulee in San Diego, and continues to set the standard for this ultimate in rich desserts.

Address: 2414 San Diego Ave • Old Town • Call for Additional Locations
Phone: (619) 291-6666
Dinner Hours: 7 Days a Week 5:30 – 10

Contemporary American - California Cuisine   see pg. 150

The restaurant that years ago introduced the concept of California cuisine to San Diego continues to flourish in Hillcrest. This small, smartly decorated eatery, which boasts a quiet courtyard for dining in clement weather, may in fact have helped to make Hillcrest the trendy neighborhood that it is today. Chef Chris Walsh cooks in a clever, knowing way, combining ingredients in fashions that wouldn't occur to ordinary cooks but seem ultimately sensible when tasted. Freshness is emphasized, seafood presentations are triumphs, and presentations are stunning — sometimes one hates to disturb the colorful arrangements which Walsh has so painstakingly lain upon the plates. The wine list is extremely well chosen.

Address: 1027 University Ave • Hillcrest
Phone: (619) 543-0790
Dinner Hours: Tue – Sun 5 – 10

A gloriously eclectic menu characterizes this extremely popular restaurant in Hillcrest's lively Uptown District. Pate is juxtaposed with meatloaf, and summertime barbecue dinners contrast nicely with delicate French specialties. The creation of restaurateurs Piret and George Munger, Canes holds a particular place in the affections of practicing foodies; the decor consists of canes contributed by admirers of the towering George Munger, who occasionally requires a bit of ambulatory assistance. Menu specials follow the seasons, and the food is of reliably high quality.

Address: 1270 Cleveland Ave, Ste K • Hillcrest
Phone: (619) 299-3551
Dinner Hours: Sun – Thurs 4 – 10, Fri – Sat 4 – 11

More a complex than a restaurant, this establishment occupies a prime Gaslamp Quarter spot and extends both up Fifth Avenue and down F Street. The brainchild of savvy restaurateur Ingrid Croce, widow of singing legend Jim Croce, it encompasses several dining venues as well as a nightclub. Talented chef Fay Nakanishi supervises the menus, which take an American-International outlook offering everything from imaginative pastas to such California-inspired treats as grilled lamb salad and a wildly good, award-winning preparation of breaded Alaskan halibut with prawns and a spicy, Indonesian nasi goreng cream sauce.

Address: 802 Fifth Ave • Gaslamp Quarter
Phone: (619) 233-4355
Dinner Hours: 7 Days a Week 4 – 12

DAKOTA
GRILL & SPIRITS

This restaurant's motto is "food to get fired up for," a coy reference to the grill from which so many of the preparations issue. Dakota is not simply located in the Gaslamp Quarter, but in the first floor and mezzanine of San Diego's original skyscraper, which currently has been transformed into a small hotel. The dining rooms are dramatic and spacious, but the mood reasonably relaxed; the kitchen is serious about food, but Dakota is far from stuffy. The emphasis is on American foods given a bit of Southwestern spice; prime examples would be the jalapeno tortellini with smoked tomato sauce, and the barbecued baby back ribs with garlic mashed potatoes.

Address: 901 Fifth Ave • Gaslamp Quarter
Phone: (619) 234-5554
Dinner Hours: Sun – Thurs 5 – 10, Fri – Sat 5 – 11

Contemporary American - Delicias

Delicias

A popular retreat in exclusive Rancho Santa Fe, this happens to be one of the most beautiful restaurants in San Diego County. Lavish fresh flower arrangements intensify the colors and effect of a decor that is already made heavily floral by richly printed tablecloths and upholstery. The menu takes its cues from contemporary California influences, which is not to say that Delicias is a purveyor of California cuisine — the emphasis is on grilled foods, elegant presentations and intense flavors. Some dishes are French, others Italian; the pizzas are elegant, and it would be hard to find better pommes frites within a 10-mile radius.

Address: 6106 Paseo Delicias • Rancho Santa Fe
Phone: (619) 756-8000
Dinner Hours: Sun 6 – 9, Tues – Thurs 6 – 9, Fri – Sat 6 – 10

DOBSON'S
Bar & Restaurant

Doubters hooted when this San Francisco-style saloon-restaurant opened south of Broadway at the end of 1983, but it quickly became the location for both power lunches and chic, after-opera suppers. Still much a place to see and be seen, it retains a uniquely comfortable environment and remains a bastion of first-rate service. Proprietor Paul Dobson, one of the more visible restaurateurs in San Diego, keeps a firm hand on the front of the house while giving full reign of the kitchen to the talented Deborah MacDonald Schneider. The menus, printed daily, offer much that is seasonal but always feature such house specialties as mussel bisque baked under a pastry coverlet. The culinary style mingles French tradition with modern California sensibilities.

Address:　956 Broadway Cir • Downtown
Phone:　(619) 231-6771
Dinner Hours:　Mon – Sat 5:30 – 11

Elario's
RESTAURANT

This long-running La Jolla institution, which sits high atop the Summer House Inn and consequently enjoys a superb view of La Jolla Cove, had come for some years to rest on its increasingly tarnished laurels. New ownership has produced a complete reverse in direction, however, and Elario's now sparkles as brightly as the sun dancing on the none-too-distant wave tops. A complete renovation has given the restaurant a handsome new look, and the culinary outlook also has been completely overhauled. The emphasis now is on the finest and freshest ingredients, cooked in contemporary French and California styles. This is yet another La Jolla restaurant that is justly famed for its wine list; another popular feature is the jazz concerts given frequently in the lounge.

Address:　Summer House Inn • 7955 La Jolla Shores Dr • La Jolla
Phone:　(619) 459-0541
Dinner Hours:　Sun – Thurs 5:30 – 9:45, Fri – Sat 5:15 – 10:45

Fifth &
HAWTHORN
Restaurant

The creation of a pair of restaurateurs who seem to have been born to the business, this intimate mid-town eatery manages to pack a sense of big city sophistication inside a rather small space. Although scaled like a neighborhood restaurant, Fifth & Hawthorn is considerably more than that, and its varied, sensibly priced menus prove especially attractive to guests attending performances at the Old Globe Theatre and other cultural venues in nearby Balboa Park. As is true of many San Diego restaurants, seafood is a specialty here, but there are also excellent appetizers and pastas; desserts tend to be deliciously rich. The service shines.

Address: 515 Hawthorn St • Downtown
Phone: (619) 544-0940
Dinner Hours: Sun – Thurs 5 – 10, Fri – Sat 5 – 11

George's
RESTAURANT
AT THE COVE
LA JOLLA

Among the first practitioners of California cuisine in San Diego County, this stylish and popular La Jolla restaurant has grown over the years to encompass an upstairs bar and now an open-air, top-deck dining terrace that serves imaginative and relatively inexpensive lunches and dinners. All venues have excellent views of La Jolla Cove — views that on a beautiful day can themselves be worth the price of admission. Celebrated chef Scott Meskan turns out a reliable cuisine in the formal but un-stuffy main dining room; all ingredients are fresh and taste it, and the seafood selections can be superb. The wine list also is worthy of special note.

Address: 1250 Prospect St • La Jolla
Phone: (619) 454-4244
Dinner Hours: 7 Days a Week 5 – 10

HARBOR S EDGE

The just-completed, $32 million renovation of the Sheraton Harbor Island Hotel resulted in the creation of a spacious new lobby restaurant, Harbor's Edge. In keeping with the hotel's new self-definition as a resort rather than a business hostelry, the mood of the room is comfortable but informal; a menu note in fact advises guests, "don't hesitate to dip into your partner's plate." And in an unusual gesture, the majority of entrees include a choice of dessert from the restaurant's extremely well-stocked bakery; breads also are baked freshly on the premises. The menu offers such hotel necessities as steaks, but takes off nicely in California-nouvelle directions with such offerings as spit-crisped duck with jalapeno mustard-almond glaze, and fresh salmon lasagne in ricotta cheese sauce.

Address: Sheraton Harbor Island • 1380 Harbor Island Dr • Harbor Island
Phone: (619) 692-2255
Dinner Hours: 7 Days a Week until 10:30

Montanas
AMERICAN
GRILL

Quite pointedly an American grill, Montanas takes the point of view that virtually every food can be grilled successfully — except, mercifully, the chocolate torte with caramel sauce, which unquestionably ranks among the five best dessert offerings in San Diego. A certain hipness pervades the decor, which reflects both the setting in trendy Hillcrest and the style-conscious clientele. The menu, however, takes its cue from rugged American cuisine, updated and reinterpreted, but based on hearty ingredients that can stand up to the intense heat of the grill. That the kitchen favors bold flavors is emphasized by such offerings as the New Mexican pork stew with jalapeno cornbread, and the clever smoked chicken with apple mustard.

Address: 1421 University Ave • Hillcrest
Phone: (619) 297-0722
Dinner Hours: Sun – Thurs 5 – 10, Fri – Sat 5 – 11

56

Stellar chef Barry Smedley has made an enormous difference at this somewhat formal, decidedly stylish dining room in La Jolla's charming Colonial Inn. Although the view is of busy Prospect Street rather than La Jolla Cove, the atmosphere bespeaks the comfortable, relaxed local life-style. The menu incorporates both classics and California cuisine-inspired creations, and dishes that have made an enormous impression upon guests include a sensational, intense lobster bisque and perfectly seasoned rack of lamb roasted to a fine, toothsome finish.

Address: Colonial Inn • 910 Prospect St • La Jolla
Phone: (619) 454-2181
Dinner Hours: Sun – Thurs 5 – 10, Fri – Sat 5 – 11

For this handsome dining room on the lower level of the Sheraton Grande Torrey Pines, Chef Doni Barnett writes sparklingly creative menus that both update old-fashioned American traditions — many of them virtually forgotten — and take advantage of seasonal produce and unusual specialty products. One triumph is the lobster chowder, made with Atlantic lobster, plenty of cream and double-smoked bacon from a boutique smokehouse. The room itself gleams with plenty of polished brass, and has the nearby Pacific as its backdrop; service is attentive and professional. The menu offers considerable variety, including some dishes influenced by the new Pacific Rim style. A pleasing feature of this menu is the wine pairing suggestions; a perfect mate has been chosen for each given dish, and in every case is available by the glass.

Address: Sheraton Grande Torrey Pines Hotel • 10950 N Torrey Pines Rd • La Jolla
Phone: (619) 450-4571
Dinner Hours: 7 Days a Week 5:30 – 10:30

One has to delve back rather far in Del Mar history, to the era of the original Inn at Del Mar, to learn that this quite stylish restaurant takes its name from a French chef (certainly the first along the coast) who planted his own herb garden in order to be able to season dishes with true Gallic panache. That insistence upon freshness and quality — and upon panache, for that matter — is maintained by the dining room of the luxurious L'Auberge Del Mar. Unquestionably the most formal room along the North County coast, Tourlas features a crisp, contemporary decor and finely tuned service; the menu emphasizes seasonal products cooked with imagination and flair. In pleasant weather, the outdoor terrace is a joy.

Address: L'Auberge Del Mar • 1540 Camino Del Mar • Del Mar
Phone: (619) 259-1515
Dinner Hours: 7 Days a Week 6 – 10

Contemporary American - Triangles

Chef Harris Golden has restructured the menus at this stylish Golden Triangle restaurant to reflect his years of work at Elizabeth Arden's Maine Chance spa and health club resort in Phoenix. The result is perhaps the first menu in San Diego that is both chic and healthy, and although more self-indulgent dishes are scattered throughout the list, the majority of offerings take a light, low-fat approach. Flavors are by no means muted, however, and frequently sparkle, thanks to Golden's free-wheeling but intelligent use of herbs and other potent condiments. A notable repository of good art, Triangles also offers a reliable level of thoughtful, attentive service.

Address: 4370 La Jolla Village Dr • Golden Triangle
Phone: (619) 453-6650
Dinner Hours: Sun – Fri 4 – 10, Sat 5:30 – 10

This nationally acclaimed restaurant occupies perhaps the oddest location of any in San Diego, since it is housed in a commercial warehouse district. But the address does nothing to deter loyal fans, who crowd into the quietly luxurious dining room to feast upon chef-proprietor Doug Organ's frequently brilliant creations. Solid French foundations underlie Organ's preparations, which change regularly but have included such masterworks as grilled duck livers with wild rice waffles and pan-roasted whitefish with shrimp ravioli. Desserts similarly are among the best around, and there are those who would name this the city's top restaurant. An exquisite wine list only adds to the many pleasures of a dinner here.

Address: 9550 Waples St • Sorrento Mesa
Phone: (619) 450-9576
Dinner Hours: Tues – Sun 5:30 – 10

Contemporary French - Belgian Lion, The

Unquestionably one of San Diego's finest restaurants, The Belgian Lion tends to be overlooked by some, thanks to a deliberate lack of glitter and a location in less-than-fashionable Ocean Beach. However, the interior has the look and charm of a Belgian country inn, and the staff, all members of the Coulon family, strives to make every dinner seem a memorable, Old World experience. Chefs and co-proprietors Arlene and Don Coulon prepare a menu that combines French classics with contemporary creations borrowed from some of the leading, many-starred chefs of France. This is the place to enjoy a stellar fish soup, a superb salmon in sorrel sauce and a quite lovely rabbit saute. The wine list pairs perfectly with the menu.

Address: 2265 Bacon St • Ocean Beach
Phone: (619) 223-2700
Dinner Hours: Thurs – Sat 5 – 10

Contemporary/Pacific Rim - Azzura Point

LOEWS CORONADO BAY
R E S O R T

Decorated in the easy, comfortable style of a genteel East Coast resort, the principal dining room of Loews Coronado Bay Hotel unquestionably ranks among the top five restaurants in the county. Luxurious but relaxed, Azzura Point boasts fine, attentive service and a sweeping view of San Diego Bay, but what is much more important is the presence of chef Jeff Tunks. The Missouri-born chef gives fine interpretations of contemporary cuisine, and emphasizes Pacific Rim creations. The menu changes with the seasons, and the most recent list included roasted sweet corn soup with crab fritters and crispy, Hong Kong-style whole roasted sea bass. The touches of luxury continue with the freshly baked breads in the basket and complimentary sweets at the end of the meal.

Address: Loews Coronado Bay Resort • 4000 Coronado Bay Rd • Coronado
Phone: (619) 424-4477
Dinner Hours: 7 Days a Week 6 – 10

Contemporary/Pacific Rim - Banzai Cantina

This most enjoyable, one-of-a-kind restaurant not far from Old Town teaches the lesson that cultural collisions can result in tasty new cuisines. Chef and co-proprietor Jose Kelley, of Mexican and American descent, studied art in Japan before turning to the kitchen full-time; the result of these influences is a wildly original cuisine that combines Mexican spice, American bounty and Japanese subtlety. Unusual creations include spicy sea scallops bedded on a crisp potato pancake, as well as Japanese paella and sushi rolls as only Kelley could envision them. These creations are served by a hip staff in a casual but enjoyably decorated environment.

Address: 3667 India St • Near Old Town
Phone: (619) 298-6388
Dinner Hours: Sun – Thurs 5 – 10, Fri – Sat 5 – 11

This extremely good-looking, extremely hip restaurant in the Golden Triangle's stylish Aventine complex actually is operated by the nearby Hyatt Regency La Jolla hotel; the arrangement gives hotel guests, as well as savvy locals, the opportunity to enjoy extraordinary Pacific Rim cuisine outside the hotel setting. The look of the place is contemporary Japanese, reinforced by a giant Tengu mask in the bar and a sushi bar that serves up vibrantly fresh offerings. The best feature, however, is the standing menu, which cleverly combines Western and Asian cuisines to achieve such triumphs as the Thai pork and Japanese eggplant on crisp sweet potato slivers, and wood-roasted duckling with plum sauce and tortillas.

Address: 8960 University Center Lane • Golden Triangle
Phone: (619) 450-3355
Dinner Hours: Mon – Sat 6 -10

Woefully overlooked by hotel-wary San Diegans, The Grill actually is one of the city's better outposts of imaginative Pacific Rim and Southwestern nouvelle cooking. Located in the Pan Pacific Hotel in the many-towered Emerald Center, the room has a crisp, sophisticated, contemporary decor that minimizes the impression of hotel dining. The menu caters to the health conscious by offering several approved "heart healthy" dishes, as evidenced by such dishes as the grilled salmon with tortilla salad and tomato vinaigrette. The Sunday brunch, if a touch on the extravagant side, steers a wonderfully luxurious course and just may be the best in town.

Address: Pan Pacific Hotel • 400 West Broadway • Downtown
Phone: (619) 338-3640
Dinner Hours: 7 Days a Week 5 – 10

61

Contemporary/Pacific Rim - Pacifica Del Mar

The flagship creation of energetic San Diego restaurateurs Kipp Downing and Deacon Brown, Pacifica Grill occupies richly view-endowed quarters in Del Mar's ultra-fashionable, ultra-hip Del Mar Plaza. A temple of California-Pacific Rim cuisine, the menu offers wonderfully imaginative interpretations of fresh seafood as well as hearty meats and clever salads that can quite easily double as entrees. Chef Jacky Sloane-Donaldson recently expanded the offerings to include a special, lighter and less expensive menu in the new Mustard Bar, which has become a relatively hot gathering spot for the younger segment of the clientele. Service is top-notch.

Address: Del Mar Plaza • 1555 Camino Del Mar #321 • Del Mar
Phone: (619) 792-0476
Dinner Hours: 7 Days a Week 4 – 10:30

Continental - Cafe Eleven see pg. 142

Cafe Eleven This Hillcrest institution is one of several local restaurants that have discovered the secret to a long life: through newsletters and frequent promotions, Cafe Eleven fosters strong clientele loyalty. In fact, it probably has as many regulars as any establishment in the city. Very much a bistro at heart, this restaurant serves traditional and updated French cuisine in several small, attractively decorated rooms. Mid-week and holiday specials vie with the regular menu, which tends to be priced in a diner-friendly manner. Cafe Eleven also makes a point of searching out quality wines that can be offered to guests at unusually reasonable prices.

Address: 1440 University Ave • Hillcrest
Phone: (619) 260-8023
Dinner Hours: Tues – Sun 5 – 11

Few restaurants foster a sense of intimacy quite so well as this charming Coronado eatery, which occupies a finely restored residence in the heart of the downtown district and within proximity of Hotel del Coronado and other hostelries. The small dining rooms, unobtrusive artwork and quietly attentive service almost suggest dining at home — at least if home happens to be equipped with a skilled chef-proprietor who cooks a carefully updated menu of French and Continental classics. Seafood is prepared with particular flair here, and courses flow with reason and rhythm; the wine list seems to have been chosen with special care.

Address: 1132 Loma Ave • Coronado
Phone: (619) 435-0661
Dinner Hours: 7 Days a Week 5:30 – 10

Continental - L'affaire

Few restaurants in the county seem to have quite so loyal a following as does this Encinitas establishment, and the reasons seem clear: The menu is a definite crowd-pleaser, in terms of both offerings and prices. A large variety of daily specials, chalked on a blackboard that is carried to each table, supplements the standing menu, which on its own is by no means short on choice. There are also a dozen or more chicken options, ranging from a simple saute in lemon butter to the elaborate, curry-flavored Chicken Bombay. Entrees include veal cordon bleu, pork tenderloin in green peppercorn sauce and even steak Diane, which is a rather complicated dish to prepare in so busy a restaurant. Like the rest of the menu, the desserts are of Continental inspiration, and rather on the rich side.

Address: 267 North El Camino Real • Encinitas
Phone: (619) 436-4944
Dinner Hours: Sun – Thurs 5 – 9, Fri – Sat 5 – 9:30

Continental - Le Fontainebleau

The Westgate Hotel

Long recognized as one of San Diego's leading "prestige" restaurants, this principal dining room of the elegant Westgate Hotel serves well-dressed guests in a setting of period grandeur; everything that looks antique probably is. That a harpist entertains on weeknights gives some suggestion of the serene mood fostered by this room. The menu runs to French classics, prepared with considerable attention to detail; both meats and seafood are extremely well done. This also is a particularly popular spot for Sunday brunch, since the buffets groan under lavish loads and specialty stations offer made-to-order omelets and other treats.

Address: Westgate Hotel • 1055 Second Ave • Downtown
Phone: (619) 557-3655
Dinner Hours: Mon – Sat 6 – 10

Continental - Mister A's   see pg. 232

MISTER
A's
RESTAURANT

Recognized nationwide as one of San Diego's premiere "prestige" restaurants, this 30-year-old establishment occupies the 12th floor of an office building that overlooks Balboa Park to the east, and the city and San Diego Bay in other directions. As the sort of place in which a gentleman never would be caught without a necktie, the decor is one of old-fashioned opulence, and the Old World service matches it perfectly. The proximity to the park makes Mister A's popular with diners en route to performances at the Old Globe Theatre, although other diners find the Continental menu, much of which is prepared at table, sufficiently theatrical to provide a full evening's entertainment. Luxury rules this list, which features rich meat and seafood preparations in both French and Italian styles. The wine list takes a point of view as lofty as the restaurant.

Address: 2550 Fifth Ave • Downtown   **Phone:** (619) 239-1377
Dinner Hours: 7 Days a Week 6 – 10:30

Thee Bungalow
Continental Cuisine

Over the years, chef-proprietor Ed Moore has crafted a very special kind of restaurant in this Ocean Beach location; the clientele is extremely loyal because Moore carefully tailors his menu and prices to match their moods and needs. The aspect of the place is formal, but the mood is relaxed, and the cuisine takes its cues from both French and Continental cuisine. Moore is known for his roast duck, and also for value-priced mid-week and Early Bird dinners. A recently constructed patio allows guests to enjoy Moore's light, flavorful cooking in the open air. The wine list is particularly well written and worth a careful perusal.

Address: 4996 West Point Loma Blvd • Ocean Beach
Phone: (619) 224-2884
Dinner Hours: 7 Days a Week 5:30 – 9:30

Continental - Triple Crown Restaurant   see pg. 292

Triple Crown

As the formal dining room of the Del Mar Hilton, Triple Crown specializes in a stylish, thoughtfully considered menu that reflects the vast produce and seafood resources of San Diego County. Intimate and elegant, this room has been the scene of more than a few celebrations following big wins at the nearby Del Mar racetrack; a large number of horse owners and pony fanciers spend the racing season at the hotel. The culinary bent reflects Continental inspiration, and meats, seafood and poultry all are cooked with definite elegance and style; the wine list suits the menu quite well indeed.

Address: Del Mar Hilton Hotel • 15575 Jimmy Durante Blvd • Del Mar
Phone: (619) 792-5200
Dinner Hours: Thurs – Sun 5:30 – 9

The ChickeNest

If you like chicken, this is your place. This small, comfortable, neighborhood-style eatery operates along the lines of a traditional, big-city Jewish delicatessen, but the bird's the word here. An open-to-view, flame-powered rotisserie twirls constantly near the entry, bearing a cargo of plump, dripping fowl that can be ordered as is or in endless combinations and permutations. The sliced chicken sandwiches on a choice of home-baked egg, rye and sourdough breads are superlative; ditto the fresh, moist, nut-strewn chicken salad. In true deli style, portions verge on the daunting. The full menu begins with traditional breakfast treats and continues at dinner with such comfort foods as stuffed cabbage and meatloaf.

Address: 7200 Parkway Drive • La Mesa
Phone: (619) 589-0088
Dinner Hours: 7 Days a Week 3 – 9

Perhaps the only Jewish-style delicatessen in San Diego that could be said to have a genuine urban location, this Hillcrest institution is popular with noshers from early in the morning until late at night; the restaurant in fact serves until 2 a.m. on weekends, which makes it quite the San Diego rarity. Foods are freshly prepared on the premises and strive, when possible, toward a low-fat content. Much of the menu, including the knishes, blintzes, stuffed cabbage rolls, beef brisket and lox platters, comes straight from Jewish tradition, but there is also a good deal of hearty, all-American food, including surprisingly good Southern fried chicken.

Address: 535 University Ave • Hillcrest
Phone: (619) 295-2747
Dinner Hours: Sun – Thurs until 12, Fri – Sat until 2 a.m.

D.Z. Akin's
restaurant • delicatessen
bakery • fountain

Several years ago, Debi and Svika Akin created San Diego's most quintessentially Jewish delicatessen restaurant, and the place gradually has multiplied in size since then. Even so, it often seems crowded; the impression may be magnified by the scores of celebrity photographs that peer down from the walls. If it should be served at a deli, it is probably on D.Z. Akin's menu; choices start in the morning with eggs, smoked fish platters and dozens of other options, including matzoh brei and potato pancakes. Sandwiches are clever and well-stuffed, and the selection is vast; at night choose from a list that includes roasted beef brisket and stuffed cabbage. Pastries are baked on the premises and delicious.

Address: 6930 Alvarado Rd • College District
Phone: (619) 265-0218
Dinner Hours: Sun – Thurs 4 – 9:30, Fri – Sat 4 – 11

French - Bernard'O Restaurant

Bernard'O
RESTAURANT

A clever play on words endowed this fine Rancho Bernardo restaurant with its name, while proprietor Bernard Mougel endowed his establishment with an authentic and delightful French character. Wine dinners and other special celebrations are a frequent feature at this cozy, well-decorated establishment; not surprisingly, Bastille Day is celebrated in style with music and an elaborate three-course menu. The cooking is very French, but often updated and lightened in style, and certain California and Italian influence add breadth to the menu.

Address: 12457 Rancho Bernardo Rd • Rancho Bernardo
Phone: (619) 487-7171
Dinner Hours: Tues – Sat 5:30 – 9, Sun 5 – 8:30

French - Chez Henri   see pg. 156

A true Parisian bistro in the heart of Del Mar, Chez Henri is presided over by the gruff, pudgy, French-speaking and thoroughly lovable Henri Knafo, a chef-restaurateur of considerable talent. The look of the restaurant is intimate and cozy, and decorated in a manner that suggests a quiet neighborhood place on a Paris side street; recordings of Edith Piaf and other French giants highlight the atmosphere. Given the area's bounty, Knafo makes much of seafood, but in a thoroughly French manner; an excellent seafood soup always is available, and special bouillabaisse dinners are served on a regular basis. Simple French pleasures that simply are unavailable elsewhere abound here — and do save room for dessert.

Address: 1555 Camino Del Mar, Ste 201 • Del Mar
Phone: (619) 793-0067
Dinner Hours: 7 Days a Week 5:30 – 10

French - Cindy Black's   see pg. 160

The personal creation of nationally known chef Cindy Black, this cozy La Jolla eatery attracts a clientele less interested in La Jolla glitz and glamour than in serious eating. The dining room has a bit of French country inn flavor to it, highlighted by contemporary artworks that change periodically; the service is highly professional and highly pleasing. Black trained in a fashionable restaurant in Southwestern France, and prepares a menu that leans in that culinary direction. The Provencale chicken stew with rouille and croutons is emblematic of her style, as are the clever gratins that change nightly but accompany every dinner. Desserts are delightfully self-indulgent.

Address: 5721 La Jolla Blvd • La Jolla
Phone: (619) 456-6299
Dinner Hours: Mon – Sat 5:30 – 10, Sun 5 – 8

French - El Bizcocho

An oasis of traditional formality in the North County landscape, the main dining room of the Rancho Bernardo Inn preserves fine French traditions on a menu written by highly regarded chef Thomas Dowling. Unquestionably the finest hotel dining room in inland North County, the room is spacious and grand, and offers service on a par with the best in San Diego. While Dowling looks at cuisine from a classic point of view, he exercises a light touch; the result is a menu that lists such treasures as roasted salmon in a crust of coriander seeds, and roasted duckling in a tartly perfumed sauce of apples and Calvados. It hardly need be added that in this setting, the duck, naturally, is carved tableside.

Address: Rancho Bernardo Inn • 17550 Bernardo Oaks Dr • Rancho Bernardo
Phone: (619) 487-1611
Dinner Hours: 7 Days a Week 6 – 10:30

French - French Gourmet, The

San Diegans who have travelled to France frequently yearn for a corner establishment that will serve them a real croissant or pain au chocolate, or, for that matter, a generous wedge of fluffy quiche. The French Gourmet takes up the slack perfectly, combining the virtues of cafe and bistro at both of its small, comfortable locations. In keeping with the style, the settings are unpretentious, but the service speedy and efficient. The charms appear on the menus, which avoid the nouvelle and stick to such French traditions as pate, onion soup baked under a cheesy crust, pepper steak and sweetbreads braised in Madeira. Bakery and delicatessen counters offer wide assortments of freshly prepared, French take-out necessities.

Address: 960 Turquoise St • Pacific Beach • Call for Additional Locations
Phone: (619) 454-6736
Dinner Hours: 7 Days a Week 5 – 10

French - Grant Grill

U.S. Grant
A GRAND HERITAGE HOTEL

One of the more important establishments in downtown San Diego, the Grant Grill remains the quintessential old-style, luxury hotel dining room. A 1980s renovation produced a magnificent, club-like interior finished in rich paneling hung with fine English oils that depict the hunt and countryside. Old World servers provide a superlative level of attention, and it can be said that this restaurant is not only run the old way, but the right way. New chef Gunther Emathinger, who formerly pleased guests at the Gaslamp Quarter's now-defunct Falco, prepares a menu that steers a steady course between French luxury and newer, lighter offerings. However, certain immutable Grant Grill classics, especially the mock turtle soup and Cobb salad, remain in place and should not be missed. The cheese trolley retains the affections of those who like to conclude a meal in this very civilized fashion.

Address: U.S. Grant Hotel • 326 Broadway • Downtown
Phone: (619) 239-6806
Dinner Hours: Sun – Thurs 5:30 – 10, Fri – Sat 5:30 – 10:30

French - L'Escale

Le
MERIDIEN

The Le Meridien's informal dining room maintains the gracious standards of this luxury hotel, but in an entirely relaxed atmosphere. The indoor room is pleasant, but the terrace, which boasts a superior across-the-bay view of downtown San Diego's skyline, is much preferred. The imaginative menu presents L'Escale's unique version of California cuisine, which allows for plenty of Asian and French influences; the results of these culinary interminglings usually are quite rewarding. Such seemingly revolutionary innovations as a saltimbocca dressed with pastrami rather than prosciutto seem sensible when tasted.

Address: Le Meridien San Diego at Coronado • 2000 Second St • Coronado
Phone: (619) 435-3000
Dinner Hours: 7 Days a Week 5 – 10

Among the few classic French restaurants remaining in San Diego County, La Bonne Bouffe features specialties from la cuisine bourgeoisie and from French regional cooking. Small and charming in its decor, the restaurant features assured service and a wine list that nicely complements the menu. Hors d'oeuvres are no small affair here, and the most advisable route is to order a sampler that offers bites of many vegetable creations, as well as tastes of fine cured sausages and pates. All the old French favorites are excellent, including boeuf bourguignon, duck done in the style of the day, and fresh seafood dressed with silken sauces.

Address: 471 Encinitas Blvd • Encinitas
Phone: (619) 436-3081
Dinner Hours: Tues – Sun 5:30 – 10

The rustic charm of a French country farmhouse gives great appeal to this quiet, mid-city restaurant. The successor to the long-popular French Side of the West, Liaison maintains the tradition of offering fixed-price, multi-course dinners that give guests considerable choice at reasonable cost. The mood, service and menu all are French, a situation that is unlikely to draw arguments from many. A pairing of pate and cheese opens a meal that continues with soup or salad, sorbet, entree and dessert; particularly enjoyable options include the heady soupe de poisson, salmon in crayfish butter and such sweet desserts as tarte Tatin and iles flottantes.

Address: 2202 Fourth Ave • Downtown
Phone: (619) 234-5540
Dinner Hours: Sun – Thurs 5 – 9:30, Fri – Sat 5 – 10:30

The Marine Room made a revolutionary change in course in the summer of 1994, transforming itself from a stodgy purveyor of indifferent food to a top-notch establishment specializing in fine, contemporary French cuisine. The new chef, Bernard Guillas, has installed a menu that offers such excellent treats as sauteed foie gras with wild mushroom pancakes, mock turtle soup, an excellent Caesar salad (tossed tableside) and no end of fine, fresh seafood selections. Other hits include a veal chop crowned with Parmesan cheese souffle, and rack of lamb in an exquisite mustard-pistachio crust. As always, the waves continue to crash against the picture windows at high tide, and dancers assemble nightly for the live music.

Address: 2000 Spindrift Dr • La Jolla
Phone: (619) 459-7222
Dinner Hours: 7 Days a Week 6 – 10

One of San Diego County's top five restaurants, the luxury dining room of Coronado's elegant Le Meridien hotel is quintessentially French, from the reliably suave service to the fanciful paintings of food that decorate the walls. The menu, if extravagant, allows diners to partake of dishes that can be found nowhere else. The culinary point of view is Provencal, a cuisine adopted because of the similarity between climate and terrain in that region of France and San Diego. Degustation menus that allow samplings of various dishes, each sided by the appropriate wine, frequently are available; the standing menu sings with such offerings as sauteed foie gras with Muscat grapes and Baume de Venise wine, and lamb medallions in creamy cappuccino sauce. Wonder of wonders, pastries are baked when ordered.

Address: Le Meridien San Diego at Coronado • 2000 Second St • Coronado
Phone: (619) 435-3000
Dinner Hours: Tues – Sat 6 -10

French - Mille Fleurs

Mille Fleurs
Restaurant

This landmark restaurant in horsey Rancho Santa Fe consistently attracts national attention and is rated by many as San Diego County's premiere eatery. Everything about the place is French, from celebrity proprietor Bertrand Hug to the exquisite cuisine, fine service and comfortably elegant dining rooms — except for German-born chef Martin Woesle, who works wonders with the menus that he writes on a daily basis. Light, imaginative and lovely, Woesle's preparations (which happen to be costly, but worth it), are composed with a painter's eye. His dishes cannot be described as entrees with garnishes, since they are worked together as organic wholes in which every item makes delicious sense. This clientele can afford fine wines, and the list consequently dazzles.

Address: 6009 Paseo Delicias • Rancho Santa Fe
Phone: (619) 756-3085
Dinner Hours: 7 Days a Week 6 – 10

French - Rancho Valencia Resort & Restaurant   see pg. 254

RANCHO VALENCIA
RESORT

This glamorous tennis resort and hideaway, related to La Jolla's classic La Valencia Hotel and located in the hills near Rancho Santa Fe, has the fine scent of old money about it, even though it opened at the dawn of the 1990s. The impression of leisured gentility is especially strong in the quietly elegant dining room; the service matches the surroundings. The menu, written by Belgian-born chef Claude Poissonniez, takes a French approach lightened by contemporary Californian attitudes, and is simultaneously luxurious and clever. Examples of Poissonniez' finely considered offerings include oysters baked on a bed of spinach and apples, and glazed with a curry sabayon sauce, and pan-roasted whitefish in a whole grain mustard crust.

Address: 5921 Valencia Circle • Rancho Santa Fe
Phone: (619) 756-3645
Dinner Hours: 7 Days a Week 6 – 10

Incontestably one of the county's top "prestige" restaurants, this venerable La Jolla institution also is one of the best. Restaurateur Ron Zappardino and Chef (and La Varenne graduate) Brian Johnston work together to present a fine menu that takes French inspiration as its basis, but frequently is lightened according to contemporary sensibilities. Triumphant examples of the cooking would include the fresh duck foie gras with endive and the combination of roasted duck and duck confit. The pastry tray is irresistible. Many tables overlook La Jolla Cove; all share an environment of rich, restful luxury. The wine list wins awards on all sides and is remarkable for its breadth and depth.

Address: 1216 Prospect St • La Jolla
Phone: (619) 454-7779
Dinner Hours: 7 Days a Week 5:30 – 10:30

Kaiserhof Restaurant German restaurants attract a relatively limited audience in San Diego, but Kaiserhof has maintained a loyal following for years. This modestly sized, comfortably furnished restaurant in casual Ocean Beach caters primarily to one kind of customer — the very, very hungry. Portions in nearly all cases verge on the gargantuan, and with first courses and hefty side dishes added to the equation, meals leave guests satisfied, to say the least. The cooking is classic and offers all the German virtues of piquancy and great savor; veal rarely is treated as well as here, and the sausage platters, pork dishes and dozens of other specialties never fail to delight.

Address: 2253 Sunset Cliffs Blvd • Ocean Beach
Phone: (619) 224-0606
Dinner Hours: Sun 4:30 – 9, Tues – Sat 5 – 10

If the chicken came before the egg, then Aesop's fables predate Aesop's Tables. Even so, it would be difficult to have to choose between the Old Greek's wise tales and the wonderful evocations of Greek cuisine served at this most attractive Golden Triangle restaurant. Built in the style of a Greek country villa, the restaurant includes an outdoor terrace as well as numerous small, comfortable dining rooms. The menu is notable both for the unusually lengthy selection of mezethes — the appetizers without which no Greek menu is complete — and for the house creations that supplement the list of traditional entrees. The galactobouriko dessert is worthy of special notice.

Address: Costa Verde Shopping Center • 8650 Genesee Ave, #106 • Golden Triangle
Phone: (619) 455-1535
Dinner Hours: Sun – Mon 4 – 9, Tues – Sat 4 – 10

Located in the historic and handsomely restored Senator Building, Athens Market is a pleasant, moderately priced retreat in a posh district — neighbors include Horton Plaza, the Paladion and the plush Meridian tower. Long popular with members of the downtown legal community, this restaurant also is a favorite of San Diego Chargers owner Alex Spanos, who dines there once a week during football season. Proprietor Mary Pappas presents a comprehensive Greek menu in a comfortable, intimate space; portions are large and the quality high. Roast lamb is especially nice here. Pappas recently opened a stylish, Greek-style cafe, the Kafenio, in an adjacent space.

Address: 109 West F St • Downtown
Phone: (619) 234-1955
Dinner Hours: 7 Days a Week 4 – 11

Greek - Calliópe's Greek Cafe

CALLIÓPE'S GREEK CAFE San Diegans disagree on the pronunciation of this Hillcrest eatery's name (the tendency is to say it like the name of the musical instrument, while the proprietor sounds it out as "kal-e-o-pay-uhs"), but tend to agree rather strongly that the Greek fare is prepared with unusual subtlety. The dining room combines the cool appearance of a Mediterranean cafe with broad views of the urban carnival frequently in progress on Fifth Avenue. The virtue of the menu is that it combines thoughtful preparations of all the typical Greek dishes — moussaka, roast lamb leg, perfectly seasoned roast chicken — with a broad range of substantial salads and such less-common offerings as sauteed artichokes over pasta.

Address: 3958 Fifth Ave • Hillcrest
Phone: (619)291-5588
Dinner Hours: Mon 5 – 9, Tues – Thurs 5 – 10, Fri – Sat 5 – 11, Sun 4 – 10

Greek - Grecian Gardens

GRECIAN GARDENS Live music and entrancing belly dancing, both offered on weekends, add to the pleasures of this taberna-style Greek eatery. The decor reminds one of the Old Country, as does the service. The menu, meanwhile, extends far beyond the usuals to include a good selection of seafood dishes as well as numerous daily specials, among them such outstanding offerings as Athenian-style meatballs and braised lamb shank. The menu also is notable for its lengthy list of mezethes, the appetizers without which no Greek meal is complete.

Address: 1020 West San Marcos Blvd • San Marcos
Phone: (619) 744-3790
Dinner Hours: Sun – Thurs until 9, Fri – Sat until 10

The GREEK TYCOON

Greek restaurants are a common enough feature of the American landscape, but for some reason, San Diego seems to have less than its fair share. One of the Greek eateries that stands out (almost literally, since it is perched high above the India Street restaurant colony near the intersection with Washington Street) is The Greek Tycoon. The views are good, the menu better, and on weekends traditional entertainment is offered. The menu lists most of the Greek standards, but supplements them with the less easy-to-find specialties, such as baked seasoned shrimp and some very interesting Greek pastas. The appetizers are excellent, notably the flamed dish of kasseri cheese called saganaki.

Address: 3731 India St • Near Old Town
Phone: (619) 295-0812
Dinner Hours: Tues – Sun 5:30 – 12

MYKONOS

One associates Greece and its islands with the blue Aegean whose colors emblazon the Greek flag, and Greek cuisine never seems to taste quite so good — indeed, quite so Greek, to put it that way — as when eaten within view of the water. Mykonos occupies a small, comfortably decorated space near the yacht basin on Oceanside Harbor, and thus meets one requirement quite neatly; the cheerful service and well-written menu take care of the rest. Several seafood specialties shine here, and it can be said that the entire Greek menu is cooked exactly the way it should be — with the belief that flavors should be full, pronounced, and generous.

Address: 258 Harbor Dr South • Oceanside Harbor
Phone: (619) 757-8757
Dinner Hours: Mon – Tues 4 – 10, Wed – Sun 4 – 11

Health Conscious - Daily's Fit & Fresh Restaurant

Located in an upscale residential corner of the Golden Triangle, this may be the only health-conscious fast food restaurant in the United States operated by a leading cardio-vascular surgeon. Dr. Pat Daily opened the place in response to needs vocalized by his patients; the surprise is that the food, carefully designed to minimize fat and sodium content, also tastes quite good. The decor, clean and contemporary, seems more like that of a cafe than a fast food establishment; in the same vein, while meals are cooked quickly and picked up at a counter, everything is made to order from fresh ingredients. The grilled eggplant and zucchini sandwich dressed with red pepper spread proves that what is good for you also can simply be good.

Address: 8915 Towne Centre Dr, Ste 103 • Golden Triangle
Phone: (619) 453-1112
Dinner Hours: Mon – Sat until 9, Sun until 8

Indian - Star of India   see pg. 272

With three locations, Star of India dominates Indian cuisine in San Diego County, and with good reason — flavors tend to be pronounced and exciting, and the range of dishes available is comprehensive. Each restaurant is decorated in a distinct style; the Gaslamp Quarter establishment, which is the smallest, also is the most intimate and sophisticated. Indians take bread seriously, and this restaurant offers a particularly fine selection of baked-to-order items, notably the richly stuffed onion kulcha. In addition to curries and assorted vegetarian specialties, the Star of India restaurants feature Tandoor ovens that turn out moist, succulent meats cooked at volcanic temperatures that seal in juices and flavors.

Address: 1000 Prospect St • La Jolla • Call for Additional Locations
Phone: (619) 459-3355
Dinner Hours: 7 Days a Week 5 – 10

78

ALBERT'S RESTAURANT

In August, 1949, a four-month-old named Albert took up residence at the famed San Diego Zoo. The silver-backed lowland gorilla ultimately became the zoo's most famous denizen, endearing himself to the public with a rather majestic demeanor moderated by what seemed to be — at least for a gorilla — a rather sharp sense of humor. In any case, when the San Diego Zoo opened its first restaurant in 1992, it named the attractive space in honor of Albert, and arranged for a menu that honors the lands of birth of many zoo creatures. Included are such things as an African-style corn chowder, a variety of pastas, pizza-like creations based on chewy Ethiopian injera bread, salads and formal entrees. Albert's makes for a fine meal break in the heart of the zoo.

Address: 2000 Zoo Dr • Balboa Park
Phone: (619) 685-3200
Lunch, Dinner Hours: Seasonal, Please Call

Avanti

Known as the home of one of La Jolla's livelier bars, this restaurant also features an elaborate and notably cosmopolitan decor; the mirrored black ceiling always causes first-time guests to spend half the evening staring upwards. Piano music drifts into the dining room as servers deliver a wide variety of freshly made pastas, many based on original house recipes. The menu leans toward the subtleties and rich finishes of Northern Italian cooking; both veal and seafood are well-prepared here. Avanti also is known as a good bet for a late-night bite.

Address: 875 Prospect St • La Jolla
Phone: (619) 454-4288
Dinner Hours: Sun – Thurs 5 – 11, Fri – Sat 5 – 1

Baci Ristorante

This fine Italian restaurant occupies an unobtrusive location that is easy to drive by, but once most guests have had a taste of the excellent pastas and delicate veal preparations, they beat repeated paths to the door. As unprepossessing as the exterior may be, Baci features a rather elegant decor and stylish mood; the small, alcove-like back room is both especially intimate and a favored spot in which to dine. The service similarly maintains a high tone. The menu includes both Northern and Southern Italian specialties, and it is difficult to decide with which the restaurant can be said to show greater virtuosity; both are cooked with considerable flair.

Address: 1955 West Morena Blvd • Morena Boulevard District
Phone: (619) 275-2094
Dinner Hours: Mon – Sat 5:30 – 10:30

B E L L A
L · U • N · A

The name of this restaurant translates as "Beautiful Moon," and the decor of this small but chic Gaslamp Quarter establishment is indeed quite enough to leave one moonstruck. A collection of moon-themed artworks covers a couple of walls; there are nearly enough pieces to stock a small museum. The menu should leave most guests equally impressed: it is haute Italian, light, imaginative and thoroughly appetizing. Daily specials often eclipse the offerings on the standing list, but there is much to praise here, including the breaded veal chop crowned with a softly piquant blend of arugula and fresh tomato, and carciofi giudea, or baby artichokes crisped with garlic in oil.

Address: 748 Fifth Ave • Gaslamp Quarter
Phone: (619) 239-3222
Dinner Hours: Sun – Thurs 5 – 11, Fri – Sat 5 – 12

Italian - Busalacchi's

Chef-proprietor Joe Busalacchi presents a menu which makes the most of the cooking of his native Sicily, and which is pungent, sharp and appetizing in unexpected ways. If you like squid, this is the place — and if you don't like squid, Busalacchi's numerous, tasty calamari preparations might well help you acquire a taste for this leggy seafood. Specialties include a Sicilian potato salad, pasta with eggplant and an assortment of veal dishes, all served in a converted Hillcrest house that boasts one of the nicest outdoor terraces in the neighborhood.

Address: 3683 Fifth Ave • Hillcrest
Phone: (619) 298-0119
Dinner Hours: Sun – Thurs 5 – 10, Fri – Sat 5 – 11

Italian - Cafe Luna see pg. 146

This "Moon Cafe" was precisely what chain-restaurant infested inland North County needed, a small Italian eatery operated by a chef-proprietor whose interest in quality outweighs his concern for the bottom line. Small enough that it can't help being intimate, the restaurant features a light-hearted decor and thoughtful service. The best feature, however, is the menu, which holds prices down by concentrating on pastas and relatively simple chicken and veal preparations. There are some highly unusual, highly rewarding choices here, including ravioli in a creamy walnut sauce and the "tris della casa," described by the menu as "for the undecided" and consisting of the chef's daily selection of three pastas. There is also perfectly grilled chicken redolent of the savors of fresh herbs.

Address: 11040 Rancho Carmel Dr, Ste 2 • Carmel Mtn. Ranch
Phone: (619) 673-0077
Dinner Hours: Mon – Thurs 5 – 9, Fri – Sat 5 – 9:30

CALDO POMODORO
One way or another, virtually every dish at this comfortable Italian bistro in quaint downtown Carlsbad includes pasta, served in sufficient quantity to guarantee satiation of the fiercest appetite. Since this restaurant is the "Hot Tomato," there is naturally a house tomato sauce of a particularly peppery nature; this is especially good with seafood, since the spice really helps to point up the fresh, briny flavors. Much of the menu concentrates on dishes that are the Caldo Pomodoro's own, such as pasta in a sauce of Gorgonzola, cream and broccoli; there are also unusual Cajun-style pastas. The menu pays delightfully close attention to the traditions of home-style cooking, notably with a saute of homemade sausage with peppers and onions.

Address: 2907 State St • Carlsbad
Phone: (619) 720-9998
Dinner Hours: 7 Days a Week 4 – 10

Christefano's
ITALIAN RESTAURANT

This tiny gem of an eatery brings a genuine sparkle to the restaurant scene in Rancho Bernardo. Operated by a family with decided opinions on precisely how Italian food should taste, Christefano's features a menu laden with Old World offerings and flavors. The pastas are quite handsome, but it is the meat and seafood specialties that really sing, especially such dishes as the Seafood Christefano — a combination of shellfish and fin fish in a light cream sauce — and the old-fashioned brasciola of beef. The homemade cannoli should satisfy every sweet tooth at the table.

Address: 16707 Bernardo Ctr Dr • Rancho Bernardo
Phone: (619) 451-2224
Dinner Hours: Sun, Tues, Wed, Thurs 5 – 9, Fri – Sat 5 – 9:30

DOMINIC'S
italian restaurant

Designed along the lines of a casual, comfortable neighborhood eatery, Dominic's goes well beyond the norm of San Diego County's mom 'n' pop Italian houses to present a sophisticated, New York-style line-up of flavorful Italian dishes. The service is easy-going but efficient and prompt, and the mood light-hearted. This is the place to find such old-fashioned, home-style treats as eggplant parmigiana and Italian sausage sandwiches. More importantly, the menu offers such fine pastas as cappellini in a light, Sicilian-style fresh tomato sauce, and such excellent meat offerings as veal baked under a topping of fresh mushrooms. The pizzas are notable for their chewy, flavorful crusts and generously arranged garnishes.

Address: 461 College Blvd • Oceanside
Phone: (619) 630-4400
Dinner Hours: Sun – Thurs until 10, Fri – Sat until 11

CUCINA
Fio's
ITALIANA

One of the key restaurants in the Gaslamp Quarter, Fio's helped popularize this booming entertainment district and remains chic and fashionable to this day. The restaurant houses a crowd, but provides intimate settings in several small rooms, each of which is decorated with murals depicting scenes from the famous Palio horse races in Sienna. Chef Nancy Fontes keeps the clientele happy with a straightforward Italian menu that aims at light effects, and offers a few hard-to-find specialties, including stuffed, deep-fried zucchini blossoms and panzanella toscana, a diced salad made aromatic by the addition of fennel and smoked ricotta cheese. Servers are as hip as the guests, and indeed, Fio's occupies one of the most popular corners in town.

Address: 801 Fifth Ave • Gaslamp Quarter
Phone: (619) 234-3467
Dinner Hours: Mon – Thurs 5 – 11, Fri – Sat 5 – 12, Sun 5 – 10

83

Italian - Giuseppe's Italian Restaurant

GIUSEPPE'S
ITALIAN RESTAURANT & PIZZA

This charming, comfortable establishment combines the virtues of an easy-going neighborhood place with a menu that quite transcends the usual; in addition, prices are decidedly on the consumer-friendly side. Specialties include chicken tortellini in a delightful pistachio cream sauce, spinach lasagna and the veal Guiseppe, which guilds this particular lily by sauteing the meat with wine, onions, bell peppers, mushrooms and tomato sauce. This restaurant also offers several excellent seafood specialties, including halibut in a pleasant piccata treatment.

Address: 13185-I Black Mountain Rd • Rancho Penasquitos • Call for Additional Locations
Phone: (619) 484-9112
Dinner Hours: Tues – Sun 4:30 – 9:30

Italian - Il Fornaio

Il Fornaio

The outpost of a successful, Bay Area-based chain, Il Fornaio is grandly furnished with enough marble to build a church, as well as with a view of the Pacific as good as any along the North County coast. The location in chic Del Mar Plaza also is a plus. The name of the restaurant means "The Oven," and in addition to baked and spit-roasted entrees, Il Fornaio offers perhaps the best selection of breads of any eatery in the county; the pastries and desserts also excel. The menu offers fine vegetable appetizers, good pastas and some intriguing entrees, including a juicy, Florentine-style T-bone steak.

Address: 1555 Camino Del Mar • Del Mar • Call for Additional Locations
Phone: (619) 755-8876
Dinner Hours: Sun – Thurs 5 – 11, Fri – Sat 5 – 12

Italia Mia
Trattoria

Incredibly bright and colorful murals of Italian food-stuffs and dishes bring a great deal of interest to the decor of this most likable eatery. The menu specializes in three categories of dishes — pizzas, salads and pastas — and does a very fine job with each. From time to time, a baked pasta special will acquire a special character in the intense heat of the wood-burning oven, which regularly adds a special perfume to such pizzas as the fiorentina (topped with goat cheese, spinach and forest mushrooms) and the Mediterraneo, which decorates the crust with shrimp, sun-dried tomatoes, pine nuts and more. Among the pastas, the linguine fantasia is especially interesting, since it includes bean sprouts and peanut sauce, while the Caesar salad is among the best in North County.

Address: 14771 Pomerado Rd • Poway
Phone: (619) 679-9300
Dinner Hours: Sun – Thurs 5 – 9, Fri – Sat 5 – 9:30

Formerly limited largely to purveyors of Mexican cuisine, Old Town in recent years has expanded its range to include a much wider variety of dining options. Among the more recent additions to the scene is Jack & Giulio's, a friendly, down-to-earth establishment operated by a family who for decades ran one of the beach area's leading Italian houses. This restaurant takes a more casual approach (and sometimes grows a bit whimsical; the Caesar salad here is named for Brutus), and makes much of salads and pastas. A surprise find is the Waldorf salad, creamy and rich and quite old-fashioned in its goodness. Pasta choices include ziti in a light seafood sauce and an attractive, vegetarian version of ravioli. The pizzas and chicken dishes also please, and the terrace is delightful in fine weather.

Address: 2391 San Diego Ave • Old Town
Phone: (619) 294-2074
Dinner Hours: Sun – Thurs 4 – 9, Fri – Sat 4 – 10

LADER'S
ITALIAN GOURMET RESTAURANT

This restaurant belongs very much in the category of reliable neighborhood eateries. The one unusual decor feature is the vast collection of pasta that decorates the room, but otherwise Lader's displays an utter lack of interest in pretense, and is thoroughly informal. The crowd — and the place frequently is crowded — comes for a simple Italian menu that goes well beyond the cliches to such house creations as veal with Gorgonzola cheese and red wine sauce, and grilled scallops over pasta in a sauce that includes both yogurt and roasted peppers. "Gourmet" pizzas avoid tomato sauce and incorporate unexpected ingredients, such as fried eggplant and spicy Cajun sausage.

Address: 5654 Lake Murray Blvd • La Mesa
Phone: (619) 463-9919
Dinner Hours: Sun – Thurs 4 – 9, Fri – Sat 4 – 10

Lorna's
ITALIAN KITCHEN
Delivery & Catering Available

This family-style Italian restaurant gained an enormous following quite rapidly in response as much to its reasonable prices as to the thin-crusted, deliciously savory pizzas that are a notable house specialty. The fresh herbs incorporated into the pizza sauce flavor every bite, and for those who like their pizza fillings encased in dough, Lorna's offers an unusually extensive selection of calzone, or football-sized stuffed pizzas. Entrees range from the vegetarian, spinach-based lasagne florentine to sesame-flavored chicken in lemon butter sauce and veal with fresh mushrooms in a light Marsala sauce. The lengthy pasta list includes mostaciolli baked with eggplant and freshly made tortelloni.

Address: 3945 Governor Dr • Del Mar
Phone: (619) 452-0661
Dinner Hours: 7 Days a Week 4 – 10

A major hit from the day it opened on the ground floor of La Jolla's Empress Hotel, this creation of restaurateur P.J. Macaluso brought a Big Apple version of Italian dining to a town that formerly was impressed by spaghetti and meatballs. The interior is big city and sophisticated, and divided into relatively small spaces by immense aquariums populated by colorful swimmers. The servers, notably professional, take pride in serving a menu that divides between deliciously sauced pastas and handsome cuts of beef, veal and lamb; seafood offerings are cooked with style and care. The antipasto table is one of the best around and should not be ignored.

Address: Empress Hotel • 7766 Fay Ave • La Jolla
Phone: (619) 554-1444
Dinner Hours: 7 Days a Week 5:30 – 10:30

Italian - Nicolosi's Italian Restaurant

For decades one of the most popular, neighborhood-style Italian restaurants in San Diego, Nicolosi's continues the tradition in new quarters at the eastern end of Mission Valley. House creations set the tone for a menu heavy on simple Southern Italian dishes; among these original offerings are "impanata," or fresh bread dough baked with stuffings of Italian meats and cheeses. Niceties include complimentary relish dishes laden with provolone and pepperoni, and baskets brimming with freshly baked bread. The pizzas are bubbling hot, generously garnished and, quite simply, delicious.

Address: 5351 Adobe Falls Rd • Mission Valley
Phone: (619) 287-5757
Dinner Hours: Sun – Thurs until 9, Fri – Sat until 10

Italian - Old Trieste

Yet another of San Diego's old-line luxury restaurants, Old Trieste has maintained a loyal clientele for some 30 years on the basis of elegant, perfectly attentive service and simple but expert cooking. Italian and American themes mingle on the menu, and although Northern Italy officially is the inspiration of Old Trieste's cuisine, thick, butter-tender steaks always have been among its main attractions. The restaurant also does a fine job with veal, seafood, and subtle Italian preparations, and is known for the piping hot zucchini chips that arrive with the first round of drinks.

Address: 2335 Morena Blvd • Morena Boulevard District
Phone: (619) 276-1841
Dinner Hours: Tues – Sat 5:30 – 10

Italian - Old Venice Restaurante

The term "upscale Italian neighborhood eatery" perhaps best applies to this casual but stylish restaurant near the entrance to Shelter Island. Locals and visitors alike come for the ambiance and the simple but flavorful cooking, and the walled patio, which seems pleasant year-round, generally is the favored dining venue. The full-service menu offers all the Italian usuals as well as some fine house specialties, and the fresh fettuccine creations can be quite nice — the version named for the restaurant adds baby clams and other ingredients to an Alfredo-style dish. The chicken and veal preparations also please, but the pizzas should by no means be ignored.

Address: 2910 Canon St • Point Loma
Phone: (619) 222-5888
Dinner Hours: Sun – Thurs 4 – 9:30, Fri – Sat 4 – 10:30

Italian - Osteria Panevino

PANEVINO

One of the hottest spots among the flock of Italian restaurants operating in the Gaslamp Quarter, Osteria Panevino offers a menu that seems closer than many of those found in Italy. A pungent Sicilian influence pervades much of the list, reflecting the birthplace of proprietor Alessandro Minutella. The brick walls and open kitchen give a comfortable, homey feel to the place, while the terrace brings guests smack into the middle of Gaslamp street life. Especially notable are the vegetable antipasti and the focaccia, a term that here implies not bread, but "stuffed" pizzas encased in two incredibly thin, crisp disks of dough. The menu is generally as varied and interesting as the clientele.

Address: 722 Fifth Ave • Gaslamp Quarter
Phone: (619) 595-7959
Dinner Hours: 7 Days a Week 5 – 11

Italian - Pernicano's

Operated by one of the families that helped put pizza on the map in San Diego, this restaurant in Hillcrest's popular Uptown District combines the virtues of neighborhood dining — a comfortable, come-as-you-are atmosphere — with a menu that takes a more sophisticated point of view. All the basics are present and accounted for, including lasagne, cannelloni, and fettuccine Alfredo, but Pernicano's also offers a number of contemporary, lighter offerings. Pizzas probably remain the pride of the house, however, and these are honest, well-arranged pies, based on supple crusts and tasting of old-fashioned goodness.

Address: 9988 Scripps Ranch Blvd • Hillcrest
Phone: (619) 271-5250
Dinner Hours: 7 Days a Week 4 – 9

Italian - Piatti

A smash hit from the day it opened, this hip Italian house in La Jolla Shores pleases with sharp, attentive service and a whimsical decor dominated by walls painted with depictions of various foods — most of them related directly to Italian cuisine, of course. The place can be noisy at times, especially when the open kitchen is operating at full bore. Unusual specialties include flattened chicken grilled under a brick — the result is exceptionally tender and moist — and the pastas generally are laudable. As is true of most contemporary-style Italian eateries in San Diego, Piatti also serves elegant, supremely appetizing pizzas.

Address: 2182 Avenida de la Playa • La Jolla • Call for Additional Locations
Phone: (619) 454-1589
Dinner Hours: Mon – Fri until 10, Sat – Sun until 11

Italian - Prego   see pg. 250

There are dozens of ways to interpret the word "prego" (a courtesy term that combines "please" and "thank you" and a good bit more in its meaning), but San Diegans tend to think of it as synonymous with fine Italian dining. This large, villa-like restaurant in Mission Valley puts its attractions up front where guests can see them, in an open kitchen that displays rotisseries laden with gilded meats, and in cases filled with clever antipasti and sweet fantasies of desserts. Chef Nicola Calamari (his name suggests at least one menu option) prepares a cuisine that runs from a Napoleon-like arrangement of grilled eggplant and other elements to lobster agnolotti, elegant pizzas and pork chops basted with musky vinegar. This restaurant sponsors wine dinners and occasionally hosts a "Cigar Club" dinner.

Address: 1370 Frazee Rd • Mission Valley
Phone: (619) 294-4700
Dinner Hours: Sun 4 – 10, Mon until 10:30, Tues – Thurs until 11, Fri – Sat until 12

Salvatore Gangale runs the front of the house while his wife, Raffaella, supervises the kitchen of this superlative Italian restaurant located on the ground floor of downtown San Diego's Meridian condominium tower. The setting is formal and notably elegant, the service polite and prompt but not at all stiff. The menu sets the place apart, since relatively few of the dishes it presents are available elsewhere, and those that are — such as a particularly moist and rich version of lasagna — are done with special style. Grilled fish perhaps never tasted quite so good as the olive oil-and-lemon basted swordfish, and there is a wonderful play of flavors in the salad of wild mushrooms, pungent greens and Taleggio cheese.

Address: 750 Front St • Downtown
Phone: (619) 544-1865
Dinner Hours: 7 Days a Week 5 – 10

One of the delights of this somewhat formal, decidedly elegant La Jolla restaurant is the number of seating venues it offers guests. For those who truly wish to see and be seen, there is a gracious dining room furnished in considerable style, but there are also a pair of sidewalk patios that are perfect at all hours, as well as courtyard tables and a few tables (these may be best of all) tucked into the tiny, New York-style bar. The service is top-notch, which is to say that it nicely matches a menu that ranges from classic Italian antipasti to flavorful soups, crisp, bitter salads and wonderfully well-composed pastas (the fresh fettuccine in forest mushroom sauce is particularly wonderful). This menu also offers game, excellent veal dishes and such fine seafood as genuine scampi and beautifully fresh fish.

Address: 7811 Herschel Ave • La Jolla
Phone: (619) 454-1315
Dinner Hours: Sun – Thurs 5 – 10:30, Fri – Sat 5 – 11

Italian - Scalini

Scalini

During the racing season, this attractive, second-floor restaurant seems to burst with well-dressed fans from the nearby Del Mar racetrack. All the rest of the year, the casually elegant crowd is drawn from the nearby coastal towns and from exclusive Rancho Santa Fe. Everyone seems to come for the same reasons: attentive service, a soothing decor, and a menu of light, imaginative Italian fare. Scalini does a particularly fine job with its antipasto selection, which always includes numerous pungent vegetable offerings as well as meat and fish salads and other tongue-teasers. The pastas also are superb, and if one is in the mood for veal, Scalini is the place to go.

Address: 3790 Via de la Valle • Del Mar
Phone: (619) 259-9944
Dinner Hours: Sun – Thurs 5:30 – 10, Fri – Sat 5:30 – 11

Italian - Sfuzzi

SFUZZI
An Italian Bistro

A chain restaurant that seems entirely local, Sfuzzi has two San Diego locations, each decorated in a whimsical style that draws upon both ancient times and local motifs. Both places have considerable appeal for the younger crowd, especially in the bar areas, where "Frozen Sfuzzi Un-Bellini-Able" cocktails are dispensed, but the Italian menus have broad appeal that crosses generational lines. Italian cooking goes in a thousand directions, but Sfuzzi generally likes it rustic and hearty, as emphasized by such offerings as the Tuscan white bean soup with rosemary, and the winning grilled beef tenderloin with black pepper-Chianti sauce and garlic mashed potatoes. Pizzas and pastas also please.

Address: 340 Fifth Ave • Gaslamp Quarter • Call for Additional Locations
Phone: (619) 231-2323
Dinner Hours: Sun – Thurs 5 – 10, Fri – Sat 5 – 12

Sirino's RESTAURANT The latest creation of the extremely talented French chef Vincent Grumel, Sirino's is without question the finest restaurant in Escondido. Although Grumel excels with French cuisine — he was private chef to one French president — he acknowledges contemporary tastes on his menu by including primarily Italian offerings. These are done authentically, but with Grumel's sure hand, and one can sense the French boldness with seasoning in the suave marinara sauce and other dishes. The room is small but pleasant, and the service notably professional; prices are more than reasonable, especially given the quality. Grumel sneaked a few Gallic creations onto the menu, including roast duck in honey-lime sauce and sauteed salmon in creamy Champagne sauce.

Address: 113 West Grand Ave • Escondido
Phone: (619) 745-3835
Dinner Hours: Tues – Sat 3:30 – 10

This restaurant has the comfortable, easy-going feel of a neighborhood establishment, although the look is considerably more sophisticated and the menu is of such quality that patrons regularly drive over from La Jolla and other relatively distant points. The chief attraction is a culinary outlook that holds that such prosaics as pizza and spaghetti can share a menu with such wonderful offerings as fresh tortellini in porcini mushroom sauce, and veal cutlets crowned with eggplant and ham. The pizza oven works its wonders too, especially with such creations as the calzone Monte Carlo, (folded dough stuffed with cheeses, roasted pine nuts and sundried tomatoes).

Address: 4724 Clairemont Mesa Blvd • Clairemont
Phone: (619) 483-1811
Dinner Hours: Mon – Fri 4:30 – 9:30, Sat – Sun 4:30 – 10:30

Ꭶtefano's   A long-running favorite at the Hillcrest end of the
CUCINA ITALIANA   Fifth Avenue restaurant row, Stefano's has maintained the steady loyalty of guests by offering quality pastas and other
Italian fare at advantageous prices. The small downstairs room is popular;
cognoscenti find the quarters upstairs rather more spacious. In either
venue, the mood is lively and the service quite good. One popular feature
is the option that allows diners to order most dishes a la carte or, for a bit
more, as part of a full-course dinner. Pastas are sauced with authority here
and the cuisine in general can be said to maintain very high standards.

Address: 3671 Fifth Ave • Hillcrest
Phone: (619) 296-0975
Dinner Hours: Sun – Thurs 5 – 9, Fri – Sat 5 – 10:30

TRATTORIA   The new creation of youthful but notably talented restaurateur
              Michael McGeath (Fio's in the Gaslamp Quarter stands as a
              monument to his efforts), Trattoria Acqua occupies quarters in La
              Jolla's richly view-endowed Coast Walk. The staff, intensely
ACQUA   trained, is as enjoyable as the light-hearted decor of murals and
         bright fabrics. Chef Joseph Savino has expanded the primarily
Italian menu to encompass other Mediterranean cuisines, so that fried
calamari are offered with fiery Moroccan harissa sauce, and roasted Japanese
eggplant are stuffed with creamy goat cheese. Pizzas arrive bubbling from a
wood-fired oven, and are crowned with cleverly arranged toppings; there are
also pastas, and such outstanding entrees as butter-tender osso bucco.

Address: 1298 Prospect St • La Jolla
Phone: (619) 454-0709
Dinner Hours: 7 Days a Week 5 – 11

Consistently among the most popular restaurants in the Gaslamp Quarter, Trattoria La Strada attracts crowds not only with a menu of updated, generally light-style Italian dishes, but with an unusually hip environment. The restaurant takes full advantage of its busy corner location by featuring huge windows that look onto both Fifth Avenue and G Street, and thus guarantee full viewing privileges of the ever-changing street scene. The clientele tends towards the young and trendy, as does the polished service staff. The menu makes much of carpaccios and salads and offers a fine range of pastas, but the excellent, beautifully crusted pizzas should not be overlooked.

Address: 702 Fifth Ave • Gaslamp Quarter
Phone: (619) 239-3400
Dinner Hours: 7 Days a Week 5:30 – 1 a.m.

To briefly paraphrase Tolstoy, every Italian restaurant is different in its own way. Trattoria Mannino, a tiny and quite beautifully decorated restaurant in the Bird Rock district of La Jolla, veers from the usual by serving a menu in which most dishes bear a distinctive stamp. There is, for example, the spigola fra'diavolo, which features one of San Diego's favorite fish — sea bass — but finishes it in a stunning, delightfully hot tomato sauce. This may be the best bass in town. The pastas similarly go off in directions quite their own (an orange cream sauce dresses veal stuffed ravioli), and among the appetizers, the sauteed baby artichokes are a locally hard-to-find rendition of a beloved Italian classic.

Address: 5662 La Jolla Blvd • La Jolla
Phone: (619) 551-8610
Dinner Hours: 7 Days a Week 5 – 10

TUSCANY
the art of Italian dining

This fairly new establishment provided exactly what the pricy La Costa area lacked, a top-quality Italian house that features a stylish and varied menu. Since the cuisine is, to a degree, inspired by that of Tuscany, the decor also looks to that richly beautiful region of Italy. The cooking is expert and highly satisfying, and options run from simple but remarkably well-composed salads to crisp, handsomely garnished pizzas and nicely sauced pastas. The osso bucco served here is among the best in the county; simply put, Tuscany has an excellent kitchen. The service only adds to the pleasure of a dinner enjoyed in this most pleasant environment.

Address: 6981 El Camino Real • La Costa
Phone: (619) 929-8111
Dinner Hours: 7 Days a Week 4 – 11

tutto•mare

In a city that virtually makes a religion of seafood, Tutto Mare ("All the Sea") caters to this taste by offering a vast assortment of sea creatures cooked and sauced in the Italian manner. The dining room — long, low and glamorously lighted — curves around an immense display kitchen in which a good deal of the work takes place; the well-trained servers do their bit by undertaking such tasks as boning entire, roasted soles at table. This is one of the few restaurants to offer fish carpaccio, which could be considered the Italian answer to sushi. There are also elegant salads, a seafood risotto that bursts with briny flavors, and such specialties as grilled freshwater prawns and pasta with Maine lobster in spicy tomato sauce.

Address: 4365 Executive Dr • Golden Triangle
Phone: (619) 597-1188
Dinner Hours: Sun 5 – 10, Mon until 10:30, Tues – Thurs until 11, Fri – Sat 5 – 12

Italian - Valentino's

Named for the famous lover of the silent film era, this comfortable restaurant also features a low-lighted, romantic decor. The menu runs to considerable length and gives equal attention to pasta and to such formal entrees as chicken breasts in nearly a dozen guises, and veal in a zesty pizzaiola sauce. Seafood also is given considerable attention here, and options include scampi sauteed in white wine, and a cioppino of assorted shellfish. Among the pastas, such offerings as the tortellini carbonara and linguine with spicy shrimp fra diavolo make particularly happy choices.

Address: 11828 Rancho Bernardo Rd • Rancho Bernardo
Phone: (619) 451-3200
Dinner Hours: Mon – Thurs 5 – 9, Fri – Sat 5 – 10

Italian - Villani's

San Diego has so many Italian restaurants that it sometimes seems difficult to sort them all out; Villani's is memorable for a good standard of cuisine and for a spacious perch high above the rushing traffic of Interstate 8. Dinner here can, in fact, seem a bit like taking a trip, thanks to the endlessly passing caravan below; the flavors of the meal, meanwhile, suggest a vacation in Italy. In a city in which every restaurant serves Caesar salad, Villani's serves a notable version, and such offerings as the seafood fettuccine, veal saltimbocca and beef tournedos in shiitake mushroom sauce all are excellent.

Address: Regency Plaza Hotel • 1515 Hotel Cir South • Mission Valley
Phone: (619) 293-0550
Dinner Hours: 7 Days a Week 5 – 11

Italian - When In Rome Restaurant

WHEN IN ROME...
RESTAURANT

Now comfortably established on the North County coastal dining scene, When In Rome was the first truly sophisticated Italian restaurant to open in the area; the response was immediate and remains enthusiastic today. The setting, in a high-ceilinged, broad-windowed room, is gracious and relaxed, the service prompt and attentive. It is the menu that pleases most, however; opening courses are light and appetizing, and pastas are prepared with unusual flair — the spicy penne alla vodka remains a perennial favorite. The kitchen also has a fine hand with veal and chicken preparations, and the desserts are complex and ravishing.

Address: 1108 First St • Encinitas
Phone: (619) 944-1771
Dinner Hours: Sun 5 – 9, Tues – Sat 5:30 – 9:30

Japanese - Benihana of Tokyo

BENIHANA

Every American city of any size — especially those that are tourist destinations, as San Diego certainly is — boasts a minimum of one Benihana of Tokyo outlet. Founded in Japan during the time of the Tokyo Olympics, this restaurant chain created the flashy style of cooking for which it is internationally famed. Multi-course meals of chicken, steak and seafood are served at grill-tables by chefs who put on a show as they cook — knives are wielded in a manner both daring and cavalier, and bits of cooked food often are flipped some distance on to diners plates. The performances amuse, but beyond this, the flavors are typically Japanese and generally very good.

Address: 477 Camino Del Rio South • Mission Valley
Phone: (619) 298-4666
Dinner Hours: Sun – Thurs 5 – 10, Fri – Sat 5 – 11

Japanese - Kabuki Japanese Restaurant

This restaurant is one of those little jewels that good fortune may lead you to stumble upon; located in an out-of-the-way spot, it is not hard to find, but it is not all that readily noticed either. Although small, Kabuki does offer pleasant, attractive decor in both the tiny sushi bar and in the dining room; service is gracious and efficient. The menu pleases very much with the broad selection of well-prepared, traditional Japanese offerings; there is nothing notably unusual here, but everything can be said to be quite flavorful. The sushi bar also turns out excellent products, including such house specialties as the pricy but rewardingly lavish Kabuki roll.

Address: 608 Crouch St • Oceanside
Phone: (619) 721-2915
Dinner Hours: 7 Days a Week 5 – 10

Japanese - Shien of Osaka   see pg. 270

Shien of Osaka

Everybody seems to be opening branches these days, even foreign restaurant chains; this cozy, traditionally decorated establishment in Rancho Bernardo is part of a well-regarded restaurant group in Japan. The sushi bar turns out a long list of popular favorites and house specialties, and the freshness and quality are beyond reproach. What sets this menu particularly apart is the presence of dishes that rarely appear on local menus; among these would be such appetizers as the yamakake, or mountain yams with tuna, and the oroshi soba, a subtly decorated bowl of noodles. Such standards as tempura and teriyaki are prepared with considerable care.

Address: 16769 Bernardo Center Dr, #K-11 • Rancho Bernardo
Phone: (619) 451-0074
Dinner Hours: Mon – Sat 5 – 9:30

TENGU

San Diego, for some reason, is not overly endowed with full-service Japanese restaurants, but one that has maintained its popularity for years is this well-decorated, very comfortable establishment. The restaurant takes its name from Tengu, a long-nosed character in traditional Japanese theater, and the decor is dominated by a reproduction of this fierce-looking fellow. Menu possibilities range endlessly from first-rate sushi to teriyakis, tempuras, sukiyakis and all the other favorite dishes of Japanese cuisine; the quality of the cooking seems consistently high.

Address: 8690 Aero Dr • Kearny Mesa
Phone: (619) 292-0141
Dinner Hours: Mon – Fri 5 – 10, Sat – Sun 5 – 11

Latin American - Berta's Latin American Restaurant see pg. 138

Berta's

Mexican cuisine rules San Diego so thoroughly that there seems little room for other Latin cuisines, and, indeed, few have ventured into the market. Berta's, a tiny but delightful restaurant in Old Town, takes up the slack quite by itself, through the agency of a pan-Latin menu that features national dishes from as far north as Mexico and as far south as Argentina and Chile. Most of the countries in between also are represented by a rewarding, very well-cooked selection of dishes that offers Guatemalan pork casserole, Argentinean marinated steak and Brazilian pasta in peanut-coconut sauce. All these are good, but best of all is the exotic and wonderfully savory pastel de choclo, a Chilean casserole of highly seasoned minced beef topped with sweet corn souffle.

Address: 3928 Twiggs St • Old Town
Phone: (619) 295-2343
Dinner Hours: 7 Days a Week until 10

Sally's

The Hyatt Regency hotel chain noted growing consumer resistance to hotel dining rooms, and thus built this excellent restaurant next door to the gleaming new Hyatt Regency San Diego tower. The bayside location offers grand views, and the menu of chef Fabrice Poigin presents grand tastes of Spanish- and French-Mediterranean cuisine. San Diego likes seafood, a taste to which Poigin caters with perhaps the city's finest raw bar, as well as with more serious preparations such as Grenada-style paella, an oven-baked swordfish with a highly flavorful tomato-cucumber sauce, and an entire rock cod baked in a salt crust. Plates are arranged and painted to look like artworks, and indeed do appear the work of a master. This restaurant's decor is purposely less formal and stuffy than might be expected, and the service excels.

Address: Hyatt Regency San Diego • One Market Pl • Downtown
Phone: (619) 687-6080
Dinner Hours: Sun – Thurs 5:30 – 10, Fri – Sat 5:30 – 11

Mexican - Alfonso's

Alfonso's What Hotel La Valencia's restaurant's rooms are to dressy La Jolla occasions, Alfonso's is to everyday, informal dining. Several generations of La Jollans have come to treat this comfortable, brightly decorated Mexican eatery almost as a private club; the attractions extend beyond the lengthy menu of typical Mexican dishes to include large portions, moderate prices and pleasant, efficient service. The outdoor patio continues to rank as one of La Jolla's places to see and be seen — and many of those present will be observed dining on the house specialty, carne asada.

Address: 1251 Prospect St • La Jolla
Phone: (619) 454-2232
Dinner Hours: Mon – Thurs until 11, Fri – Sat until 12, Sun until 10

Mexican - Baja Beach Buffet & Cantina

A new entrant on the San Diego scene, this extremely informal eatery presents a relaxed, enjoyable atmosphere that attempts to recreate the laid-back mood common along the Baja California coast. The bar stocks a vast selection of tequilas and Mexican beers, including some unusual, hard-to-find brands. The kitchen, meanwhile, takes a modern, enlightened point of view that dictates a considerably reduced fat content in most foods; canola oil substitutes for lard, and all meats are grilled rather than fried. Specialties include tortilla soup; a unique, Baja-style lobster bisque; and soft tacos stuffed with a choice of chicken, carne asada, grilled mahi mahi or, as a vegetarian surprise, grilled eggplant.

Address: 7305 Clairemont Mesa Blvd • Clairemont
Phone: (619) 576-7009
Dinner Hours: 7 Days a Week until 11

Mexican - Carlos Murphy's   see pg. 152

An extremely popular chain with locations around San Diego County, Carlos Murphy's excels at offering typical Mexican fare at affordable prices. The menu makes it a favorite with families, and the atmosphere proves an equally strong draw for the younger set. These restaurants offer a full selection of the type of Mexican cuisine beloved in San Diego, from enchiladas that burst at the seams to rich chiles rellenos and other trans-border favorites. Salads and seafood also are given good attention here, and the cheerful decor and service make for pleasant, relaxed meals. Carlos Murphy's restaurants are known for their animated bar scenes.

Address: 3890 Twiggs • Old Town
Phone: (619) 260-0306
Dinner Hours: 7 Days a Week until 10

Mexican - Casa de Bandini Restaurant and Cantina

CASA DE BANDINI
MEXICAN RESTAURANT

One of several hugely popular establishments in San Diego's much-visited Old Town State Historic Park, Casa de Bandini is under the same management as the nearby Casa de Pico and Rancho El Nopal. Located in the venerable hacienda built by early San Diego settler Juan Bandini, the restaurant features carefully tended gardens, sparkling fountains and an attractive patio — which is the first choice of most guests, so make reservations or arrive early. The menu pays a reasonable amount of attention to seafood and otherwise concentrates on typical Mexican preparations. This is a good bet when in the neighborhood.

Address: Bazaar del Mundo • 2754 Calhoun St • Old Town
Phone: (619) 297-8211
Dinner Hours: Sun – Thurs until 9:00, Fri – Sat until 9:30

Mexican - Casa de Pico

CASA DE PICO
MEXICAN RESTAURANT

This immensely colorful restaurant occupies the focal point of Old Town's Bazaar del Mundo, a collection of shops dealing with crafts, artworks and other imports from Mexico and Central America. An extremely popular destination with visitors, this restaurant fills early and tends to stay full, but waits are usually not too bad — the efficient kitchen sends the meals out relatively quickly. The indoor dining rooms are attractive and comfortable, but by all means wait for one of the outdoor tables, since the courtyard is among the most attractive in town. The traditional Mexican menu includes all the usuals, plus such house specialties as tacos al pastor and the delicate pollo fundio.

Address: Bazaar del Mundo • 2754 Calhoun St • Old Town
Phone: (619) 296-3267
Dinner Hours: Sun – Thurs until 9:00, Fri – Sat until 9:30

El Tecolote
Mexican Restaurant

The creation of a large, culinarily talented family from Mexico City, El Tecolote is the only establishment with a center-of-town address to serve genuine regional Mexican fare. The several small rooms are decorated with an attractive collection of artifacts and artworks, and servers are prompt but gracious — as in Mexico, guests never feel hurried. The menu is the chief attraction, however, and although El Tecolote found over time that it had to yield to local tastes and offer such commonplaces as tacos and burritos, it is known much more for such items as cheese-filled cauliflower patties, beef tongue Veracruz-style and a really fine chicken in mole sauce.

Address: 6110 Friars Road West • Mission Valley
Phone: (619) 295-2087
Dinner Hours: Mon – Sat 4 – 10, Sun 4 – 9

Guadalajara Grill

Just the name of this large, popular Old Town establishment means "fun" to many loyal customers, who value this eatery as much for the lively mood as for the menu of traditional Mexican specialties. The interior reminds one of a Mexican village, and frequently the crowd is sufficiently animated to suggest a fiesta in progress. Imaginative house bar creations may help to foster this mood. The Mexican list is long and thorough-going, and notably strong in the appetizer and soup departments. The entree list similarly covers all the bases; fajitas made with a full selection of meats are a particular Guadalajara Grill favorite.

Address: 4105 Taylor St • Old Town
Phone: (619) 295-5111
Dinner Hours: 7 Days a Week 3 – 10

This small, modest restaurant in downtown Chula Vista serves a marvelous, regional Mexican menu that quite outshines any other such list in the county. The branch of a grander Tijuana establishment (one to which Tijuanans repair when they want food like mama used to make), La Fonda Roberto's offers dishes of which those accustomed to American style, two-taco-and-one-enchilada combination plates, may never have heard. This is the place to find crepes stuffed with cuitlacoche, a truffle-like fungus that grows on ears of corn; it also serves a darkly spicy chicken in mole poblana, and the triumphant filete Roberto's, a flat, pounded steak stuffed with tender nopalito cactus and dressed with a smoothly fiery chipotle sauce.

Address: 300 Third Ave • Chula Vista • Call for Additional Locations
Phone: (619) 585-3017
Dinner Hours: 7 Days a Week until 10

This large, immensely popular Coronado restaurant for years has been a home away from home for servicemen stationed on the peninsula's several Navy bases; the place also finds a following both among locals and among visitors to Coronado's many hotels. A traditional village decor that includes colorful murals, bright artifacts and thatch-roofed booths lends to this restaurant's attractions, as does warm, attentive service. Entertainment brightens the mood further on selected evenings. The menu offers a full survey of popular Mexican foods, all given authentic treatment and cooked with care; portions are meant to send guests home wondering if breakfast the next morning will be possible.

Address: 120 Orange Ave • Coronado
Phone: (619) 435-1822
Dinner Hours: 7 Days a Week 4 – 10

One of the few San Diego restaurants where guests line up patiently for tables even in the middle of the day, "Old Town Mex" (as it is locally known) packs 'em in for a simple reason: the flavors are authentic and the prices on the friendly side. Attractions include the display tortilla kitchen, from whence fresh breads issue constantly through the day and night; these are used for a multitude of purposes, among which is rolling up mouthfuls of the sizzling pork carnitas that have done so much to put Old Town Mexican Cafe on San Diego's culinary map. Despite the sometimes hectic pace, the servers perform with style; this restaurant also is known for feisty margaritas and a lively bar scene.

Address: 2489 San Diego Ave • Old Town
Phone: (619) 297-4330
Dinner Hours: 7 Days a Week until 11

PACHANGA

This Latin-themed restaurant claims that its name translates as "happy times," and without question, the decor and mood add up to a lively nightclub atmosphere. One of the most colorful establishments in the Gaslamp Quarter, Pachanga's wild look suggests a party in progress — which is usually the case in the upstairs discotheque. The menu makes a thorough survey of popular Mexican items, and adds such contemporary favorites as fajitas in a virtual rainbow of varieties; one Pachanga innovation is a platter of vegetable fajitas. Other house specialties add novelty to the menu. Despite the quick pace of the atmosphere, service is leisurely and gracious.

Address: 314 Fifth Ave • Gaslamp Quarter
Phone: (619) 235-4545
Dinner Hours: Sun – Thurs until 9:30, Fri – Sat until 11

PALENQUE
RESTAURANT

Although located in the middle of the busiest commercial strip in Pacific Beach, this unassuming restaurant is hard to notice, but well worth searching out. Walk inside and you feel much more in Mexico than in the United States; the decor mimics the interior of a tropical hut, but is quite comfortable for all that. Operated by a family from Acapulco, Palenque offers subtle, regional Mexican fare, and if it sometimes is fiery, it is hot in a way that really lets flavors sing out. Several specialty salads verge on the sublime, and there are soups of much richness and subtlety. Such spicy-delicious dishes as the tinga poblana are especially noteworthy.

Address: 1653 Garnet Ave • Pacific Beach
Phone: (619) 272-7816
Dinner Hours: Sun – Thurs 5 – 9, Fri – Sat 5 – 10

RANCHO el NOPAL
RESTAURANT &
CANTINA

Named for the tender cactuses from which Mexican cooks concoct excellent salads and other dishes, this new restaurant replaces Old Town's long-running Hamburguesa. The decor and atmosphere are designed to create the mood of the mid- to late-1880s, when several major, Mexican-owned ranches still operated in San Diego and were known for entertaining on an opulent scale. There is even a collection of historic sombreros, presumably the only collection of its kind in the area. The menu encompasses most popular Mexican snacks and entrees, but includes a "healthy dining" list as well.

Address: Bazaar del Mundo • 2754 Calhoun St • Old Town
Phone: (619) 295-0584
Dinner Hours: Sun – Thurs until 9:00, Fri – Sat until 9:30

The newest creation of noted restaurateur Paul Dobson, this comfortably casual eatery occupies a unique location alongside the curving tracks of the main San Diego Trolley station. The restaurant's theme, however, is dominated less by transportation than by coastal Mexico, which also gives direction to the menu. A bit of meat is available, but Santa Fe primarily offers seafood spiced with Mexican subtlety and piquancy, and is one of the few places on this side of the border that captures the true flavors of this exciting cuisine. The elegant seafood cocktails lead naturally into such substantial, enticing entrees as chile rellenos stuffed with scallops and shrimp, and fresh fish filets served in a variety of sauces.

Address: Broadway Cir • 600 W. Broadway Ste. 130 • Downtown
Phone: (619) 696-0043
Dinner Hours: 7 Days a Week 4 – 10

Mexican - Tony's Jacal

TONY'S JACAL

The several large, cheerful, family-style Mexican restaurants hidden on a back road in old Solana Beach have been popular for several generations, and show no signs of slowing down. Tony's Jacal may be the best of the lot, and is likeable as much for the lively atmosphere and friendly service as for the menu of traditional Mexican foods. Specialties include turkey tamales and carnitas, but, in general, everything tastes as it should, and the only caution that need be issued is that guests should not arrive without sharp appetites — Tony's believes firmly in heaped plates.

Address: 621 Valley Ave • Solana Beach
Phone: (619) 755-2274
Dinner Hours: Mon, Wed – Thurs 5 – 9:30, Fri – Sat 5 – 10, Sun 3 – 9:30

Middle Eastern - Khayyam Cuisine

Named for the famed Arab poet, this restaurant takes a rather poetic stance with the cooking of the Middle East. Flavors such as these are not offered elsewhere in the county, perhaps because of the emphasis on foods from the cuisine of Jordan, which simply is not well-known here. The decor mimics a beautiful Middle Eastern courtyard, while the plates suggest colorful fantasies from "One Thousand and One Arabian Nights". Especially good are such dishes as the upside-down curry of scallops, the spiced chicken wrapped in phyllo dough and the wonderful selection of baklava.

Address: 437 South Hwy 101, Ste 201 • Solana Beach
Phone: (619) 755-6343
Dinner Hours: Tues – Sun 5:30 – 10

Peruvian - Machupicchu Restaurant

Given the dominance of Mexican cooking in San Diego, other Latin cuisines have encountered difficulties in finding an audience. The Peruvian menu at the minuscule Machupicchu in Ocean Beach has charmed guests for years, however. The intimacy of the setting and the low prices no doubt contribute to the popularity, but the clear, fresh flavors of such dishes as the shrimp and fish ceviche would seem the major draw. The beef heart antichucos are strictly for aficionados of Peruvian cooking; everyone should enjoy the stewed chicken in nut sauce and the seco de cordero, a lamb stew flavor with cilantro and spices.

Address: 4755 Voltaire St • Ocean Beach
Phone: (619) 222-2656
Dinner Hours: Mon, Wed – Fri 5:30 – 9, Sat – Sun until 9:30

Pizza Plus - California Pizza Kitchen

This immensely popular chain is proliferating so quickly that one wonders if any corner of the county soon will be without its very own California Pizza Kitchen. The chain succeeds with a simple but rigorously observed formula that calls for a high-tech, contemporary decor to be combined with a family-friendly menu of clever salads, pizzas and pastas. If other eateries weren't taking the same approach, the menu would seem quite novel; as it is, the menu pleases with such items as Peking duck pizza, a "chopped salad" of meats, vegetables and greens, and pasta in everything from basic bolognese sauce to a Thai-style broth spiked with mint and spices.

Address: 437 South Hwy 101 • Solana Beach • Call for Additional Locations
Phone: (619) 793-0999
Dinner Hours: Mon – Thurs until 10, Fri – Sun until 11

Pizza Plus - Embers Wood-Fired Pizza

EMBERS
WOOD FIRED PIZZA

The newest creation of the dazzlingly successful Souplantation chain, Embers joins the hotly competitive pizza market with a menu based on California-style pies baked in intensely hot, wood-fired ovens. The mood of this establishment is casual and family-style, the colors are drawn from the bright palette of the Mediterranean and prices reflect the restaurant's something-for-everyone approach. The unusual menu is divided into five categories, including Italian, International and Southwestern, with salads, pizzas, and pastas unique to each included.

Address: 3924 West Point Loma Blvd • Sports Arena District
Phone: (619) 222-6877
Dinner Hours: Sun, Tues – Thurs until 9, Fri – Sat until 10

Pizza Plus - Pizza Nova

Pizza has become just a starting point for the inventive Pizza Nova mini-chain, which now offers such items as the "banana rama" dessert of mascarpone cheese, bananas and puffy pastry, and a "Ninja pizza" for kids. Decor varies among the three Pizza Nova locations, but it is safe to say that a mood of informality prevails at each; the service pleases. Because of the restaurant's self-designation as a purveyor of "California woodfired" pizzas, the menu generally takes a spicy, contemporary tone, and in addition to pizzas with such unusual toppings as bacon, lettuce, tomato and mayonnaise, there are a fine assortment of pastas, such interesting salads as a watercress-romaine pairing, and desserts that range from the simply rich to the Rockefeller rich.

Address: 5120 North Harbor Dr • Point Loma • Call for Additional Locations
Phone: (619) 226-0268
Dinner Hours: Sun – Thurs until 9:30, Fri – Sat until 10

Pizza Plus - Pizzeria Uno Restaurant & Bar   see pg. 248

The battle pitting thin-crust pizzas versus the Chicago-style, deep-dish version may rage on for all eternity, but San Diegans who frequent the city's two Pizzeria Uno locations already have signalled their allegiance to the rich, pie-like Windy City creation. As outlets of the Chicago establishment that claims to have invented the over-stuffed pizza, these eateries not only dish up wonderfully indulgent pies — topped with such house creations as a spinach-broccoli blend — but a full range of entree-sized salads as a sort of low-cal counterweight. These busy restaurants feature lively atmosphere, interesting decor and swift, professional service.

Address: 4465 Mission Blvd • Pacific Beach • Call for Additional Locations
Phone: (619) 483-4143
Dinner Hours: 7 Days a Week until 2 am

The expansion of this remarkable mini-chain from La Jolla to Del Mar and now to a location in the Gaslamp Quarter proves two things: that proprietor Sammy Ladeki has hit on the ultimate restaurant format, and that San Diegans know a bargain when they see one. Ladeki's thesis is simple enough — he offers tasty food in large portions at reasonable prices. San Diegans could ask for nothing more, so they keep asking for Sammy's supple-crusted designer pizzas, overflowing salads and clever pastas. This restaurant no longer is the only local establishment offering such (admittedly tasty) curiosities as Peking duck pizza and Thai shrimp linguine, but it does an excellent job with these, and with the menu in general.

Address: 702 Pearl St #D • La Jolla • Call for Additional Locations
Phone: (619) 456-5222
Dinner Hours: Sun – Thurs until 10, Fri – Sat until 11

Walk into this place with your eyes closed and you'll know you're in a Polish restaurant — the rich, garlicky scents of kielbasa sausage and hunter's stew that perfume the air are dead giveaways. Open your eyes and you'll swear you're in Chicago or Milwaukee; the decor reminds one exactly of cozy, happy, Polish neighborhood eateries in both these cities. Chef-proprietor Stella Zenkner cooks the old-fashioned way, with a deft touch and careful attention to detail that guarantees a crisp finish to the fine potato pancakes, and a piquant edge to the unusual — and tangy — dill pickle soup. This is not merely San Diego's sole Polish restaurant, but a fine spot for dinner by any measure.

Address: 14323 Penasquitos Dr • Rancho Penasquitos
Phone: (619) 672-3604
Dinner Hours: Sun 4 – 9, Tues – Thurs 5 – 9:30, Fri 5 – 10, Sat 4 – 10

Scandinavian - Dansk Restaurant

One of the few places that has the feel and appeal of an old-fashioned tea room, Dansk stands virtually alone in the county as a purveyor of Scandinavian fare. The La Mesa location is a natural, since the county's quiet but sizeable Scandinavian population seems to cluster in the area. Although fairly small and modest, the place exudes Old World charm, and while the menu offers numerous Danish and Swedish treats, it actually is rather broad and encompasses many American-style favorites as well.

Address: 8425 La Mesa Blvd • La Mesa
Phone: (619) 463-0640
Dinner Hours: Fri – Sat 5 – 9

Scandinavian - Särö Restaurant   see pg. 266

You have to speak Swedish to be able to pronounce the name of this stylish downtown restaurant, but you need merely appreciate the subtleties of Scandinavian cuisine to enjoy such Särö trademarks as the "toast skagen," a luxurious open sandwich of toast topped with dilled shrimp and golden caviar. The decor is Swedish modern, from the highly polished wooden floors to the intimate mezzanine, while the menu takes an international direction and includes Asian-inspired chicken dishes alongside the traditional Swedish meatballs and salmon baked in puff pastry. This is the only place in town to sample punsch, a unique and thoroughly wonderful Swedish beverage.

Address: 926 Broadway Cir • Downtown
Phone: (619) 232-7173
Dinner Hours: Mon – Sat 5 – 11

 Among the best-established and longest-running prestige restaurants in San Diego, Anthony's Star of the Sea is the flagship of the immensely popular, family-operated Anthony's chain of seafood eateries. The Star of the Sea is itself part of a complex that includes more modest Anthony's outlets. Located on the Embarcadero, and less than a stone's throw from the historic, iron-clad Star of India merchantman, this waterside restaurant serves elegant seafood presentations in a setting of considerable formality. Sole Admiral, a dish of some complication, remains a house specialty. And if abalone, increasingly rare and costly, is available anywhere in town, Anthony's usually will have it.

Address: 1360 North Harbor Dr • Downtown
Phone: (619) 232-7408
Dinner Hours: 7 Days a Week 5:30 – 10:30

 For more than a dozen years, this popular La Jolla restaurant has defied the odds of an off-street location to attract crowds night after night. The wonderful view of La Jolla doesn't hurt (the restaurant is located downstairs in the Coast Walk collection of boutiques), nor does the colorful, comfortable Hawaiian theme, which dresses the dining room in warm colors and specifies that servers be professional but friendly. The menu works wonders with salads and highly flavored, quite attractive appetizers; seafood receives close attention and is very well done. The massive desserts invite sharing.

Address: 1298 Prospect St • La Jolla
Phone: (619) 454-9587
Dinner Hours: Sun – Thurs 5:30 – 10, Fri – Sat 5 – 10:30

When the small, top-quality Fish Market chain opened its first San Diego County location in Del Mar, it marked something of a revolution in terms of local seafood houses. Now also located in a huge establishment on San Diego Bay, this restaurant chain offers menus that read like shopping lists of everything that swims or crawls beneath the waves. Preparations tend to be relatively simple, which suit such ultra-fresh seafood perfectly. In environments built to resemble the (admittedly comfortable) crew quarters of fishing vessels, guests enjoy raw shellfish, smoked fish, luxurious seafood cocktails, pasta specialties, seafood salads and a daily list of fresh fish, mostly broiled over mesquite, that can run to 20 and more choices. The mood at both restaurants is casual, and the service attentive and caring.

Address: 750 North Harbor Dr • Downtown • Call for Additional Locations
Phone: (619) 232-3474
Dinner Hours: Mon – Thurs until 9:30, Fri – Sat until 10:30

TOP OF THE MARKET

Located on the upper floor of downtown San Diego's cavernous The Fish Market, this formal restaurant looks over San Diego Bay and a passing parade of vessels ranging from kayaks to aircraft carriers. The list of seafood options is even more extensive than in the downstairs dining room, and preparations also are considerably more complex; selections run upwards to such extravagances as Beluga Malossal caviar. The menu, printed daily, offers dozens of interesting possibilities that usually include cioppino enriched with Dungeness crab; the pasta with lox is another favorite. The service matches the menu, and the wine list has been chosen with particular care to provide a galaxy of possible pairings with the fine seafood dishes.

Address: 750 North Harbor Dr • Downtown
Phone: (619) 234-4TOP
Dinner Hours: Mon – Thurs until 9:30, Fri – Sat until 10:30

Trendy restaurants generally have a far shorter shelf life than this chic outpost on the eastern edge of Del Mar, which announces in its name — cilantro is the favorite herb of both Mexico and the American Southwest — a culinary bent that interprets border cuisine in a contemporary manner. The look of the dining room invites silk shirts and stylishly tumbled coiffures, while the menu offers the option of dining either on a progression of clever appetizers or on such substantial fare as spit-roasted chicken with chipotle aioli and roasted garlic and peppers. In general, flavors are as bold as the restaurant's decor, and timid tastes should be checked at the door.

Address: 3702 Via de la Valle • Del Mar
Phone: (619) 259-8777
Dinner Hours: Sun – Thurs 5 – 10, Fri – Sat 5 – 10:30

The Del Mar Plaza offspring of the popular Cilantro's, Epazote offers what its parent restaurant cannot, a stunning view of the Pacific enjoyed from one of the nicest outdoor terraces in the county. Like Cilantro's, Epazote is named for one of the principal herbs in Mexican cooking, although the menu tends more towards the Southwestern in style. A hip gathering spot for the North County young, Epazote also offers serious food for the serious diner; serious bibbers will take a long look at the list of house Margaritas before deciding just which of these hand-shaken, perfectly composed beauties to order.

Address: 1555 Camino Del Mar • Del Mar
Phone: (619) 259-9966
Dinner Hours: Sun – Thurs 5 – 10, Fri – Sat 5 – 11

Named for the ceremonial rooms constructed inside Southwestern Indian pueblos, Kiva Grill purveys an unusually beautiful, contemporary Southwestern cuisine. The setting, warmly earth-toned and crowded with plantings, matches the style of the menu, while much excitement takes place in the display kitchen that opens along one side of the room. Tortillas are cooked fresh constantly and served hot with several excellent salsas, and are wonderful for scooping up bites of the superb queso fundido, a blend of cheese, chorizo sausage and salsa that servers mix. Elegant variations on Mexican themes supplement the Southwestern side of the menu, which offers a baked corn crepe torte and the shellfish-enriched pozole verde.

Address: 8970 University Center Lane • Golden Triangle
Phone: (619) 558-8600
Dinner Hours: Sun – Thurs 5 – 10, Fri – Sat 5 – 11

As the first restaurant in San Diego County to offer tapas, a term that encompasses a multitude of Spanish appetizers, La Gran Tapa occupies a special place on downtown San Diego's restaurant row. Enormously popular with guests bound for performances at both Symphony Hall and the Civic Theatre, this darkly paneled, artifact-decorated restaurant serves what could be called twin menus: one a long list of tapas, the other a survey of more substantial Spanish specialties. The cooking in both cases is quite up to par, and it must be added that the pleasure inherent in a meal made up of nothing but snacks can have special appeal on almost any occasion.

Address: 611 B St • Downtown
Phone: (619) 234-8272
Dinner Hours: 7 Days a Week until 11

An early favorite in the Gaslamp Quarter's restaurant sweep-stakes, Olé Madrid proved so popular with the younger crowd that it moved from smallish quarters to an immense, fancifully restored building on Fifth Avenue. The decor seems to take the surrealist approach of such painters as Picasso and Dali; in any case, there is much to keep the eye occupied. The mouth will be busy enough with a lengthy list of hot and cold tapas, or appetizers, which extends from the classic Spanish potato omelet called tortilla espanola, to tuna empanadas and calamari served swimming in their own ink. There is also an excellent selection of salads and hot entrees, and if you happen to like sangria, you can't go wrong with Olé Madrid's version.

Address: 755 Fifth Ave • Gaslamp Quarter
Phone: (619) 557-0146
Dinner Hours: Tues – Sat 5 – 11

Yo España
Café and Restaurant

This relatively new restaurant was precisely what Pacific Beach needed: a relaxed but stylish eatery that offers dining options ranging from light meals to snacks. Brightly colored murals add life to a scene that already seems lively enough, especially when the place is crowded; the servers handle their duties with wit and aplomb. The Spanish theme defines but does not limit the cuisine, which features numerous attractive specials. The tapas list is extensive, and allows guests to have a single snack as an accompaniment to a glass of wine, or to dine regally on a procession of these small, appetizing plates. Major productions include paella and juicy roast pork.

Address: 1050 Garnet Ave • Pacific Beach
Phone: (619) 274-0990
Dinner Hours: 7 days a Week 5:30 – 12

Thai - Five Star Thai Cuisine

The striking, contemporary decor at this excellent restaurant makes up for a location in a less-than-favorable stretch of Broadway. Fanciers of Thai cuisine agree that this is among the best San Diego has to offer, especially in terms of noodle dishes, curries and salads that combine sweet, salty and hot flavors. Be sure to inquire about specialties not listed on the menu, and also pay close attention to the daily chef's specials, since these can be quite exciting. Some Thai restaurants pay lip service to the concept of spicy-hot food, but this one takes the issue seriously, so don't order your food hotter than you really want it.

Address: 816 Broadway • Hillcrest • Call for Additional Locations
Phone: (619) 231-4408
Dinner Hours: Mon – Sat 5 – 9:30

Thai - Karinya Thai Cuisine see pg. 204

Before Karinya rolled into Pacific Beach, there was not a scrap of authentic Thai cuisine to be found in San Diego. This pleasant restaurant did more than set a culinary tone, however; opened by a Thai architect, it features an elegant, intricate decor that makes it one of the most attractive restaurants in the neighborhood and has inspired succeeding Thai eateries also to opt for highly stylish interiors. The cooking is delicate and subtle, and the flavors quite bright; Karinya moderates heat to suit, but one shouldn't be too conservative with the thermal units in such dishes as the beef Panang curry, a particularly flavorful preparation that shows this restaurant's skills to great advantage.

Address: 4475 Mission Blvd • Pacific Beach
Phone: (619) 270-5050
Dinner Hours: Mon – Sat 5:30 – 10, Sun 5:30 – 9:30

Thai - Royal Thai Cuisine

Part of a popular Southern California chain, Royal Thai serves the traditional foods of Thailand in a stylish environment in the heart of La Jolla's downtown "village." The food is spicy or mild according to the demands of the dish and the diner's mood, but if you specify a reasonable degree of heat, the kitchen will comply. Noodle dishes and soups are very well done, and the kitchen seems to have a particularly good handle on the preparation of squid — which can be very interesting when cooked according to the many imaginative Thai recipes.

Address: 737 Pearl St, #110 • La Jolla • Call for Additional Locations
Phone: (619) 456-2063
Dinner Hours: Sun – Thurs 5 – 10, Fri – Sat 5 – 11

Thai - Sala Thai

One of the better, neighborhood-style Thai restaurants, Sala Thai joins its peers in offering good service and a pleasant, cheerfully decorated environment. The menu presents a comprehensive survey of Thai cuisine, and the daily specials can feature some quite unexpected surprises — who, for example, would expect to find snails at a Thai eatery? Like most Thai establishments, this restaurant will moderate heat to suit diners' tastes, but if you do like it hot, try the bracing tom ka kai chicken soup, and the "Hot #1" curry with seafood.

Address: 6161 El Cajon Blvd • College District
Phone: (619) 229-9050
Dinner Hours: Mon – Sat until 10

Thai - Siam Restaurant

SIAM
●RESTAURANT●

To know Thai cuisine is to love it — at least if you're the fire-breathing type, as so many fans of this exciting cuisine happen to be. Siam will moderate the heat of any dish to suit, but chilies, used the right way, can bring out flavors in an almost magical way, as they do with such Siam specialties as the larbnauh, a wonderful ground beef salad, and the shrimp Panang curry. At the newer Siam on Midway Drive, the decor is comfortable but stylish; service at both establishments is attentive and caring.

Address: 3545 Midway Dr, Ste N • Sports Arena District • Call for Additional Locations
Phone: (619) 523-5203
Dinner Hours: Sun – Thurs 5 – 10, Fri – Sat 5 – 11

Thai - Spices Thai Cafe

Unquestionably the most stylish Thai restaurant along the North County coast, this also is one of the best to be found anywhere in San Diego County. The menu entices with such starters as larb kai, a spicy salad of minced chicken with fresh mint leaves and multiple seasonings, and the delicate stuffed dumplings. The menu offers an especially good selection of vegetarian dishes and noodle preparations, but excels with such unusual entrees as the sizzling Siamese spareribs and the choo-chee duck, a roasted bird dressed with a particularly aromatic curry sauce.

Address: 3810 Valley Center Dr, Ste 903 • Del Mar
Phone: (619) 259-0889
Dinner Hours: 7 Days a Week until 10

Á ĐÔNG Restaurant This could be considered the restaurant that popularized Vietnamese cuisine in San Diego, and one that continues to present authentic and exciting flavors. The neighborhood that surrounds A Dong has slipped somewhat, but the restaurant itself is comfortable and well-maintained, and service is prompt and attentive. As is common at Vietnamese restaurants, the menu is of nearly astonishing length and presents an encyclopedic compendium of Vietnamese dishes that may be daunting to Westerners. There is an easy way of dealing with this situation, however, by sticking primarily to the "specialties" page, which offers such delights as beef barbecued inside sheets of pig's caul, beef fondu, shrimp paste on sugar cane and crab shells stuffed with a mixture of spiced crabmeat.

Address: 3874 Fairmount Ave • East San Diego
Phone: (619) 298-4420
Dinner Hours: 7 Days a Week until 10

LE BAMBOU As perhaps the only formal Vietnamese restau-
RESTAURANT rant in the county, this long-established Del Mar
favorite serves in a setting of some style. Ameni-
ties that sometimes are ignored by local Asian restaurants, such as gracious service and a decent wine list, are very much available here. The cooking also is excellent, and the menu is sufficiently limited in its scope that the process of choosing a meal is relatively easy — and a definite pleasure. French refinements give distinction to many dishes, and the flavors tend to be subtle and elegant; Le Bambou could be said to practice a very fine cuisine.

Address: 2634 Del Mar Heights Rd • Del Mar
Phone: (619) 259-8138
Dinner Hours: Tues – Sun 5:30 – 9:30

Some restaurants feature elegant decor, but Phuong Trang is not among them. This small but busy eatery on Convoy Street's Asian restaurant row expends all its energies in one direction — the preparation of what many agree is some of the best Vietnamese cooking in San Diego. The exhaustive selection of dishes runs to more than 230 items; to read the menu thoroughly would require more time than most diners are willing to invest. A good tip, therefore, would be to spend most of your time perusing the appetizer and specials pages, upon which a good many of this restaurant's culinary gems will be found. The beef fondu, cooked by diners at table, is both tasty and fun to prepare.

Address: 4170 Convoy St • Kearny Mesa
Phone: (619) 565-6750
Dinner Hours: 7 Days a Week until 9:30

This may be the only San Diego restaurant to take the shape of a perfect cube, but otherwise, there is nothing square about Saigon Restaurant. Hip in the style of modern, booming Asia, the restaurant features wall-mounted video machines that boom out pop tunes and display lyrics for those inclined to sing along. Tables are set for action with canisters of chop sticks and piles of tiny dishes to hold the various (and mild to hot) chili sauces offered as optional dips. The menu covers all the Vietnamese bases, from beef noodle soups (there are 20 varieties) to steamed broken rice dishes, porridges, stir-fries and more. The specialties page offers exciting choices, notably the seven-course beef dinner.

Address: 4455 El Cajon Blvd • East San Diego
Phone: (619) 284-4215
Dinner Hours: 7 Days a Week until 11

94TH AERO SQUADRON
A RESTAURANT TO REMEMBER

Appetizers

CRAB STUFFED MUSHROOMS 6.95

POTATO SKINS 5.95

COMBINATION PLATTER 10.95
*Escargot, crab stuffed mushrooms with
zucchini, calamari and potato skins*

Entrees

*All entrees are served with fresh baked cracked wheat bread, soup or salad and your choice of
baked potato, rice pilaf, fresh vegetables or buttered noodles*

AUSTRALIAN LOBSTER TAIL
*Oven broiled and served with drawn butter
and lemon. Single or twin*
MARKET PRICE

COCONUT SHRIMP
*Coconut battered and deep fried. Served
with orange mustard horseradish sauce*
14.95

CHICKEN MEDITERRANEAN
*Grilled chicken breast with tomato basil
cream sauce and fresh vegetables*
12.95

CRAB STUFFED SHRIMP
*Jumbo shrimp, stuffed with crabmeat,
wrapped in bacon and broiled. Served with
beurre blanc sauce*
15.95

VEAL OSCAR
*Sauteed medallions of fresh veal topped with lump crabmeat,
asparagus and bearnaise sauce*
16.95

Combinations

FILET OR PRIME RIB AND SCAMPI
*Broiled filet mignon or prime rib with
jumbo scampi style shrimp*
17.95

FILET AND CRAB STUFFED SHRIMP
*Charbroiled filet mignon with our jumbo
crab stuffed shrimp with beurre blanc sauce*
17.95

FILET OR PRIME RIB AND AUSTRALIAN LOBSTER TAIL
*Charbroiled filet mignon or prime rib au jus with a broiled lobster tail.
Served with drawn butter and lemon*
MARKET PRICE

Pastas

Served with fresh homemade cracked wheat bread and your choice of soup or salad

SHRIMP AND SCALLOPS WITH BOWTIE PASTA
Shrimp and scallops tossed with bowtie pasta and fresh tomato basil sauce
14.95

PASTA CALIFORNIA
Fresh linguini sauteed in butter with fresh vegetables, herbs and garlic cream
9.95

Steaks and Prime Rib of Beef

All of our beef selections are U.S.D.A. Choice, midwest cornfed and aged to our specifications

Prime Rib of Beef, Au Jus

Slow roasted and served with creamed horseradish and au jus

Regular Cut 10 oz. 13.95   Large Cut 14 oz. 15.95   Commander's Cut 16 oz. 18.95

Broiled Steaks

Center cut and served with onion crisps

FILET MIGNON
The most tender cut of beef with bearnaise sauce
7 oz. **14.95**   10 oz. **16.95**

NEW YORK STRIP
The king of steaks
10 oz. **14.95**   14 oz. **16.95**

TOP SIRLOIN
Our most flavorful cut
12 oz. **14.95**

TERIYAKI TOP SIRLOIN
Our full flavor cut, charbroiled and basted with teriyaki sauce
12 oz. **14.95**

PORTERHOUSE STEAK
The best steak in town
20 oz. **19.95**

PEPPERCORN STEAK
Ten ounce New York steak seared with cracked black pepper, served over a sauce of brandy, cream, demi-glace and green peppercorn
15.95

N.Y. STEAK RICKENBACKER
Ten ounce New York steak pan fried and served with sauteed bell peppers, onions and mushrooms
15.95

DOUBLE PORK LOIN CHOPS
Twin center cuts, lightly breaded and pan fried with ginger apples
15.95

DOUBLE DOMESTIC LAMB CHOPS
Twin center cut loin chops marinated with rosemary, thyme and olive oil. Charbroiled and served with mint sauce
16.95

For additional information see page 24.

MEZETHES

The traditional *small plates of many tastes* served in Greece and all through the
Mediterranean as appetizers or light meals. We encourage sharing!

SAGANAKI
sauteed Kasseri cheese flamed at your table with Ouzo. Served with Greek bread   6.50

TARAMASALATA
creamy red caviar dip served with pita   small 4.95   large 6.95

MELIZANASALATA
*marinated grilled eggplant, tomato, red onion and pine nuts in
spicy Moroccan vinaigrette   4.39*

CALAMARI
deep fried squid served with red pepper mayo   7.50

LOUKANIKA AND MERGUEZ SAUSAGE
*charbroiled orange and cumin flavored Greek sausage along with spicy
Moroccan lamb sausage   6.50*

B'STILLA
*tender chicken and almond filling baked in a filo shell and topped with powdered sugar
and cinnamon. To be shared and eaten with your fingers Moroccan style   7.50*

ASSORTED MARINATED SALAD PLATE
*portions of eggplant salad, broad beans, tabouleh, cold dolmades, marinated artichoke
hearts and mushrooms   7.50*

SANDWICHES

GYROS IN PITA
*Our own blend of lamb and beef and spices, sliced off vertical rotisseries and
stacked on warm pita. Topped with onions and tomatoes, served with
Tzatziki sauce and red potatoes   6.75*

FALAFEL IN PITA
*middle eastern vegetarian patties on warm pita topped with marinated cucumbers,
lettuce and tomatoes. Served with sesame lemon sauce and red potatoes   6.25*

SALATAS

GREEK SALAD
Romaine topped with tomatoes, feta, olives, cucumber, onion and Aesop's vinaigrette
small 3.89   large 6.95

HORIATIKI
village salad with chunks of cucumber, bell pepper, tomato, feta, olives, artichoke hearts,
red onions and anchovy   small 4.25   large 7.25

GRILLED CHICKEN SALAD
charbroiled chicken breast served on Romaine with feta and toasted walnuts   7.75
substitute tuna for chicken   1.00

ENTREES

All entrees include your choice of Greek dinner salad or freshly made homestyle
soup and warm pita bread.

GYROS PLATE
a large portion of GYROS served on a dinner plate with pilaf,
tomatoes and onions   9.95

MOUSSAKA
the most requested dish from Greece. Layers of ground lamb and beef and tender
eggplant baked en casserole with a topping of bechamel sauce and freshly grated cheese
and a scoop of pilaf   11.95

DOLMADES
grape leaves with a meat and rice filling topped with egg lemon sauce and pilaf   9.95

ROAST LEG OF LAMB
slow roasted spiced leg of lamb served with red potatoes and vegetable   14.95

KOTOPITA DIJON
boneless breast of chicken sauteed with cream and dijon mustard, wrapped in filo pastry
with broccoli spears and baked   13.95

GRILLED SALMON IN GRAPE LEAVES
salmon filet in grape leaves, grilled, topped with a Mediterranean salsa.
Served with pilaf   13.95

VEGETARIAN COMBINATION PLATE
portions of hummos, tabouleh, falafel and spanakopita   10.95

PASTA AND "PITZA"

Pasta and "Pitza" is served with your choice of soup or salad.

SAUSAGE PITZA
spicy lamb sausage with feta cheese, artichoke hearts, walnuts and red onion   8.95
(may be prepared vegetarian with eggplant and zucchini)

CHICKEN PITZA
grilled chicken breast with basil pesto, red bell pepper, feta and kasseri cheese   8.95

PASTITSIO
rich casserole of seasoned ground lamb and macaroni, topped with bechamel sauce,
grated cheese and a special tomato sauce. With soup or salad   9.95

For additional information see page 75.

127

A L I Z É

Menu Changes Monthly

As a first course, we will serve you this week's selection of a specialty Appetizer from the Carribean Islands of Guadeloupe & Martinique enhanced by a touch of personality from our Chef Olivier.

You will as a second course have a choice of the Salade "Alizé" or a traditional Soup which your server will describe.

The third course is your choice of entree.
The fourth course will be your choice of dessert.

"Zouritte" $18.50

Sliced calamari sauteed with onion, a touch of saffron, garlic and a little ginger. From Reunion to the Mauritius Islands, Guadeloupe or Martinique, this divine recipe is prepared by all the gourmet chefs of the creole world.

Seabass Arachides $19.50

A filet of seabass brushed with a blend of grilled peanuts, carribean spices and a touch of soy   sauce and topped with laurel and thin slices of lime. This entree, baked wrapped in a corn husk, is another pride of the carribean cuisine.

Shrimp "Alizé" $20.50

Six large shrimp flambé in rum, then sauteed in fresh tomatoes, garlic, a touch of ginger, cilantro and a squeezed lime.

"Blaff" of Salmon $20.50

Filet of salmon marinated and simmered in lime juice with a blend of cracked pepper, spices, onion, garlic, white wine and thyme. Originally, the name "Blaff" was given to this recipe for the sound of the fish falling in the boiling water.

The Paladion • 777 Front Street, Ste 430 • Downtown • (619) 234-0411

BROCHETTE $21.⁵⁰
An assortment of marinated seabass, halibut and salmon, grilled with herbs and spices, served with a side of our three "Alizé" sauces. An avocado mayonnaise, a spicy tomato and a caribbean vinaigrette.

SEA SCALLOPS $22.⁵⁰
Seven large sea scallops served grilled with a sweet citrus sauce.

SWORDFISH GRILLED "LOLO" $25.⁵⁰
Six ounce filet of swordfish simply grilled with caribbean spices, the style for the fishermen of "Petit Havre" in Guadeloupe, served with a side of spicy caribbean vinaigrette.

LOBSTER "CLARA" $26.⁵⁰
One pound lobster simmered in light cream of lobster sauce with saffron and vegetables, the bouillabaisse of the islands!

CHICKEN AND SHRIMP "KARY" $18.⁵⁰
A chicken breast and a few small shrimp simmered in fresh tomatoes with garlic, a touch of ginger, cilantro, onions, spices and curry. Originally from Mauritius Islands, this recipe is now found everywhere in carribean cuisine.

BIFTEK A LA CREOLE $20.⁵⁰
Eight ounces of thinly sliced filet mignon marinated in a carribean dressing of olive oil, garlic, vinegar and spices then grilled and served topped with a small serving of curry flavored butter with parsley. This delicious recipe from the Lesser Antilles has probably been influenced by the cuisine of Venezuela, geographically very close.

LAMB LOIN "SAINTE ANNE" $21.⁵⁰
This recipe, named after the city of Sainte Anne, features a grilled filet of lamb loin served cut in medaillons over succulent tropical sauces.

RACK OF LAMB "CARAIBE" $26.⁵⁰
A rack of lamb stuffed with a blend of paprika, mustard, harissa, olive oil and spices, baked with a hint of aged rum.

ALL OF THE PRICES ABOVE INCLUDE APPETIZER, SALAD OR SOUP, YOUR CHOICE OF ENTREE AND YOUR CHOICE OF DESSERT. A FOUR COURSE MEAL, WE HOPE WILL BE A PLEASANT DISCOVERY OF THE FLAVORS AND SPICES OF THE FRENCH WEST INDIES.

For additional information see page 42.

THE ATOLL

Menu Changes Seasonally

Appetizers & Salads

Caesar Salad with Shaved Reggiano Parmesan $5.00

Lobster and Scallop Salad
Orange - Fennel Vinaigrette **$12.50**

Scottish Smoked Salmon
Arugula, Capers, Red Onions and Asiago Cheese **$9.25**

Spicy Crab Cakes
Lime Ginger Butter Sauce **$8.50**

Brazilian Style Seafood and Coconut Soup
with Lobster and Rock Shrimp **$7.50**

Salad Nicoise
*Freshly Broiled Ahi Served Rare over Green Beans,
Steamed Red Potatoes, Calamata Olives, Nicoise Style Dressing* **$9.50**

Pizza

Three Cheese Pizza
Ricotta, Mozzarella, and Gorgonzola Cheeses **$6.00**

Spanish Pizza
Smoked Chicken, Bell Peppers and Smoked Cheddar Cheese **$6.50**

Spicy Shrimp Pizza
Pesto, Chile Flakes, Tomato and Marinated Shrimp **$7.50**

Pasta

Linguini with Mussels, Shrimp and Scallops
in a Creamy Lobster Sauce   **$10.50**

Papaddela with Lamb Sausage, Santa Barbara Olives
Sundried Tomato Pesto   **$8.00**

Penne Pasta
Roasted Peppers, Sauteed Mushrooms, Asparagus and Garlic
in a Spicy Tomato Sauce   **$7.50**

Paella
Soft Shell Crab, Mussels and Sea Bass with
Risotto in a Saffron Broth   **$12.95**

Entrees

Pan Fried John Dory
Cool Rice Noodle Sesame Salad, Thai Flavor Dipping Sauce   **$18.00**

Grilled Opakapaka Mediterranean Style
Artichoke, Orange, Black Olives, Garlic and Basil   **$18.00**

Blackened Ahi on a Bed of Linguini
Roasted Peppers, Wild Mushroom - Balsamic Vinegar Sauce   **$17.00**

Seared Salmon
Fermented Black Beans and Braised Baby Bok Choy   **$17.00**

Grilled Swordfish with Curry Sauce
Topped with Plum, Apple, Ginger Chutney   **$17.00**

Grilled Chili Rubbed Beef Tenderloin, Corn and Pepper Sauce
Topped with Crispy Parsnip   **$19.00**

Sauteed Veal Scallopini with Tomatoes, Calamata Olives, Capers,
Garlic, Oregano and Feta Cheese   **$19.50**

Broiled Noisette of Lamb
on a Bed of White Beans with a Natural Sauce   **$18.50**

Roasted Half Chicken with Natural Rosemary Sauce
on a Bed of Wild Mushroom Risotto   **$16.00**

For additional information see page 25.

Menu Changes Seasonally

Starters

Baked Brie, Smoked Salmon & Walnut Pesto, wrapped in Puff Pastry - Nicely Garnished with the Freshest Available Berries 5.75

Camembert Garlic Caviar Fondue Served with Garlic Toast Tips .. 5.75

Pate Avalon - Appropriately Garnished 4.25

Chesapeake Crab Cakes - Served with a Dill Creme Fraiche 5.75

Eggplant Rollatini, stuffed with Mascarpone & Basil, baked with sauce Bechamel & Marinara ... 4.95

Russet Skins Stuffed with Avocado, Shrimp, Sharp Cheddar & Brie 4.95

Pastas

Linguine Rustico, Fresh Tomatoes, Roasted Garlic, Basil, Zucchini & Baby Peas 11.95

Fettuccini Fra Diaviolo with Taiwanese Lobster Tails 16.95

Homemade Cheese Ravioli in a Creamy Tomato Sauce with Prosciutto and Baby Peas 12.50

Ziti, tossed with Roasted Peppers, Gorgonzola, Olive Oil, Garlic, and Vodka 12.95

Fettuccine, Shrimp, Pistachio Pesto, Sun-Dried Tomatoes & Cream 13.95

Seafood Posillioppo with Linguini, Shrimp, Scallops, and Calamari sauteed in a light White Wine Tomato Sauce 14.95

Fettuccine with Scallops & Shrimp in a Light Alfredo Cream, Flavored with Dry Vermouth, Shallots & Fresh Thyme 14.95

Linguine White Clam with Sauteed Calamari, Capers, Olive Oil and Artichokes 14.95

Entrees

Served with House Salad

Pork Schnitzel Burgerstock, Onion Confit, Mashed Potatoes
and Sauerkraut.. 14.95

Top Sirloin - Sauteed Mushrooms with Rosemary Sweet butter &
Dickel Bourbon 15.95

Paula's Curry Chicken - Hot Chilies, Pineapple, Coconut Milk & Curry,
with Sour Plum Chutney 12.95

Hawaiian Ono - Brushed with Honey Mustard and Pine Nuts Pan
Jus Lie... 14.95

Monk Fish (Poor-mans Lobster) - Drawn Butter and Lemon 14.95

Beef Goulash with Buttered Sesame Noodles 13.95

Shrimp Parmesan with Home Made Cheese Ravioli 16.75

Chicken Parmesan with Penne Marinara 12.95

Swordfish Portofino Placed on a Bed of Julienne of Carrots, Peppers & Celery
Root, topped with Shrimp, Sauce Veloute & Lattice Potatoes.................. 16.95

Shrimp Panache - Sauteed with Lemon Butter, Garlic & Crushed
Chili Pasilla 14.95

Grilled Pork Chop Served with a Cassoulet of Black Beans Topped with
Avocado, Sharp Cheddar and Shredded Cabbage..................................... 12.95

Chicken Gismonda - Served with Mashed Potatoes, and Mushroom Gravy .. 12.95

Grilled New York Sirloin - Accompanied with a Lime, Cilantro,
Garlic, & Chili Ancho Relish 14.95

Jumbo Gulf Shrimp & East Coast Scallops, surrounded by Potato Puree
held in a Fortress of Light Puff Pastry, Sauce Americaine 15.95

Herbed Roast Chicken, French Fries 12.95

Fish & Chips Avalon, Confetti Slaw 12.95

Grilled Marinated Chicken Breasts, topped with hot Cherry Peppers,
Lime, and Avocado 12.95

Broiled White Fish basted with Olive Oil, Lemon and Tarragon,
Beurre Blanc 12.50

Dessert Selection   2.95

For additional information see page 50.

Avanti

Menu Changes Seasonally

Le Ostriche Fresche   **$9.95**
Fresh Oysters from Fanny Bay, Wash. You can have them in the raw,
or Rockefeller, fresh spinach, a touch of Pernod and Hollandaise sauce.

Mozzarella e Pomodori con Basilico   **$5.95**

Prosciutto di Parma e Melone   **$6.95**
Imported Prosciutto wrapped around seasonal melon.

Carpaccio Avanti   **$7.95**
Black Angus sirloin, arugola, parmesan, mushrooms, extra virgin
olive oil. Served with a dijon mustard dipping.

****

Minestrone Milanese   **$3.50**
With a touch of pesto.

Insalata Di Franco   **$5.95**
Baby lettuce, red bell peppers, fresh mozzarella, onions, black olives,
fresh basil, extra virgin olive oil and balsamic vinaigrette.

Insalata di Arugola, Uova e Funghi   **$6.95**

****

Cappellini Pomodoro   **$10.95**
Angel hair pasta with fresh tomato, garlic, basil and extra virgin olive oil.

Tortellini Avanti   **$11.95**
Our creation, Spinach Tortellini in a walnut, mushroom and cream sauce.

Rigatoni Ai Quattro Formaggi $11.95
A creamy blend of Parmesano, Pecorino, Fontina and Gorgonzola.

Paglia e Fieno $11.95
Spinach and Egg Fettuccini with Ham, Peas, Parmesan cheese sauce.

Linguini Vongole $14.95
Fresh manila clams, white wine, parsley, garlic, extra virgin olive oil.

Fettuccine Pescatora $14.95
Rock shrimp, clams, mussels, fresh fish. Red or white sauce.

****

Quaglie alla Griglia con Risotto ai Porcini $16.95
Grilled quails served with Risotto with Wild Porcini Mushroom.

Pollo Valdostana $14.95
Breast of chicken stuffed with ham, spinach, fontina cheese.
Sliced and served with a light rosemary cream sauce.

****

Salmone Norvegese $18.95
Sautéed and served with a chardonnay dill cream sauce.

Scampi Alla Karina $18.95
Sautéed, served with a garlic butter white wine sauce over linguini.

****

Filetto di Bue al Pepe $22.00
Select choice, in a peppercorn Brandy sauce.

Ossobucco Milanese $21.00
Braised Veal Shank with vegetables in a traditional Northern
Italian recipe, served with Risotto.

Costolettine di Agnello alla Griglia $19.95
Grilled Baby Lamb chops brushed with olive oil and garlic,
grilled to perfection.

For additional information see page 79.

Baci Ristorante

Baci
Ristorante Italiano

Menu Changes Seasonally

Antipasti

Carpaccio di Manzo
*Filet Mignon, Dijon, olive oil,
parmesan cheese, garlic, capers*
$8.95

Lumache Alla Guido
*Escargot sauteed with pernod,
in the shell, garlic and butter*
$6.95

Prosciutto e Melone
Parma ham with melon
$7.95

Calamari Fritti
Fried Squid with house marinara
$6.50

Zuppa del Giorno
$3.00

Insalata

Caesar Salad
$4.95

Hearts of Palm
$4.95

Paste

Bucatini Matriciana
Tomatoes, Pancetta peppercorn, onions
$10.95

Cannelloni Bolognese
*Crepes stuffed with veal, parmesan
chicken, Besciamella*
$11.95

Penne Quattro Formaggi
*Gorgonzola, parmesan, fontina,
mozzarella, cream*
$11.95

Linguini Pescatore
*Linguini with tomatoes, seafood
clams, mussels, calamari*
$15.95

Linguini Zingarella
*Tips of veal, tomatoes,
mushrooms and peas*
$14.95

Tortellini con Presciutto
Sage, cream, parmesan
$13.95

1955 West Morena Blvd • Morena Boulevard District • (619) 275-2094

136

Vitello

Saltimbocca alla Romano
*Medallions of veal, prosciutto,
sage, white wine*
$16.95

Valdostana alla Baci
*Stuffed veal, cream cheese, prosciutto,
porcini, wine, cream*
$17.95

Lombata Porcini
Porcini, cognac, shallots, cream
Market Price

Veal Marsala
Mushrooms, Marsala wine, shallots
$16.95

Vitello Francese
*Veal sauteed with shallots,
artichokes and mushrooms, cream*
$16.95

Veal Parmigiana
*Tender veal cutlets sauteed with a blend
of Italian cheeses and marinara sauce*
$16.95

Veal Chop Lamberti
Broiled veal chop in a roasted garlic sauce
Market Price

Pollo

Pollo Toscano
*Baked chicken, gorgonzola, fontina,
prosciutto, sage, wine sauce*
$15.95

Chicken Rusticana
*Sauteed chicken, artichokes, mushrooms,
garlic, white wine*
$15.95

Pesce

Sea Bass Livornese
*A light tomato sauce, white wine,
capers, black olives*
$16.95

Calamari Marinara
Sauteed squid with marinara

Scampi Conca d'Oro
*White wine, garlic, olive oil,
mushrooms*
$18.95

Calamari Fritti
Fried squid
$14.95

Fish of the Day
Market Price

Carne (Meats)

Filet Mignon au cognac
Cognac, shallots, mushrooms, brandy
$23.95

New York Steak
Broiled to perfection
$21.95

For additional information see page 80.

Menu Changes Annually

TAPAS

Ensalada de Naranja
Green Sicilian olives, oranges, parsley, garlic and red onion $3.95

Tortilla a la Española
Traditional Spanish potatoes with eggs, onions and herbs,
sauteed in olive oil. With fresh tomato salsa... $2.95

Anticucho de Pollo
Chicken marinated with lemon and cayenne pepper with
garlic mayonnaise sauce $4.50

Empanadas de Queso
Chilean cheese turnovers $1.50

Colombian Tostones
Fried plantain banana flavored with fresh garlic $3.50

Spanish Pincho Moruno
Lamb marinated with garlic, parsley, oregano,
saffron, onion and black pepper $4.75

ENTREES

Spanish Paella
Valencia style! Seafood medley served on a bed of saffron rice,
cooked with wine, herbs, fish stock & Spanish chorizo.
Served with green salad $12.95

Venezuelan Arepas
A thick patty of masa harina with cheese, sauteed in butter, topped with
sour cream & red salsa. Served with black beans & green salad $7.50

Guatemalan Shrimp
Shrimp smothered in a spicy salsa made with baked tomato, Jalapeño,
green onion & garlic. Served with rice & green salad $9.95

Tallarines Vatapa
Pasta with Brazilian peanut coconut sauce made with ginger,
tomatoes & chiles. Served with green salad $7.95

Peruvian Red Snapper
Sauteed snapper with a touch of lemon vinaigrette. Served with
red potatoes, cabbage salad, & onions $9.50

Venezuelan Pavellon
Marinated strips of flank steak with fried plantain & fresh tomato salsa.
Served with black beans, rice & green salad $10.95

Bolivian Beef special
Tender, spicy marinated beef served with fresh Garlic Pasta
(tomato & onion topping) and green salad $9.50

Costa Rican Casado
Black beans & rice with sauteed bananas. Served with cabbage salad,
corn tortilla & tomato salsa.. $7.50

Chilean Pastel de Choclo
Fresh corn & beef pie with olives, raisins, hard-boiled eggs & onion.
Served with green salad $9.95

Guatemalan Chilimal
Traditional pork casserole with chiles, tomatoes, masa harina,
vegetables, coriander, clove, and annatto seed. Served with
red potatoes & green salad $9.50

Molé Poblano
Grilled chicken breast with spicy chile almond chocolate sauce.
Served with rice & green salad.. $10.50

Peruvian Pollo a la Huancaina
Grilled chicken breast with a spicy feta cheese sauce.
Served with rice & green salad... $9.75

Pollo en Chipotle
Grilled chicken breast with sauce of smoked jalapeños, cilantro &
tomatillos. Served with black beans, rice & green salad $9.75

Vatapa, Brazilian Seafood Especial!
A variety of seafood with tomatoes, peanuts, ginger, coconut &
chile sauce. Served with rice & green salad $12.95

Columbia Bandeja Paisa
Served with beef, plantain, rice,
pinto beans, Arepa, avocado & salad $12.95

For additional information see page 100.

𝕭𝖚𝖑𝖑𝖞'𝖘

LUNCHEON SPECIAL .... Ask waitress for Daily Selections
PRIME RIB Open Face Sandwich 8.95
MARINATED "NOONER" STEAK 7.50
NEW YORK STEAK SANDWICH Open Face 9.95
"BARBECUE" BEEF RIB BONES 5.95
BABY BACK RIBS .... FULL RACK .....13.95 .... HALF RACK ...9.50
FRENCH DIP SANDWICH 6.95
CALAMARI SANDWICH...5.95
CHICKEN BREAST SANDWICH 6.95
CHARBROILED CHICKEN One Breast 6.75
COLD CRACKED CRAB PLATE...9.95

All Lunch Entrees are Served with Your Choice of French Onion Soup, Soup du Jour or a Garden Salad, and
Your Choice of Rice Pilaf, Cottage Cheese, Sliced Tomatoes or Frech Fries. Cheese on Soup $1.00 extra.

EGGS & OMELETTES

STEAK AND EGGS 8 oz. New York 9.95
MARINATED STEAK & EGGS 7.95
BACON & EGGS 5.25
HAM & EGGS...5.25
ITALIAN SAUSAGE & EGGS...5.25
EGGS & POTATOES 4.25
OMELETTES: SPANISH .... 5.25   HAM & CHEESE.............5.50
                      CALIFORNIA .... 5.95   CRAB 6.50

All Egg Dishes include 3 Eggs Served with Home Fried Potatoes,
Choice of Hot Muffin, English Muffins, Sourdough, Wheat or Rye Toast

SALADS

CHEF'S SALAD....................... 5.50   CAESAR SALAD Ala Carte 4.50
CHICKEN BREAST SALAD ... 6.25   CHICKEN CAESAR............... 7.95
CRAB SALAD.......................... 6.75   Choice of Broiled or Cajun. Served with Garlic Bread
           SHRIMP CAESAR 8.95
           Choice of Broiled or Cajun. Served with Garlic Bread

---

FRENCH ONION SOUP 4.25
Served with Thick Toast and Mozzarella Cheese and Small Green Salad
SOUP DU JOUR 4.25
Served with Thick Toast and Small Green Salad
SANDWICH OF THE DAY 5.75
with Soup or Salad (With Fries, Add .75)

DINNER MENU

All Dinner Entrees are Served with Your Choice of Homemade French Onion Soup or Soup du Jour or a
Garden Salad, Fresh Baked Bread and Your Choice of Baked Potato, French Fries, Rice Pilaf or Spanish Rice.

APPETIZERS

GARLIC BREAD	1.50	PEEL AND EAT SHRIMP	6.95
CALAMARI STRIPS	4.95	SAUTEED MUSHROOMS	4.25
STEAMED ARTICHOKE	3.95	CHICKEN FINGERS	5.50

CRAB STUFFED MUSHROOMS..........6.50

SALADS

CAESAR SALAD	4.50	SHRIMP CAESAR	8.95
CAESAR SALAD In Place of	2.50	Choice of Broiled or Cajun. Served with Garlic Bread	
Soup or Salad with Dinner		CHICKEN CAESAR	7.95
		Choice of Broiled or Cajun. Served with Garlic Bread	

PRIME RIB - STEAKS - RIBS

BULLY'S PRIME RIB (FULL CUT) 17.95
BULLY'S PRIME RIB (FULL CUT For Two) 19.95
   Includes Extra Salad, Baked Potatoe or French Fries or Rice Pilaf or Spanish Rice
BULLY'S PRIME RIB (HALF CUT) 12.95
PORTERHOUSE 16.95
FILET MIGNON 15.95
NEW YORK STEAK 15.95
TOP SIRLOIN 11.95
TERIYAKI TOP SIRLOIN 11.95
BABY BACK RIBS .... FULL RACK.....13.95 .... HALF RACK .. 9.50

COMBINATIONS

STEAK & LOBSTER	25.95	PRIME RIB & LOBSTER	26.95
STEAK & CRAB LEG	21.95	PRIME RIB & CRAB LEG	22.95
STEAK & SHRIMP	15.95	PRIME RIB & SHRIMP	16.95
CARNE ASADA &		HALF RACK BABY BACK RIBS &	
ENCHILADAS	9.95	B-B-Q CHICKEN BREAST...	12.95

SHELLFISH, FISH & CHICKEN

AUSTRALIAN LOBSTER - 1 Tail .... MARKET PRICE
ALASKAN KING CRAB 20.95
SHRIMP SCAMPI 13.95
BREAST OF CHICKEN (2) (Choice of Teriyaki or BBQ Sauce) 11.95
FRESH FISH OF THE DAY (Prepared with Choice of White Wine and Lemon or Garlic Butter)

SANDWICHES

BULLY-BURGER .... 5.75 ....WITH CHEESE 5.95
CHICKEN BREAST SANDWICH 7.50
FRENCH DIP SANDWICH 6.95
NEW YORK STEAK SANDWICH (Open Face) 9.95

For additional information see page 37.

Cafe Eleven

Appetizers

Cold

Smoked Salmon Smoked salmon with herb cheese,
  capers and toast points — $7.50

Carpaccio Thinly sliced tenderloin, cured in cognac and
  shallots with herb oil and capers — $5.75

Hot

Mussels Fresh mussels poached in white wine, garlic butter and basil — $6.95

Brie Cheese Brie cheese in a puffed pastry shell,
  served with fresh fruit and walnuts — $6.50

Pasta Sarah Fresh angel hair pasta tossed with smoked
  salmon, fresh dill, and cream — $6.50

Linguine LeVan Fresh Pasta tossed with olive oil, tomato,
  pine nuts, fresh basil, California chilies and grated parmesan — $6.95

Shrimp Rufel Shrimp and mushrooms sauteed with garlic,
  cream, herbs and sherry — $5.95

Entrées

Served with soup or salad

Filet of Beef Brittingham Filet mignon, rubbed with fresh
  garlic and thyme, served in a demiglacé, flavored with
  brandy and mushrooms — $15.95

Green Peppercorn Duck Long Island duck; roasted with apples
  and onions, served with a green and pink peppercorn sauce — $12.95

Lamb Chops Seasoned and pan fried, served with a dijon and
  horseradish créme fouettée — $16.95

1440 University Ave • Hillcrest • (619) 260-8023

142

Veal Sweetbreads Sautéed in olive oil, served in a port wine sauce
with black olives $13.95

Red Snapper Georgia With a light lime and tequilla cream
topped with toasted pecans $11.95

Pork Chops Two thick center-cut pork chops, broiled, then
crowned with spicy sweet and sour black cherry sauce $13.95

Chicken Julie Chicken breast topped with crabmeat, artichoke
hearts, and hollandaise sauce, then sprinkled with fresh dill $12.95

Chicken Eleven Chicken breast, stuffed with brie, Black Forest ham,
and black olives, topped by a light cream sauce, delicately flavored
with a hint of dijon mustard $11.95

Rack of Lamb Seasoned with fresh herbs, roasted and served
with Rosemary demiglacé $17.95

Chicken Wellington Chicken breast with spinach, buttered
almonds and herb cheese, wrapped in puff pastry and baked.
Served on a raspberry sauce $14.95

Patio Menu
Served 9pm to 11pm

House Cured Carpaccio of Filet Mignon served with
asparagus spears, olives, olive oil, Asiago cheese and
fresh lemon zest $8.95

Smoked Salmon Plate of herb cheese, hearts of palm, capers,
egg, red onion, and toast points $9.95

Country Cracked Black Pepper Paté with toast points,
capers, tomato, onions and olives $7.25

Chicken Caesar Salad of Romaine greens tossed with Caesar
dressing, grilled chicken, Asiago cheese and fresh croutons $10.95

New Zealand Mussels with lots of garlic, piquant herbs and
fresh tomato on angel hair pasta $11.95

Ravioli stuffed with Herbed Ricatta Cheese in a light lemon beurre
blanc with wilted spinach and pine nuts $7.95

Mushrooms a la Sheri stuffed with scallops, topped with
Swiss and Asiago cheese and broiled. Served with
house greens salad or soup $8.95

Seabass Crepes on braised fennel bulb with a sauce of cognac,
cream, garlic and lemon $11.95

For additional information see page 62.

Cafe Japengo

Menu Changes Seasonally

STARTERS

Grilled Teriyaki Chicken Skewers and Fried Maui Onions 6.75
Hot and Sour Tomatillo Soup with Crisp Tortillas, Creme Fraiche 4.75
Dry Marinated Seared Sea Scallop with Kimchee, Crisp Ginger 8.75
Grilled Sake Shrimp in Kataifi Crust, Melon-Mango Chutney 9.75
Curry Fried Calamari on Clear Noodles, Grapes,
Mint and Thai Lime Vinaigrette 7.75
Japengo Potstickers with Coriander-Mint Pesto 6.50
Roast Eggplant with Red Miso, Ground Chicken, Roasted Pinenuts 6.75
Spicy Grilled Pheasant Sausage on Cucumber Salad,
Smoked Tomato Mayonnaise 7.25
Warm Duck Salad on Tender Greens with Tart Apples,
Red Currant Vinaigrette 6.75
Seared Rare Ahi Napoleon, Crispy Wontons and Avocado, Wasabi Aioli 9.75
Mixed Baby Lettuce, Daikon Sprouts, Enoki Mushrooms,
Miso-Soy or Roast Shallot Vinaigrette 4.75

WOK

Ten Ingredient Fried Rice 15.95
Vegetarian Fried Rice 13.00
Thai Pork, Japanese Eggplant, Cabbage and Basil, Crisp Potatoes 14.75
Shrimp and Scallops with Dragon Noodles, Roast Peppers,
Shiitake Mushrooms, Black Sesame Butter 18.95
Alaskan Rock Shrimp with Roast Garlic, Daikon and
Tofu in Jungle Curry Sauce, Jasmine Rice 16.75

PACIFIC GRILL AND SPECIALTIES

Crisp Whole New Zealand Snapper Japonaise 19.75
Grilled Beef Filet on Wilted Spinach with Roast Pepper,
Garlic-Chili Mashed Potatoes, Chinese Black Bean-Sherry Sauce 24.00
Salmon in Ligh Sesame Crust, Tempura Mushrooms and Red Onions
on Arugula, Lemon Basil Vinaigrette 19.50
Grilled Swordfish with Wild Mushrooms, Smoked Bacon, Soy Beans,
Rich Herbal Broth 18.50
Chicken, Small Beans, Sun-Dried Tomatoes, Scallion Sticks, Gobo Root and
Herbed Potato Dumplings with Brown Vinegar Sauce 16.50

WOOD ROASTED OVEN

Slow Roasted Duckling with Crisp Vegetables,
Fresh Plum Sauce and Tortillas 17.95
Tamarind Glazed Grilled Lamb Chops, Roast Fennel and
Watercress Risotto, Natural Jus 23.00
Roast New Zealand Venison, Potato-Parsnip Cake, Braised Greens with
Coriander Seed, Merlot Sauce 21.75
Katsu Marinated Mahi Mahi, Grilled Rice Cake,
Woked Baby Bok Choy, Lemon Grass-Shallot Essence 16.95

ENDINGS

Banana Flan with Macadamia Nut Brittle 5.00
Orange Muscat Mousse, with Warm Peach Crisp, Chocolate Sauce 5.75
Sesame Macaroon Cookie with Mango Sorbet, Passion Fruit Coulis 5.50
Flourless Chocolate Bombe with Sour Cherry Ice Cream 5.50
Warm Apple Fritters, Ginger Sabayon, Plum Compote 5.50
Homemade Rich Ice Creams, Roasted Banana,
Cardamom, Toasted Coconut 4.00

For additional information see page 61.

CAFE LUNA

Menu Changes Seasonally

Dinner Menu

Antipasti

Marinate	Eggplant, zucchini & roasted peppers in a tangy vinaigrette	4.95
Caprese	Fresh tomatoes topped with buffalo mozzarella, extra virgin olive oil & fresh basil	4.95
Italiano	Mixed greens, sun-dried tomatoes, prosciutto, coppa, olives & cheese	6.95

Insalate

Della Casa	Mixed greens in a balsamic vinaigrette	1.95
Siciliano	Diced tomato, cucumber & onion in a light vinaigrette	2.95
Di Caesare	Classic Caesar salad (perfect for 2)	4.95
Di Spinaci	Fresh spinach leaves, egg, tomato in a honey bacon dressing	4.95

Pasta

Spaghetti di Nona	Spaghetti & Meatballs (Grandma really makes these)	9.95
Spaghetti Alla Norma	Tomato Sauce, eggplant, basil & mozzarella cheese	8.95
Lasagna	Layers of thin noodles baked in a bolognese sauce with mozzarella, bechamel & Parmesan	8.95

Penne All' Arrabbiata	Pasta tubes, fresh tomato sauce, garlic & chile peppers	8.95
Rigatoni alla Matriciana	Paste tubes, tomato sauce, pancetta, chile peppers	8.95
Tortellini Alla Panna	Cheese filled tomato, spinach & egg pasta in a light cream sauce	8.95
Fusilli Umbriaco	Spiral shaped pasta, tomato cream sauce, pancetta & a touch of vodka	9.95
Manicotti	Homemade crepes stuffed with ricotta cheese & spinach in a light tomato sauce & bechamel	8.95
Ravioli con Noci	Cheese and spinach stuffed noodles in a light cream sauce with ground walnuts	8.95
Capelli D' Angelo	Angel hair pasta, fresh tomato & basil	8.95
Capelli Alla Putanesca	Fresh tomato, black olives, capers, garlic & anchovies	9.95
Rosetta	Thin noodles rolled with ham, Swiss cheese and bechamel baked in a light cream sauce	9.95
Tris Della Casa	Sampler Plate (for the undecided)	10.95

Carni
~All meat dishes served with fresh pasta of the day~

Pollo Alla Griglia	Marinated in olive oil, lemon, garlic, white wine, fresh sage, & rosemary. Grilled to perfection.	10.95
Pollo De La Costa	Boneless breast of chicken sauteed in cream with mushrooms, onions, carrots, lemon and dijon	12.95
Pollo Marsala	Boneless breast of chicken sauteed in Marsala wine & cream topped with mozzarella	12.95
Veal Limone	Scallopini lightly floured, sauteed in butter & lemon	12.95
Veal Marsala	Scallopini sauted in Marsala wine, cream & mushrooms	13.95
Saltimbocca	Scallopini topped with prosciutto, mozzarella & sage in a burnt white wine sauce	14.95

For additional information see page 81.

CALDO POMODORO

Menu Changes Seasonally

Appetizers

Sicilian Style Sautéed Mushrooms $5.95
Branci's Shrimp Scampi (Tiger Shrimp) .... $7.95   Calamari $6.95
Side of 1 Meatball or 2 Sausages $2.50
Sicilian Style Pickled Veggies Salad (olives, carrots, celery, garbanzo beans,
    eggplant in Italian seasoning) 5.95

Complete Dinners served with Soup or Salad & Garlic Bread
Entrées Only served with Garlic Bread

Pastas

Choice of Pasta

Linguini • Angel Hair • Fettuccine • Penne Rigate

Choice of Homemade Sauce

	Entrées Only	Complete Dinner
Pasta Aglio & Olio (Garlic & Olive Oil) anchovies by request	$ 6.95	$ 8.95
Fresh Tomatoes, Basil, Garlic with Olive Oil & Capers	$ 7.95	$ 9.95
Pasta Gorgonzola & Broccoli (Cream Gorgonzola Cheese & Broccoli)	$ 7.95	$ 9.95
Pasta al Pesto (Fresh Basil, Garlic, Cream & Cheese	$ 7.95	$ 9.95
Branci's Mushroom Pasta (Mushrooms sautéed in Olive Oil, Garlic & Wine)	$ 7.95	$ 9.95
Pasta alla Puttanesce (Marinara Sauce, Garlic, Anchovies, Olives, Cheese, & Olive Oil)	$ 7.95	$ 9.95
Aribiata (Hot & Spicy Marinara Sauce, Cheese, Capers & Wine) over Penne Rigate	$ 7.95	$ 9.95

Branci's Cajun Corner

Served Over Your Choice of Pasta

Linguini • Angel Hair • Fettuccine • Penne Rigate
Medium Hot • Hot • Extra Hot

	Entrées Only	Complete Dinner
Shrimp Linguini (Tiger Shrimp sautéed in a Special Cajun Sauce over pasta)	$13.95	$15.95
Chicken Linguini (Sautéed in a Special Cajun Sauce over pasta)	$10.95	$12.95
Calamari Linguini (Sautéed in a Special Cajun Sauce over pasta)	$10.95	$12.95

148

House Specialities

	Entrées Only	Complete Dinner
Ravioli Alfredo (Pasta filled with Ricotta Cheese and covered with Cream Sauce)	$ 8.95	$10.95
Lasagna (Pasta layered with Ricotta and Mozzarella Cheese and covered with Tomato Sauce)	$ 8.95	$10.95
Sicilliani Style Sausage Peppers, Onions & Marinara Sauce over Pasta	$10.95	$12.95
Sicilian Style Eggplant Parmesan (Eggplant layered with cheese, breadcrumbs and marinara sauce, served with pasta)	$10.95	$12.95
Veal Piccata (Veal sautéed in olive oil, lemons, capers, & garlic served with pasta)	$12.95	$14.95
Sicilian Style Marinated Steak (Steak cut up into pieces and marinated in Italian seasoned sauce served with pasta and marinara sauce)	$12.95	$14.95

Seafood

Served Over Your Choice of Pasta
Linguini • Angel Hair • Fettuccine • Penne Rigate

	Entrées Only	Complete Dinner
Pescatore (Fresh clams, tiger shrimp, mussels, calamari and scallops sautéed in red, hot or spicy, or clear sauce)	$16.95	$18.95
Shrimp Piccata (Tiger Shrimp sautéed in a lemon, capers, & garlic sauce over pasta)	$13.95	$15.95
Shrimp Alfredo (Tiger Shrimp sautéed in white cream sauce & cheese over pasta)	$14.95	$16.95
Calamari Linguini (Calamari sautéed in a marinara sauce over pasta)	$10.95	$12.95
Fresh Clams and/or Mussels (Sautéed in red, Hot & Spicy or clear sauce)	$12.95	$14.95

Chicken

Served Over Your Choice of Pasta
Linguini • Angel Hair • Fettuccine • Penne Rigate

	Entrées Only	Complete Dinner
De Rita's Chicken Cacciatore (Chicken breast, onions, peppers, olives, mushrooms, Italian herbs & spices with marinara sauce over pasta)	$10.95	$12.95
Chicken De Lite (chicken sautéed with mushrooms, wine, soy sauce, oil, lemon & garlic over pasta)	$10.95	$12.95
Branci's Chicken Caldo Pomodoro (Chicken breast sautéed in Caldo's Hot & Spicy Marinara Sauce over pasta)	$10.95	$12.95

Specialty Pizzas

Pizza Palermo (Sundried Tomatoes, Calamatti Olives & Italian seasoning)		
Reg. or Hot	$ 9.95	$12.95
With Chicken	$10.95	$13.95
With Shrimp	$12.95	$15.95
Seafood Pizza (Calamari and Shrimp with marinara or hot & spicy sauce)	$13.95	$16.95
Cajun Chicken Pizza	$10.95	$13.95

For additional information see page 82.

California Cuisine
RESTAURANT & CATERING

Menu Changes Daily

APPETIZERS

tomato bean soup	3.50
curried oyster stew with wild rice, asparagus and pernod	4.00
grilled japanese eggplant with garlic goat cheese	4.50
pinenut crusted calamare steak with sesame-red bell pepper vinaigrette	5.00
fried polenta triangles of three cheeses and sun dried tomatoes with olive tapenade	4.75
black and white sesame seed seared ahi with hot and sour raspberry sauce	6.00
phyllo triangles of escargot, roasted garlic and fresh herb butter	5.00
new zealand greenlip mussels with saffron, tomatoes, garlic and white wine	6.00
quesadilla of smoked turkey & sonoma pepper jack with salsa fresca	5.00
snowcrab and shrimp chili relleno with black bean sauce and cilantro creme fraiche	6.00
crispy veal sweetbreads with wild mushroom duxelle and balsamico glaze	5.75
pork potstickers with plum dipping sauce	5.00

SALADS

california cuisine's warm chicken salad	8.50
caesar salad	5.00
winter greens with jicama, tomatoes and fresh herb vinaigrette	4.50

warm asparagus salad with montrachet crouton and vinaigrette
   of basil, roasted bell peppers, fennel and green peppercorns   5.75
wilted organic greens with apple wood smoked bacon,
   leeks and champagne vinaigrette   5.00

PASTAS
linguini with braised rabbit, sunflower sprouts,
   sugar snap peas & walnut brown butter   10.75
cappellini with seafood, crumbled feta, basil
   and extra virgin olive oil   11.75
penne primavera with sundried tomatoes   9.50
fettuccine with grilled chicken, roasted garlic, broccoli
   and extra virgin olive oil   11.75

ENTREES
breast of chicken stuffed with roasted bell peppers
   and feta cheese with jalapeno tsatsiki   13.50
grilled quails with baked butternut squash
   and nutmeg-maple marsala glaze   15.75
paprika grilled atlantic salmon with sherried
   pumpkin-garlic sauce and toasted pistachios   15.75
grilled mahi mahi with passionfruit-mango vinaigrette   14.00
blue nose seabass baked with meaux mustard cream
   and tomato-fresh oregano coulis   14.75
filet of beef tenderloin with saga blue cheese
   and cabernet sauvignon glaze   16.25
veal osso bucco with creamy herb polenta   15.25
new zealand venison with montrachet mashed potatoes
   and rosemary-madeira and green peppercorn glaze   16.00
grilled prarieland veal chop with cassis and dijon glaze   20.75
almond and black pepper crusted new zealand lamb loin
   with sherry glaze   15.00
pork tenderloin scallopini with wild rice pancakes
   & port, shiitake, sour cherry glaze   15.00

For additional information see page 51.

APPETIZERS

Beef or Chicken Nachos   **$6.99**
Freshly grilled sirloin or chicken, sliced and piled on top of our
crisp corn tortilla chips, then smothered with melted cheese and toppings.

Iguana Eggs   **$4.25**
Golden fried jalapeños stuffed with cream cheese.
Served with our delicious sweet chile sauce.

Red Hot Wings   **$4.25**
A dozen wings sautéed in a spicy red pepper sauce. Served with Mexican
cheese bread, carrot and celery sticks and bleu cheese dressing.

SOUP & SALADS

Chicken Tortilla Soup   **$3.99**
Our house specialty. Grilled chicken breast served in a rich broth
with fresh diced avocados, tomatoes and cilantro.

Tostada Suprema   **$6.99**
Your choice of marinated grilled sirloin or chicken in a crisp flour
tortilla shell with lettuce, cheese, sour cream and guacamole.

Chicken Caesar Salad   **$6.99**
Freshly chopped romaine, tossed with parmesan cheese and
Carlos' special dressing. Served in our flour tortilla shell topped with
grilled chicken, corn tortilla strips and tomatoes.

BARBECUE

Baby Back Ribs
A generous half-slab or a grande full-slab of tender pork ribs, double basted
with our special barbecue sauce. Served with Carlos' steak-cut fries and
Mexican cheese bread.

Half · $9.99   Full · $13.99

HOUSE SPECIALTIES

Sizzling Fajitas $9.99
Our fajitas made us famous! Marinated grilled sirloin, chicken breast,
or a combo of the two served sizzling atop a mountain of sautéed bell
peppers, onions and tomatoes. Wrap everything in our warm homemade
flour tortillas with Carlos' rice, refried beans, salsa, guacamole,
sour cream, cilantro and shredded lettuce.

Shrimp Fajitas $11.99
Half a pound (before cooking) of succulent marinated shrimp and
our sizzling fajita vegetables. Served with Carlos' rice, salsa, refried beans,
guacamole, sour cream, cilantro and shredded lettuce.

Chiles Rellenos $8.45
Fresh anaheim or poblano chiles, filled with cheese and gently fried
to a golden brown.

Grilled Fish Tacos $8.25
Ono, a great-tasting southern Pacific game fish, is marinated and
charbroiled, then wrapped in soft flour tortillas with shredded cabbage,
jack and cheddar cheese, cilantro and our tomatillo mayonnaise.

MEXICAN FAVORITES

Chimichanga Crispa $8.25
Your choice of seasoned beef or chicken, with jack and cheddar cheese
and refried beans, inside a crispy fried tortilla. Covered with ranchero sauce,
shredded lettuce, diced tomatoes, and scallions.

Ultimate Steak or Chicken Burrito $8.45
Marinated grilled sirloin or chicken breast rolled up in a grande-size
flour tortilla with guacamole and salsa, then covered with
Carlos' ranchero sauce and grated cheeses.

El Gordo Shrimp Burrito $9.25
Plump shrimp, marinated and sautéed, then wrapped in a large flour tortilla
with fajita vegetables. Topped with ranchero sauce and cheese.

BURGERS & TORTAS
All burgers and tortas are served with steak-cut fries.

Carlos Fajita Melt $5.75
Charbroiled sirloin or chicken stacked on a grilled torta roll with
jack cheese, avocado, fajita vegetables and sliced tomatoes.

Barbecue Pork Torta $5.75
Tender shredded pork smothered in our savory BBQ sauce,
then piled high on a toasted cheese torta roll.

For additional information see page 102.

CHANG
■ CUISINE OF CHINA ■

Menu Changes Seasonally

Appetizers

Chang's Specialties

CRAB LAGOON (6)..5.95
Crab meat and cream cheese wrapped in egg flour skin,
deep fried and served with sweet & pungent sauce.

SEASONED SHRIMP 13.95
Lightly breaded shrimp sprinkled with seasoned salt and
red chili pepper seeds then deep-fried to a golden brown.

SEASONED CHICKEN 7.95
Lightly breaded breast of chicken slices, sprinkled with pepper, seasoned salt and
red chili pepper seeds then deep-fried to a golden brown.

Traditional

VEGETABLE SPRING ROLLS (2) 3.50
PAPER WRAPPED CHICKEN (6) 4.95

Soups
By Quart

WOR WONTON SOUP 4.95
Wonton soup with Shrimp, Chicken, Roast Pork, and Eggs.

BEAN CURD SPINACH SOUP 3.95
A Vegetarian Soup.

MANDARIN SOUP..5.50
Soup Made of Minced Chicken and Crab Meat.

Chang's Choice

ORANGE CHICKEN 8.95
Lightly breaded white meat chicken blended with juicy orange flavored sauce.

HONEY CHICKEN 8.95
Lightly breaded white meat chicken, fried and mixed in honey and vinegar sauce.

BLACK PEPPER STEAK 10.95
Steak cuts marinated in our own special sauce and prepared in a black pepper sauce.

Chicken
Served with bowl of fried or steamed rice

IMPERIAL CHICKEN*..7.95
Sliced white meat chicken with minced mushrooms, water chestnuts & ginger.
All gently simmered in spicy tomato paste sauce.

CHICKEN WITH CASHEW NUTS..7.95
Diced chicken cooked in homemade red brown sauce with toasted cashew nuts.

Duck

PEKING DUCK 25.00
Long island Duckling, processed in a real Peking manner. Served with pancakes.

CRISPY DUCK (Whole) 20.00
(Half) 11.00
Long island Duckling marinated in condiments, steamed and fried crispy. (Served with fried or steamed rice.)

Beef
Served with bowl of fried or steamed rice

YU-HSIANG BEEF* 7.95
Shredded prime beef with bamboo shoots and green pepper sauteed in spicy vinegar sauce.
MO-SHU BEEF 7.95
Tender beef mixed with vegetable, eggs, bamboo shoots, and mushrooms. Served with four pancakes or rice.

CRISPY BEEF* 7.95
Shredded prime beef quickly fried with celery and carrots then cooked with hot & spicy sauce.

Pork
Served with bowl of fried or steamed rice

MO-SHU PORK 7.95
Tender shreds of pork mixed with cabbage, eggs, bamboo shoots, and mushrooms. Served with four pancakes or rice.

TWICE COOKED PORK* 7.95
Sliced pork with cabbage, green onion, bamboo shoots, and mushrooms in hot pepper sauce.
MONGOLIAN PORK 7.95
Sliced pork sauteed with hearts of green scallions in natural sauce.

BARBEQUED PORK WITH SNOW PEAS 7.95

Seafood
Served with bowl of fried or steamed rice

KUNG PAO SHRIMP* 14.95
Shrimp with green onions cooked in spicy red chili pepper sauce. Garnished with peanuts.

CHOW SAN SHEIN 9.95
A combination of shrimp, beef, and tender chicken with broccoli, water chestnuts and bamboo shoots in brown sauce.

DOUBLE HAPPINESS 10.95
A combination of shrimp and scallops with green peppers and carrots in a white sauce.

LOBSTER PEKING STYLE 16.95
Lobster meat with broccoli and snow peas in a garlic and white wine sauce.

Vegetables
Served with bowl of fried or steamed rice.

BUDDHA'S DELIGHT 6.95
A mixture of vegetables in light brown sauce.

MUSHROOM BEAN CURD 6.95
Fried bean curd sauteed with black mushrooms, bamboo shoots and snow peas in brown sauce.

EGGPLANT SZECHUAN STYLE* 7.50
Traditional hot & spicy Szechuan dish, cooked with red chili pepper.

*Indicates Hot & Spicy

For additional information see page 43.

CHEZ HENRI
· French Cuisine ·
DEL MAR · PARIS

✧ Hors-d'oeuvres - Appetizers ✧

Saumon Fumé Mariné aux Senteurs de Provence
(Smoked & marinated salmon in herbs of Provence) 6.50

Carpaccio de Viande
(Thinly sliced beef marinated in olive oil, garlic, & basil) 6.50

Jambon de Parme (Imported smoked ham with slices of melon) 7.50

Cuisses de Grenouilles à la Provençale
(Lightly sauteed frogs legs with a tomato, garlic, and herb sauce) 9.00

✧ Soupes - Soups ✧

Soupe à l'Oignon (Onion Soup) 4.50

Soupe de Poisson (Fish Soup) 5.50

✧ Salades - Salads ✧

Salade d'Avocat aux Crevettes
(Avocado salad garnished with bay shrimp) 6.95

Salade "Chez Henri"
(Assorted greens topped with smoked duck & melted goat cheese on toast) 6.95

Entrées

EVERY TUESDAY—CASSOULET FOR TWO 29.50
EVERY THURSDAY—BOUILLABAISSE FOR TWO 29.50

✧ Viandes - Meat ✧

Escalope de Veau Normande (Veal in a creamy mushroom sauce) 16.00

Pièce de Boeuf sauce Grand Venuer et fois gras
(Filet of beef tenderloin with Grand Veneur sauce & goose liver) 19.50

Carré d'Agneau à la Provençale (Rack of lamb à la Provençale) 19.50

✧ Volailles - Poultry ✧

Canard à l'Orange
(Half a roast duck with an orange sauce) 16.50

Suprême de Poulet au Citron (Breast of chicken with a lemon sauce) 13.50

Escalope de Volaille Jurassienne
(Breast of chicken with asparagus, parmesan, & gruyère cheese) 14.50

✧ Poissons - Fish ✧

Poisson au Sel (A house specialty, ask your waiter for details) 19.50

Saumon sauce Basque (Fresh salmon cooked in a Basque sauce) 16.50

Gambas Provençales (Prawns sauteed & served with a Provençale sauce) 16.50

Linguini du Pêcheur
(Linguini with mussels, clams, shrimp, fish of the day, & fresh tomatoes) 16.50

✧ Four Course Dinner ✧

"Prix Fixe" $16.50	"Prix Fixe" $21.50
Soup of the day	Lobster Bisque
House Salad	Caesar Salad
Your Choice of...	Your Choice of...
Beef Bourguignon	Filet Mignon with a Green Peppercorn Sauce
or	or
Coq au Vin	Escalope de Veau with a Caper Sauce
or	or
Fish of the Day	Swordfish with a Pesto Sauce
Dessert	Dessert

For additional information see page 68.

Chez Loma
Restaurant
Menu Changes Seasonally

First Courses

Escargots à la Niçoise
*Chez Loma tradition - snails simmered in vermouth,
tomatoes, garlic, herbes de Provence and butter*
$5

Salade d' Agneau Grillé
*Fresh spinach, grilled leg of lamb, roasted pinenuts, peppers
cumin vinaigrette*
$7

Roulade D'Aubergine
*A roulade of grilled eggplant, montrachet goat cheese and tapenade
served chilled with a roast pepper coulis*
$6

Terrines du Chef
*A selection of the Chef's homemade country paté,
served with cornichons and mustards*
$5

Pissa du Canard Fumé
*French style Pizza, confit of onions, smoked duck sausage,
spinach, parmesan and sweet red peppers*
$6

Brie et Crevettes en Phyllo
*Shrimp, Brie cheese, basil and sun-dried tomatoes wrapped and
baked in phyllo dough, finished with a tomato coulis*
$6

Entrées
Entrées include your choice of todays soup or our salade maison

Poulet Montrachet
Sheltons free-range chicken breast with Montrachet goat cheese, finished braised leeks and Kalamata olives in a tomato broth
$18

Linguini aux Brocolis
Fresh broccoli, linguini, garlic and sun-dried tomatoes tossed with olive oil, peppers, roasted pinenuts and parmesan
$15

Saumon Piquant
Roast Atlantic salmon fillet, horseradish crust, smoked tomato vinaigrette
$20

Côtes de Veau Madeira
Large free-range veal rack chop, madiera wine sauce with forest mushrooms
$24

Filet de Bouef Mediterranée
Certified Angus filet mignon steak, demi glace sauce with fresh mushrooms, sweet red peppers, drizzled with Danish blue cheese
$24

Fruits de Mer Cassoulet
Greenlip mussels, shrimp and salmon, tomato lobster coulis with saffron white beans, topped with cornbread and gratineéd
$19

Canard Rôti Façon Chez Loma
Chez Loma's traditional roast duckling served with a choice of three sauces; spicy green peppercorn, lingonberry-cherry port wine and a burnt orange sauce
$18

Agneau Grillé de Provence
New Zealand lamb loin grilled, roast garlic Español sauce with provencial herbs
$20

For additional information see page 63.

CINDY BLACK'S

Menu Changes Seasonally

Appetizers

House Hors d'Oeuvre Plate 6.25

Grilled Portobello Mushroom in Rosemary Oil 7.95

Chilled Vegetable Plate, Sweet Pepper Vinegar & Creme Fraiche 5.95

Arugula Salad with Grilled Shrimp, Roasted Pepper & Fresh Mint 6.95

Gratin of Spinach Gnocchi in Gorgonzola Cream 5.75

House Salad Vinaigrette 3.95

Special Soup

Steamed Garlic Clams with Green Chile "Rouille" 7.50

Rice, Pastas, etc.

Vegetable Risotto 9.50

Green Linguine with Shellfish in Garlic Wine Sauce 16.25

Spaghetti & White Beans in Chianti with Oregano,
Ripe Tomatoes & Olive Oil 10.50

5721 La Jolla Blvd • La Jolla • (619) 456-6299

Entrees

Grilled Chicken & Leeks 15.95

Whole Dover Sole Meuniere (Market Availability) ...

Broiled Large Shrimp Stuffed with Mushrooms,
Roasted Peppers & Spinach 21.95

Grilled Salmon Filet, Tomato Marmalade & Tarragon 17.95

Provencale Chicken Stew, Rouille, Croutons & Gruyere 12.50

*All
Entrees
Served With
House Gratin*

Cilantro Peppercorn Filet of Beef Flamed in
Armagnac 23.00

Rolled Loin of Lamb with Parsley Bread Crumbs 21.95

Grilled Duck "Two Ways," Crispy Carrots & Leeks, Basil Sauce 18.50

Fritto Misto with Lemon Sauce 16.75

Desserts

Plate of Assorted Cookies 3.75

Belgian Chocolate Brownie with Homemade Caramel Ice Cream 4.25

Raspberry Crepes 5.50 House Souffle (allow 10 min.) 5.25

Frozen White Chocolate and Hazelnut Torte 4.50

Warm Lemon Curd Tart with Glazed Pears 4.75

For additional information see page 68.

Menu Changes Seasonally

Appetizers

Honey Roasted Chicken Wings $6.95
10 Broiled chicken wings seasoned with cayenne pepper and drizzled with honey. Served
with bleu cheese dipping sauce.

Fish Tacos $4.95
Fresh red snapper, battered and deep fried, served in a grilled corn tortilla with fresh lime
coleslaw. Garnished with fresh cilantro, sour cream, guacamole, diced tomatoes and
lime. 2 per order.

Calamari Rings $8.95
Lightly battered, deep fried calamari served on a bed or lettuce with a spicy cocktail
sauce, old bay mayonnaise and fresh lemon.

Chef's Special Salads

Grilled Vegetable Salad $6.95
Iceberg, romaine and red leaf lettuce tossed with a creamy mint lime cilantro vinaigrette
and topped with grilled seasonal vegetables and tomato wedges.

Embassy Cobb $8.95
Iceberg, romaine and red leaf lettuce topped with julienned smoked turkey and Monterey
Jack cheese, bay shrimp salad, curried chicken salad and tomato wedges and fanned
avocado. Served with your choice of dressing.

Sandwiches

All sandwiches served with your choice of seasoned steak fries, homemade potato salad,
fresh coleslaw, seasonal fruit salad, pasta or grilled marinated vegetables.

Philly Steak Sandwich $7.95
Thinly sliced prime rib grilled with red and green bell peppers and onions, topped with
melted jack cheese and tomato basil sauce. Served on a french roll.

Nature's Best $5.95
Avocado, cucumber, tomato, alfalfa sprouts, lettuce and dill havarti cheese on toasted
7-grain bread.

Pasta Bar

All you can eat. Freshly tossed Caesar salad, garlic bread, and cooked-to-order entree with your choice of pasta, sauce, chicken, seafood and vegetables.

Lunch		Dinner
Monday thru Friday	Kids under 10	Tuesday thru Saturday
$8.95	$6.95	$10.95

Entrees

All entrees served with fresh baked sourdough rolls and butter, your choice of soup or salad, fresh steamed vegetables and a choice of seasoned steak fries, baked potato, steamed red potatoes, pasta of the day or saffron rice.

Vegetarian Lasagna $12.95
Mushroom pesto lasagna topped with fresh tomato basil sauce. Served with garlic bread.

Grilled Beef, chicken and Vegetable Brochettes $13.95
Tender chunks of beef tenderloin marinated in a ginger soy sauce, chunks of chicken breast marinated in lemon and olive oil, and fresh zucchini, yellow squash, red and green bell pepper, onion, tomato and mushroom caps, all grilled separately and served on a bed of saffron rice.

Shrimp Scampi $15.95
Four jumbo shrimp sauteed with fresh garlic, butter, white wine and cayanne pepper, served on a bed of saffron rice.

Linguini in Clam Sauce $10.95
Olive oil, garlic and basil sauteed with clams and your choice of red or white sauce over linguini. Served with garlic bread.

After 5:00's

Tournedos of Beef   19.95
Tenderloin medallions with artichoke bottoms sauteed in a rich cabernet, shallot sauce, served on a bed of saffron rice. The chef's specialty.

Chicken Oscar $13.95
10 oz broiled chicken breast topped with steamed crab meat, asparagus spears and bearnaise sauce.

Filet Mignon $18.95
an 8 oz filet grilled to order, topped with a mushroom cap.

Junior NY Strip $16.95
a 10 oz cut, grilled to order and topped with a mushroom cap.

Prime and Pasta

Freshly tossed Caesar salad, garlic bread, a junior cut of prime rib and pasta primavera. Available at the Pasta Bar, Tuesday through Saturday, 5:00pm - 9:00pm
$13.95

For additional information see page 26.

CRABCATCHER

Menu Changes Seasonally

STARTERS

CRAB STUFFED MUSHROOMS $5.95
A blend of blue crabmeat, sourdough crumbs, jack cheese, scallions and sweet sherry stuffed into mushroom caps, topped with melted jack cheese.

PASTA FAGGOLI $4.95
Puréed Tuscan beans in a rich chicken broth with bits of tomato and crispy fried cappellini.

FIRE SHRIMP $6.95
Jumbo shrimp coated with serrano, ancho and anaheim chili paste and pan grilled with caraway potato mash.

GRILLED OYSTERS $7.95
Fresh oysters on a half shell, topped with a roasted leek and lemon mascarpone and flame broiled.

CLAM CHOWDER $3.95
Traditional New England style.

SALADS

FLAME-GRILLED SWORDFISH CAESAR SALAD $11.95
Slices of warm, flame-grilled swordfish on our large Boston caesar salad.

WATERCRESS SALAD WITH PAN-SEARED SCALLOP CHIPS $8.95
Served with a pancetta sun-dried tomato vinaigrette.

WARM BEAN SALAD $4.95
Cannellini beans tossed with grilled corn, bell peppers, fennel and onions on a grilled crostini.

1298 Prospect St • La Jolla • (619) 454-9587

PASTA

GRILLED CHICKEN CANNELLONI.. $14.95
*Roasted vegetables and grilled chicken breast stuffed into a fresh egg sheet pasta
in a basil tomato cream sauce.*

DUCK RAVIOLI $16.95
*Broken ravioli, duck confit and roasted peppers with ricotta, wrapped with beet pasta
and charred under a flame with fontina cheese.*

AVOCADO AND KING CRABMEAT $15.95
*Avocado, seared onions and tomatoes in a light cream sauce with grilled King crabmeat,
tossed with penne.*

ENTREES

FRESH CATCH OF THE DAY .... MARKET PRICE
Our waitperson will describe today's fresh selection.

SALMON $16.95
*Fresh salmon, pepper-crusted and grilled, served with leeks and fennel in a shrimp broth
with red lentils.*

CATCHER'S MIX GRILL $18.95
A combination of three grilled seafood items of the chef's choice.

GIANT TIGER PRAWNS $19.95
*Giant freshwater shrimp, dusted with sourdough crumbs, char-grilled and served with
a risotto timbalo and homemade ketchup.*

SEARED BEEF TENDERLOIN.. $18.95
*A filet of beef, pan seared, with black olives, arugula, lemon and extra virgin olive oil;
with garlic mashed potato.*

GRILLED DUNGENESS CRABCAKES $17.95
Grilled and served with a fried pasta cake and spicy mango chili salsa.

CRAB STUFFED FISH $17.95
*Our daily choice of fresh fish with our special blue crab and sourdough stuffing,
topped with bell pepper relish.*

CHAR-BROILED LAMB CHOPS $18.95
Flame-grilled and served with a lamb stock and roasted tomato sauce, with grilled pasta.

For additional information see page 114.

CROCE'S

RESTAURANT & JAZZ BAR

Menu Highlights

—STARTERS & SALADS—

Risotto D'Ortaggi with fresh vegetables and shiitake mushrooms. 7.95

Szechuan chicken pizza with hoisin barbeque sauce, grilled peppers and gouda. 8.95

Poached calamari salad with sweet peppers, cilantro, tomatoes and water chestnuts,
served with orange jicama relish. 8.95

—PASTA—

Shrimp and wild mushroom raviolis sautéed with chicken-cashew sausage and
water chestnuts in a madeira cream. 15.95

Tagliatelle Pomodoro with roasted garlic, vine-ripened tomatoes and fresh basil. 11.95

Penne with breast of chicken and broccoli in a gorgonzola cream tossed with pancetta. 16.50

Linguini with Manilla clams and arugula. 16.50

—ENTRÉES—

Charcoal grilled ahi served with a chilled avocado tomato concassé and vegetables. 18.50

Coulibiac—Salmon baked in delicate puff pastry, layered with kasha, mushroom duxelle
and fresh spinach, finished with lemon hollandaise. 16.50

Chef Fay's Award-Winning Alaskan Halibut with Japanese-style panko crumbs,
garnished with a sautéed prawn and finished with a spicy Nasi-Goreng cream. 18.95

Simply Chicken with lemon, garlic and cracked black pepper, served with Buchanzi rice pilaf. 12.95

Pacific Rim Tamales—Mousseline of baquetta seabass laced with shiitake mushrooms,
water chestnuts and fresh ginger. Served with spicy guacamole and Tahitian salad. 17.95

Garlic glazed culotte steak served with creamy mashed potatoes. 18.95

FREE Live Jazz and Rhythm & Blues with purchase of a dinner entrée.

802 Fifth Ave • Gaslamp Quarter • (619) 233-4355

Croce's

Ingrid's Wild West Cafe

Menu Highlights

—Breakfast—

Blue corn pancakes with sweet whipped butter and maple syrup. 4.95

Polenta del Pueblo with chorizo, fresh tomatoes, scallions, yellow corn,
melted jack and blackened tomato sauce. 6.50

Pappas Fritas with chilies, scallions and jack. 5.95   Croce's Five Star Eggs Benedict 8.95

—Lunch—

Crab and avocado quesadilla served with papaya mint salsa. 7.95

Ingrid's Southwest Vegetarian Lasagne with polenta, corn, chilies, ricotta,
mozarella and jack, finished with a marinara mole. 10.95

Ingrid's Caesar Salad with char-grilled chicken, tossed with our chile Caesar dressing. 8.95

Roasted Pepper Sandwich with grilled onions, mozzarella, provolone, fresh basil and
vine-ripened tomatoes on toasted herb focaccia bread. 7.50

—Pasta & Dinner Entrées—

Spinach fettucini with chicken in a roasted garlic sauce with grilled eggplant,
sundried tomatoes and peppers. 15.95

Linguini with prawns and chicken in a blackened tomato cream. 17.95

Alaskan Halibut Pescadero with avocado lime mousseline. 17.95

Char-Grilled Mission Chicken served with a spicy black bean purée and Spanish rice. 12.95

Saged rubbed rack of lamb with chile molido, accented with a chipotle mole demi glaze. 21.95

Santa Fe Wellington with a spicy sausage-raisin filling, served with jalapeño hollandaise. 16.50

Cowboy Rib Steak with spicy wild west onion rings, garlic mashed potatoes
and roasted pepper salad. 19.95

FREE Live Jazz and Rhythm & Blues with purchase of a dinner entrée.

For additional information see page 52.

D.Z. Akin's
restaurant • delicatessen
bakery • fountain

Appetizers

Debi's Chopped Liver 5.95
Served with Bread

Smoked Salmon (Lox) 9.95
Tomato, Onion, Bagel and Cream Cheese

Potato Latkes (3 Pancakes) 6.50
Served with Sour Cream or Applesauce

Blintzes (4) (Cheese or Blueberry) 5.95
Served with Sour Cream and Preserves

Potato Knish 3.25
Delicate Pastry Dough stuffed with Potatoes and Fried Onions

Kasha Varnishkes 5.95
With Gravy and served with Bread

Stuffed Derma (Kishka and Gravy) 5.25
Served with Bread

Matzoh Ball Soup 3.25

Oldies But Goodies

Hot Corned Beef	6.25	Hard Salami	6.50
Hot Pastrami	6.25	Cold Baked Meat Loaf	6.25
Hot Brisket	6.25	Fried Salami and Egg	6.25
Fresh Turkey Breast or		Jack Cheese	5.25
Smoked Turkey	6.25	*Served with Lettuce and Tomato.*	
Pepper Beef	6.25	Swiss Cheese	5.25
Hot Pickled Tongue	7.25	*Served with Lettuce and Tomato.*	
Baked Ham	5.95	Smoked Salmon (Lox)	9.95
Salami	5.95	*Served on toasted Bagel*	
Bologna	5.95	*and Cream Cheese.*	
Chopped Liver	5.95	Smoked Whitefish	9.95
Liverwurst	5.95	*Served on toasted Bagel and Cream Cheese*	
Kosher Salami	6.25	*with Tomato and Onion.*	

𝒟𝒾𝓃𝓃𝑒𝓇𝓈

Served from 4:30 p.m. Dinner price includes Cup of Soup and Tossed Green Salad, Bread and Butter, Choice of Potato, Kasha, Cottage Cheese or Sliced Tomato—unless otherwise specified. We Invite You to Share a Meal at $2.00 Extra Charge

	Ala Carte	Dinner
Roasted Brisket of Beef	8.95	11.95

Tender slices of Brisket served with our delicious Beef Gravy.

Baked Meat Loaf 8.95   11.95
Our very own Meat Loaf baked in a delicious Tomato Sauce and savory Spices.

Grilled Beef Liver Steak 7.95   10.95
Grilled to your perfection and smothered with Onions.

Mushroom Chicken 8.95   11.95
Half of a juicy Chicken smothered in our fresh Mushrooms and Onion Gravy.

Stuffed Cabbage Rolls 11.95   14.95
Two large Cabbage Rolls in our own special Sweet and Sour Sauce.

Corned Beef and Cabbage 9.95   12.95
A mound of sliced Corned Beef served with a quarter Cabbage and boiled Potatoes.

𝒟. 𝒵.'𝓈 𝒮𝓅𝑒𝒸𝒾𝒶𝓁𝓉𝒾𝑒𝓈

D.Z.'s Smoked Fish Brunch 42.95
(Serves 3–4) Sumptuous portions of Smoked Salmon, Whitefish and Codfish; served with heaps of Cream Cheese, fresh Vegetables, Greek Olives, garnish and complemented with six Bagels.

D.Z.'s Ethnic Sampler 19.95
For those who crave ethnic delights, D.Z. has created this special platter for you. Stuffed Cabbage Roll, Potato Knish, Stuffed Kishka, Kasha Varnishkes and fresh Rye Bread.

Bernie's Deli Platter 21.95
(Serves 2-3) Sliced White Meat of Turkey, Salami, Corned Beef, Pepper Beef, Swiss Cheese; Served with Potato Salad, Cole Slaw, fresh Vegetables and choice of Bread.

𝒟𝑒𝓈𝓈𝑒𝓇𝓉𝓈

Chocolate Chip Cheesecake .. 3.25	Bread Pudding 2.95
7 Layer Rum Cake 3.25	Cream Puff 3.25
Rice Pudding 2.95	Eclair 3.25

Double Chocolate Cherry Cheese Squares.......3.25

For additional information see page 67.

DAKOTA
GRILL & SPIRITS

Menu Changes Seasonally

STARTERS

RED CHILE ONION RINGS	$4.95
with house-made ketchup	
WILD MUSHROOM FAJITA	$5.95
with a port wine and fresh herb sauce	
JALAPEÑO POPPERS	$5.95
spicy peppers stuffed with cream cheese, lightly deep fried, Santa Fe ranch dip	
ANCHO HONEY GLAZED LAMB CHOPS	$6.95
mesquite smoked with orange chipotle sauce	
ROASTED GARLIC	$3.95
served with caramelized onions on a gorgonzola pizza bread	
CRAWFISH ENCHILADA	$5.95
with tomatillo and garlic salsa	

SOUP & SALAD

OUR OWN BLACK BEAN SOUP	$3.50
vegetarian, served with sour cream and smoked tomato salsa	
DAKOTA MIXED GREENS	$3.95
organically grown locally, with aged jack cheese, glazed walnuts and dijon vinaigrette	
SOUTHWEST CHOPPED SALAD	$4.95
mixed greens, roasted turkey, tasso ham, fresh corn, red bell peppers, cotija cheese, orange dijon vinaigrette	
CACTUS CHICKEN SALAD	$4.95
napa cabbage, grilled chicken, nopales, carrots, spicy peanuts with ancho honey vinaigrette	

WOOD-FIRED PIZZA
made with honey-whole wheat dough

WILD MUSHROOM	$8.50
Oyster, Portobello, Crimini, sun-dried tomatoes, garlic, fresh herbs, jarlsberg	
FOUR CHEESE	$7.95
basil pesto, fresh roma tomatoes, provolone, mozzarella, jarlsberg, cotija	

901 Fifth Ave • Gaslamp Quarter • (619) 234-5554

DAKOTA BBQ CHICKEN $8.95
house-made BBQ sauce, red onion, cilantro and smoked gouda

ITALIAN SAUSAGE and HOT SALAMI $8.95
mozzarella, provolone and fresh oregano

GRILLED SEASONAL VEGETABLE $7.95
fresh tomato herb sauce, mozzarella, fresh basil (may be prepared without cheese)

TAOS CHICKEN $8.95
black beans, red bell pepper, corn, cilantro, scallions and jalapeño jack

P A S T A

PENNE with SPICE-CHARRED SHRIMP $10.95
with scallions, cilantro, fresh lime, in a white wine sauce

NEW MEXICO LINGUINE $8.95
spit-roasted chicken, roasted peppers, scallions, spicy tomato cream sauce

PEPPERED FETTUCCINE with WILD MUSHROOMS $8.95
roasted garlic, in a brandied cream sauce

BASIL GARLIC LINGUINE with STEAMED MUSSELS $10.95
tomatoes and fresh herbs

VEGETARIAN LASAGNA $8.95
meatless, seasonal vegetables, pesto, ricotta and provolone

BLACK BEAN LINGUINE $8.95
with sun-dried tomatoes, artichoke hearts, broccoli florettes, garlic oil
and fresh parmesan

G R I L L & R O T I S S E R I E
served with chef's accompaniment and seasonal vegetables

PEPPERED FRESH ATLANTIC SALMON $15.95
mesquite grilled to medium rare (or to your liking)

SHRIMP TASSO $15.95
sauteed with Tasso Cajun ham & sweet peas in an ancho chile cream

SPIT-ROASTED CHICKEN $12.95
orange chipotle glaze or Dakota BBQ sauce

SAGEBRUSH CHICKEN BREAST $11.95
with chile lime marinade and grilled pineapple salsa

K.C. STRIP STEAK $14.95
spice-charred with cilantro vinaigrette and grilled scallions

CATTLEMAN'S CUT RIB CHOP market
22 ounces, served with BBQ black beans, and blackened tomato salsa

BBQ BABY BACK RIBS $14.95
mesquite smoked, then grilled to order, fresh jicama slaw

GRILLED PORK CHOPS $13.95
with mango habenero sauce

For additional information see page 53.

DOBSON'S
Bar & Restaurant

Menu Changes Daily

A P P E T I Z E R S

Dobson's Mussel Bisque En Croute	6.00
Malapeque Oysters On the Half Shell	8.50
Broiled Oysters With Caviar	10.50
Cold-Smoked Scottish Salmon Plate With Capers, Onions, Egg, Cream Cheese	10.50
Truffled Duck Liver Pate	8.50
Escargots Bourguignonne	8.00

F I R S T   C O U R S E S

SPOONLEAF SPINACH (TAT SOI) With Blue Cheese, Apple, Candied Walnuts	6.50
GIANT SHIITAKE MUSHROOMS Grilled With Olive Oil, Garlic & Herbs	7.00
SPINACH & CHEESE TORTELLONI With Smoked Salmon, Blue Cheese & Pignolias	8.00
ROASTED GARLIC & PESTO-LAYERED POLENTA With Marinara Sauce	5.95
FRENCH BRIE Whole Small Brie Baked With Pesto In Puff Pastry, Fruit	8.95

E N T R E E S

SPICY SHRIMP & MUSSELS MARINARA With Cappellini, Basil, Sundried Tomatoes	16.00
GRILLED ATLANTIC SALMON On Vine Ripe Tomatoes, Basil, Balsamico, Olive Oil	18.00
ALASKAN HALIBUT With Shrimp Sauce, Lemon & Dill	18.00
SPICY CRAB CAKES With Three Sauces (Roasted Tomato/Wasabi/Citrus)	17.00

---

956 Broadway Cir • Downtown • (619) 231-6771

CHICKEN & MUSHROOMS IN PUFF PASTRY	15.00
With Madeira Sauce With Asparagus	
SOUTHWESTERN CHICKEN SAUSAGES	14.00
With FRESH FAVA BEANS & Herbs	
VEAL FLANK STEAK	16.00
Marinated In XV Olive Oil & Herbs, With Pesto Polenta	
RIBEYE STEAK Grilled, With Grilled Red Onions & Shallot Butter	18.00
CITRUS-MARINATED DUCK BREAST	17.00
Grilled Medium, Raspberry Sauce & Berries	
NEW ZEALAND VENISON LOIN	18.00
Peppercorn Seared, With Chestnut Puree & Raspberry Sauce	
TOURNEDOS & LOBSTER Grilled Filet & Slipper Lobster Tail, Two Sauces	21.00
DOBSON'S MIXED GRILL With Filet Medallion, Double Lamb Chop, Sausage	21.00
PRIME VEAL LOIN CHOP Grilled With Herbs	28.00
NEW ZEALAND FRESH RACK OF LAMB	19.00
Roasted, With Ratatouille, Roast Garlic	

D O B S O N ' S   S U M M E R   P R I X   F I X E   M E N U

Four Courses $21.95
(Includes glass of house wine or coffee)

Mussel Bisque En Croute
***
Baby Lettuce Salad With Goat Cheese

OR

Caesar Salad With Garlic Croutons
***
PLEASE CHOOSE ONE:

GRILLED SALMON FILET With Vine Ripe Tomatoes, Basil, Balsamico,
Olive Oil, White Beans

RISOTTO WITH SEAFOOD Fish, Shrimp, Mussels, White Wine,
Fresh Tomato, Parmesan

CITRUS-MARINATED DUCK BREAST Grilled Medium,
With Raspberry Sauce & Fresh Berries

VEAL FLANK STEAK Grilled With Extra-Virgin Olive Oil & Fresh Garlic,
With Pesto-Layered Polenta

CHICKEN BREAST Stuffed With Spinach & Cheese In Puff Pastry, Demiglace

DESSERT: Creme Brulee, Double Chocolate-Walnut Brownie OR
Fresh Nectarine & Pear Crumble w/Ice Cream

For additional information see page 54.

DOMINIC'S
italian restaurant

ANTIPASTI

CAPONATA 4.95
Sauteed onions, capers, celery, green olives, eggplant, tomato sauce,
balsamic vinegar, pine nuts and basil

CALAMARI FRITTI 5.00
Fried baby squid

INSALATE E ZUPPE

INSALATA CAPRESE 5.50
Sliced tomato, fresh mozzarella, fresh basil and extra virgin olive oil

INSALATA MEDITERRANEA 5.25
Red onion, artichoke hearts, fresh tomato, feta cheese and black olives
served with a balsamic vinaigrette

LE PASTE
All dishes include: soup or salad and fresh baked bread sticks

LINGUINE VESUVIO 12.95
Shrimp in a spicy tomato sauce

FETTUCCINI PRIMAVERA 8.50
Fresh garden vegetables in a light cream sauce

SPAGHETTINI ALLA MATRICIANA 9.50
Onions, pancetta, tomato sauce and pecorino cheese

PENNE AL PESTO 8.95
Fresh basil, pine nuts and garlic

MANICOTTI AL FORNO 8.95
Crepes stuffed with ricotta and mozzarella

---

461 College Blvd • Oceanside • (619) 630-4400

IL POLLO

POLLO AL MARSALA 11.95
Chicken breast sauteed with mushroom and marsala wine sauce

POLLO ALLA CACCIATORE 10.50
Chicken breast simmered with onion, green pepper, peas, black olives
and mushrooms

IL VITELLO

VITELLO MILANESE 12.95
Breaded veal in a lemon wine sauce

VITELLO SALTIMBOCCA 14.95
Veal with prosciutto, sage and mozzarella cheese sauteed in a white wine sauce

IL PESCE

SCAMPI AL PESTO 15.50
Shrimp in fresh basil, garlic and pine nuts

SCAMPI AL VINO BIANCO 14.95
Shrimp sauteed in white wine, lemon and garlic

*Above entrees served with salad or soup, side of pasta,
fresh breadsticks and seasonal vegetables*

CALIFORNIA STYLE PIZZA
All pizzas have mozzarella cheese unless otherwise stated

ROASTED GARLIC CHICKEN 8.50
Roasted garlic, grilled chicken, onions, chopped parsley, and
white wine lemon-garlic butter

ARTICHOKE, OLIVE AND CAPER 7.50
WITH ANCHOVIES 8.50
Baby artichoke hearts, Mediterranean olives and capers with tomato sauce

PESTO 8.50
Fresh tomatoes, olives, sun-dried tomatoes and homemade pesto sauce

For additional information see page 83.

RESTAURANT

SOUPS AND STARTERS

Grilled Asparagus   *Fresh asparagus is marinated in balsamic* $4.50
vinegar and grilled, served with a toasted pecan hollandaise

Sherried cream of wild mushroom soup en croute $4.95
Rich wild mushroom soup baked with a delicate puff pastry cap

Elario's French onion soup   *with melted swiss and parmesan* $4.95

Smoked trout   *smoked over applewood, served with crisp toasts* $5.95
and horseradish cream

Japanese style Calamari   *Calamari squid steak is lightly breaded* $5.95
in Japanese panko crumbs and pan-fried, with a sweet and spicy
plum dipping sauce

Sesame seed seared ahi   *Freshest ahi tuna is crusted with black and* $6.50
white sesame seeds and flash-seared, with a hot & sour raspberry sauce

Oysters on the Half Shell   *Our Chef chooses the market's freshest* $7.95
oysters and serves them on the half-shell, with a spicy cocktail sauce

Oysters Pocholas   *Fresh-shucked oysters are baked with a* $8.75
cilantro pesto and finished with red wine cilantro hollandaise

SALADS

Spring Salad   *Baby seasonal greens with French burnt walnuts,* $4.95
crisp pippin apples and fresh herb vinaigrette

Spinach Salad   *Fresh spinach leaves tossed with oranges,* $5.50
red onions and a sesame-ginger vinaigrette

Caeser Salad   *Prepared tableside, for two* $9.95

PASTA

Elario's Pasta   *Angelhair pasta tossed with wild mushrooms,* $14.95
fresh basil, sundried tomatoes and port wine cream sauce

Penne with Scallops   *Penne pasta with sea scallops,* $16.95
roma tomatoes, scallions and a light lemon saffron cream

ENTREES

Citrus Grilled Chicken Breast   *Boneless breast of chicken is* $14.95
marinated with orange liqueur and lime and char-grilled, with a
sweet and hot jalapeno chutney

Seared Seabass with panfried potatoes   *Filet of bass is seared* $20.95
and served on a bed of pan-fried potatoes and applewood-smoked bacon,
with wilted greens and crispy onions

Grilled Salmon with fresh chive beurre blanc   *Grilled salmon* $21.95
on a bed of julienne vegetables with a chardonnay-chive butter sauce

Veal loin medallions with Wild Mushrooms   *Sauteed with* $22.95
fresh wild mushrooms, shallots, veal stock and madeira wine

Five-pepper Filet mignon   *With garlic mashed potatoes &* $22.95
peppery cognac cream

Aged Angus Culotte Steak   *Baseball cut top sirloin steak, grilled,* $22.95
with a shallot-cabernet glaze, garlic mashed potatoes and crisp red onions

Roasted Venison Loin   *With raspberry-peppercorn sauce &* $23.95
crisp pancetta

Beef Wellington   *An Elario's classic, with duxelle of mushrooms* $24.95
and fois gras, wrapped in puff pastry, with port wine glaze

Rack of New Zealand Lamb   *Marinated with olive oil,* $25.95
rosemary and garlic and oven-roasted, with a port wine honey glaze

Steak Diane   *Filet mignon prepared with shallots, cognac,* $22.95
mustard, and veal stock at your tableside

DESSERTS

You may choose from this evening's selection of desserts from our pastry tray
or your server will prepare one of our specialties tableside.

For additional information see page 54.

Emerald Chinese Seafood Restaurant

EMERALD

Menu Changes Seasonally

APPETIZERS

	Small	Large
Emerald Combination Platter	12.00	30.00
Roasted Duckling	8.50	16.00
Soy Sauce Braised Chicken	8.50	16.00

SOUP

	Small	Large
Emerald Seafood Soup	7.25	9.75
Shredded Duck with Orange Peel Soup	6.85	9.25
Abalone Chicken Soup	7.50	10.00

SHARK FIN & BIRD'S NEST

Braised Shark Fin with Brown Sauce	25.00
Shark Fin with Crab Meat Soup	10.00
Bird's Nest Chicken Soup	10.00

CONCH, OYSTER & CLAM

Steamed Oysters Whole in Black Bean Sauce	8.50
Conch with Fresh Vegetables	13.00
Clam in Ginger and Scallion Sauce	9.50

SQUIDS

Squid in Black Bean Sauce	7.50
Squid with Shrimp Paste Sauce	7.50
Sautéed Dry Squid with Yellow Leek	7.50

ABALONE & SEA CUCUMBER

Abalone with Fresh Vegetables	25.00
Abalone with Sea Cucumber	25.00
Sea Cucumber with Duck Webs	20.00

LOBSTER & CRAB

Lobster with House Special Sauce	Seasonal
Lobster with Ginger and Scallion Sauce	Seasonal
Crab with Curry Sauce	Seasonal

FISH

Whole Flounder Emerald	26.00
Sweet and Sour Rod Cod Filet	9.25
Rod Cod Filet with Black Bean Sauce	9.25
Steamed Flounder	20.00

SCALLOPS & SHRIMP

Shrimp with Walnut	14.95
Shrimp with Lobster Sauce	10.00
Scallops with Black Pepper Sauce	12.75

POULTRY

Peking Duck (Two Courses)			whole	28.00
Braised Duck Buddhist Style			half	12.00
Steamed Chicken with Ham and Fresh Vegetables			half	14.00
Braised Chicken with Ginger and Scallion	half	10.00	whole	20.00

BEEF & PORK

Steak Cantonese Style	11.75
Beef with Ginger and Pineapple	8.25
Baked Pork Ribs with Special B.B.Q. Sauce	7.00

VEGETABLE & BEAN CURD

Straw Mushrooms with Snow Peas	7.25
Bean Stalk Topped with Crab Meat	14.95
Fried Creamy Bean Curd with Crab Meat Sauce	11.50

RICE & NOODLES

Fried Rice Topped with Duck & Vegetables	12.00
Pineapple Stuffed with Fried Rice	12.00
Diced Chinese Sausage and Broccoli Fried Rice	7.50

For additional information see page 44.

Fifth &ss
HAWTHORN
Restaurant

Menu Changes Daily

Relaxed, cozy, intimate. A favorite in-spot with old globe actors and famous writers. Rub elbows with Hal Holbrook, Elizabeth Montgomery, Sada Thompson. Compare notes with Joseph Wambaugh, who featured Fifth & Hawthorn in his latest thriller, *Finnegan's Week*. Each night a newly-printed menu features fresh seafood, inventive pastas, chicken and what has been called "The Best Filet Mignon in San Diego."

APPETIZERS

Escargot - 5.95
sauteed with mushrooms in a spicy Chinese black bean sauce

Baked Oysters - 6.95
1/2 spicy bacon and tomato herb Parmesan and 1/2 with cilantro pesto

Steamed Clams - 7.50
white wine, thyme and roasted garlic butter

Hanalei Roll - 5.95
a sushi roll of salmon, cream cheese and avocado done tempura style

Gravlax Sushi - 5.50
fresh salmon cold cured with whole white pepper and dill

Spicy Calamari Stirfry - 9.50
with radicchio, mushrooms, baby corn and stirfried
with spicy hoisin sauce on a bed of fresh greens

Rock Shrimp Quesadilla - 4.95
a traditional quesadilla with rock shrimp

515 Hawthorn St • Downtown • (619) 544-0940

ENTREES
include choice of soup or salad

Salmon - 16.95
baked in shredded potato and served with lemon butter sauce

Ahi - 16.95
grilled medium rare, served with pine nuts, soy and fresh basil cream

Alaskan Halibut - 16.95
grilled and served with a ginger lemon butter

Swordfish - 17.95
grilled and served with a warm avocado and tomatillo salsa

White Sea Bass - 15.95
steamed with ginger, cilantro and scallions

Chicken Breast (Pollo de Nayarit) - 14.95
sauteed in wine, fresh garlic, tomato, mushroom and bell pepper

Filet Mignon - 18.95
sauteed with green peppercorns, cabernet and
brandy, side of mango chutney

Catfish - 14.95
marinated in mustard and Cajun spices, lightly breaded and sauteed

Mahi Mahi - 14.95
dusted with cracked pepper, sauteed
with tamarind cabernet sauce, pineapple salsa

Calamari - 14.95
"abalone style", lightly breaded and served with a Grand Marnier sauce

Duck Breast, boneless - 17.50
sauteed in a black cherry sauce and served with wild rice crepes

Fettucine and Chicken - 14.95
sauteed with mushrooms, tomatoes and Espagnol sauce

Tortellini - 14.95
stuffed with ricotta cheese, tossed with bay scallops in parmesan cream

For additional information see page 55.

CUCINA

Fio's

ITALIANA

Menu Changes Seasonally

ANTIPASTI

MELANZANE ALLA FORNAIA   5.95
*Stuffed baby eggplants in our woodfired oven
with roasted peppers, goat cheese, pinenuts and a fresh tomato-basil sauce.*

CARPACCIO   6.75
*Thinly sliced raw beef accented with spicy mustard,
cracked black pepper, capers and shaved parmigiana cheese.*

CALAMARI FRITTI   6.95
Deep-fried calamari served with a spicy marinara sauce and lemon.

COZZE ALLA TARANTINA   7.50
Mussels steamed with garlic, white wine, olive oil and parsley.

INSALATA

INSALATA DI MICHIELLE   8.95
*Mixed baby greens, red onions, grilled shitake mushrooms, artichoke hearts and
shrimp served on sliced tomatoes and fresh asparagus with lemon-lime vinaigrette.*

INSALATA DI POLLO   6.95
*Wilted salad of spinach, roasted chicken, tomatoes, bacon and parmigiana cheese,
with an herb dressing.*

INSALATA DI FIO'S   4.50
*Crisp greens with pinenuts, golden raisins, goat cheese and
mushrooms, with a balsamic dressing.*

PIZZA E FOCACCIA

PIZZA RUSTICA   9.95
Roasted chicken, pinenuts, pesto, sundried tomatoes and basil.

801 Fifth Ave • Gaslamp Quarter • (619) 234-3467

PIZZA QUATRO STAGIONE   10.50
Quartered with wild mushrooms, prosciutto, spicy eggplant and marinated artichoke hearts.

PIZZA CON SALSICCIA   10.75
Hot Italian sausage, spinach, roasted tomatoes, ricotta cheese, black olives and garlic bread crumbs.

PASTA

	Appetizer	Entrée

FETTUCCINE CARBONARA CON ASPARAGO   7.50   11.50
Fettuccine in cream sauce with eggs, pancetta, onions, asparagus and parmesan cheese.

RAVIOLI ALL' ARAGOSTA   8.95   12.95
Lobster ravioli with a sauce of roasted tomatoes, rosemary and butter.

CAPELLINI AL BASILICO CON POLLO   6.95   10.95
Angel hair pasta with pesto, pinenuts, sundried tomatoes, roasted chicken and parmigiana cheese.

TUTTO MARE   7.95   11.95
Black linguine pasta with shrimp, calamari, clams and mussels in a spicy tomato sauce.

SPECIALITA

BRODINO AI FRUTTI DI MARE   14.75
Shrimp, scallops, clams and mussels in a spicy tomato broth. Served with pizza bread.

POLLO ALLA FIORENTINA   13.50
Stuffed chicken breast with mushrooms, spinach, cheese and sundried tomatoes. Served with a green peppercorn sauce.

POLLASTRELLA RIPIENO AL FORNO   13.95
Roasted game hen stuffed with Italian cheeses, artichoke hearts, pancetta, black olives and chopped almonds from the pizza oven.

COSTIGLIETTE DI AGNELLO   17.95
Oven baked rack of lamb with an herb and garlic breadcrumb crust served with pan juices and mashed potatoes.

OSSO BUCO   14.95
Veal shank braised with vegetables, porcini mushrooms and lemon zest. Served over mushroom risotto.

For additional information see page 83.

Menu Changes Daily

PASTA APPETIZERS

PASTA RUSTICA 4.25

PASTA CON PESTO 5.50

PASTA CON NOVA 6.25

SMOKED FISH

(FROM OUR OWN SMOKER)

IDAHO RAINBOW TROUT 5.75

PACIFIC ALBACORE 4.95

CANADIAN NOVA LOX 7.90

ENTREES

All entrées include your choice of au gratin potatoes, parsley potatoes, french fries, or fishwife rice and freshly made coleslaw, cottage cheese or cherry tomatoes.
Always included are sourdough bread and butter, fresh lemon, and our tartar sauce.

MESQUITE CHARBROILED

FRESH HAWAIIAN HEBI 12.80

FRESH OREGON PETRALE SOLE 12.50

FRESH PACIFIC MAHI MAHI (Dorado) 15.05

FRESH PACIFIC LINGCOD 10.20

FRESH ALASKAN HALIBUT 13.85

FRESH HARPOONED CATALINA SWORDFISH 16.95

FRESH PACIFIC RED SNAPPER 7.75

FRESH HAWAIIAN ONO 14.10

FRESH FLORIDA YELLOWFIN TUNA (Ahi) 14.95

FRESH ALASKAN TROLL CHINOOK SALMON 12.10

FRESH MISSISSIPPI FARM RAISED CATFISH 10.45

FRESH IDAHO FARM RAISED RAINBOW TROUT 9.20

FRESH CALIFORNIA THRESHER SHARK 9.65

FRESH MEXICAN WHITE SEABASS 13.55

NEW ZEALAND ORANGE ROUGHY 12.90

ALASKAN KING CRAB LEGS 22.75

FRESH WHOLE CANADIAN DUNGENESS CRAB 17.75

AUSTRALIAN ROCK LOBSTER TAIL (10 to 12 oz.) 26.50

LIVE MAINE LOBSTER - 1.75 to 2 lbs. 29.35

SKEWERED:

> COMBINATION - **FRESH** PACIFIC RED SNAPPER, **FRESH** EASTERN SEA SCALLOPS, PACIFIC SHRIMP, BELL PEPPER, ONION 10.95
>
> **FRESH** EASTERN SEA SCALLOPS WITH BACON 10.25
>
> **FRESH** TERIYAKI SWORDFISH K-BOB w/PINEAPPLE 15.95
>
> **FRESH** EASTERN SEA SCALLOPS & SHRIMP WITH BACON . 10.95
>
> MAZATLAN PRAWNS 16.50

GRILLED:

PANKO CALAMARI STEAK 9.15

PANKO **FRESH** MARYLAND SOFTSHELL CRABS 13.50

NON-SEAFOOD ENTREES:

CERTIFIED ANGUS RIB EYE STEAK 13.25

TERIYAKI OR ROSEMARY **FREE RANGE** CHICKEN 9.25

For additional information see page 115.

GOLDEN GARDEN RESTAURANT

Menu Changes Seasonally

APPETIZERS

PUPU PLATTER .... (For Two) 8.60
Served Flaming On The Table........................ (Each Additional) 4.30
*Combination Of Egg Roll, Fried Wonton, Chow-Chow Beef, Fried
Shrimp, Barbecued Ribs, Paper Wrapped Chicken.*

RUMAKE (6) 4.50

CHICKEN SALAD... 4.25

BEEF TERIYAKI STICK (4) 4.95

CHEF'S SPECIALTIES (GRAND STYLE)
(Served with Steamed Rice, Fortune Cookies)

SIZZLING BEEF A LA MANDARIN*.. 8.95
Tender Slice Beef with Chinese Vegetables Cooked in Spicy Barbecue Sauce.

SEAFOOD COMBINATION 12.95
*Combination of Shrimp, Crab, Scallops, in Special Brown Sauce with
Fresh Chinese Vegetables.*

PLUM TREE BEEF* 8.95
Chunk Tender Beef Deep-Fried & Cooked with Hot Sauce.

SESAME TRIPLE DELIGHT* 8.95
*Lightly Battered Giant Shrimp, Tender Beef & Chicken Stir-Fried with
Spicy Honey Sauce.*

SZECHWAN SCALLOPS & SHRIMP*... 11.95
*Scallops, Shrimp, Water Chestnuts, Green Onions, Bamboo Shoots &
Mushrooms in Szechwan Spicy Sauce.*

DOUBLE HAPPINESS 11.95
*Sauteed Scallops with Shrimp, Broccoli & Snow Peapods in Special
White Sauce.*

CRISPY GARLIC CHICKEN... 8.95
Sliced Breaded Chicken Served with Garlic Hot Sauce.

SUBGUM SIZZLING PAN FRIED NOODLES 8.95
*Shrimp, Beef & chicken Sauteed with Brown Sauce Over
the Pan Fried Noodles in a Sizzling Hot Plate.*

HUNAN BEEF* 8.95
*Sliced Steak Sauteed with Onion & Bell Pepper in
Famous Hunan Sauce.*

GOLDEN GARDEN TRIPLE DELIGHT 9.95
*Shrimps, Chicken, BBQ Pork, Mushrooms, Bamboo Shoots,
Water Chestnuts, Snow Peapods & Broccoli, in a Savory Sauce,
with Golden Fried Crispy Rice on the Top.*

SNOW HILL (Beef or Chicken)* 8.95
*Sliced Tender Chicken or Beef, Cashew Nut in a Mildly Spicy Sauce,
with Fried Rice Noodles Underneath.*

LOVER'S NEST 11.95
*Tender Chicken, Shrimp, Broccoli, Straw Mushroom, B.B.Q. Pork,
Cabbage, & Snow Peapods with Chef's Special Sauce in an
Edible Basket.*

DRAGON & PHOENIX 11.95
*Sliced Chicken, in special White Sauce, Sauteed Shrimps in
Chili Tomato Sauce.*

KUNG POA THREE INGREDIENTS* 9.95
*Shrimp, Chicken, & Beef Sauteed with Green Onion & Peanuts
in Spicy Sauce.*

HON-HON SHRIMP* 10.95
Crispy Shrimp Sauteed in Sweet & Pungent Sauce.

SWEET PUNGENT SCALLOPS* 10.95
Crispy Scallops Sauteed in Sweet & Pungent Sauce on Broccoli Bed.

MANDARIN THREE TASTES 9.95
*Jumbo Shrimp, Sliced Beef & Chicken Sauteed with Broccoli,
Snow Pea, Mushroom, Chef's Special Brown Sauce.*

TANGERINE CHICKEN* 8.95
Sliced Chicken Dry-Style Cooking with Tangerine Sauce.

SPICY HONEY CHICKEN* 7.50

Hot Spicy

For additional information see page 45.

The GREEK TYCOON

MEZETHES
(APPETIZERS)
COLD SELECTIONS

TARAMASALATA 3.95
*Red Caviar, Whipped into a Prize Winning Spread, Served with
Grilled Pita Bread*

TZATZIKI 3.95
*Yogurt, Cucumber, Fresh Garlic and Fresh Herbs, Blended together in a
Delicious Dip, Served with Grilled Pita Bread*

MELITZANOSALATA 4.50
*Whipped Eggplant salad with a Touch of Garlic, Parsley, Fresh Tomato,
Olive Oil and Herbs. A Taverna Favorite, Served with Grilled Pita Bread*

TABOULI 4.50
*Cracked Wheat, Lemon Juice, Parsley, Green Onions, Fresh Tomato,
Fresh Herbs and Olive Oil*

HOT SELECTIONS

KEFTEDAKIA 4.95
Tiny Greek Meat Balls, Served Hot with Tzatziki Yogurt Sauce

DOLMATHAKIA 5.95
Stuffed Grape Leaves, Served Hot with Avgolemono Sauce

LOUKANICO 6.95
Greek Sausage, Spicy and Delicious, Served Hot with Fresh Lemon

SAGANAKI 6.95
Flaming Kasseri cheese in Lemon-Butter Sauce, served Hot with Pita Bread

GYROS (Yee-Ros) 5.75
*Sandwich In Pita Bread with Lettuce, Tomatoes, Onions, Tzatziki Yogurt
Dressing, Served with Garnitures.*

ENTREES

Served With: Roasted Potatoes or Rice Pilaf and Fresh Vegetable

SPANAKOPITA **9.95**
Greek spinach and Feta Cheese Pie in Filo Dough, Baked Meatless Treat

ROAST CHICKEN RIGANATI **9.95**
Seasoned with Fresh Lemon Juice, a Touch of Garlic, Oregano and other Herbs

MOUSAKA **10.95**
Alternate Layers of Sliced Eggplant with Seasoned Meat Filling, Topped with Bechamel Cream Sauce and Baked

SHRIMP AEGEAN ISLES **14.95**
Shrimp Baked with Shallots, Scallions, Tomatoes, White Wine and Seasonings, Topped with Feta Cheese and Served with Rice

STUFFED GRAPE LEAVES **9.95**
Tender Leaves Stuffed with Ground Meat, Rice, Fresh Dill, Spring Onions, and Other Seasonings, Served with Avgolemono Sauce

LAMB YOUVETSI **11.95**
Baked Lamb Shank with Orzo Pasta, Baked Together in a Mild Greek Provincial Sauce, Natural Lamb Juice, Fresh Tomato and Herbs

SOUVLAKI (Lamb Shish Kebab) **14.95**
Tender Chunks of Lean Lamb, Marinated and Skewered with Green Peppers, Onions and Mushrooms, Broiled and Served with Rice

LAMB CHOPS A LA GREQUE **14.95**
Char-Broiled and Seasoned with Herbs, Touch of Garlic and Fresh Lemon

PASTA SPECIALTIES

PASTITSIO **9.95**
A Classic Greek Dish - Layers of Ziti Pasta and Delicately Spiced Meat Filling, Topped with Bechamel Cream Sauce and Baked

HILOPITES RODOS STYLE **10.95**
Imported Fettuccine Pasta with Shrimp, Tossed in a Fresh tomato and Basil Sauce

FIDES PIQUENTE **9.95**
Island of Corfu Favorite! Angel Hair Pasta Tossed in a Delicious Sauce of Fresh Tomatoes, Smoked Ham, Fresh Basil, and Tiny Capers

LINGUINI SALONICA STYLE **9.50**
Imported Linguini Pasta Tossed with Fresh Dill, Feta and Parmesan Cheeses and a Touch of Cream

For additional information see page 77.

Guadalajara Grill

Menu Changes Seasonally

Appetizers

Quesadilla	Guacamole
4.95	5.75
Guadalajara Nachos	Ceviche Acapulco
5.25	5.95
Taquitos	Cilantro Cheese
5.25	5.95
Queso Fundido	B.B.Q. Ribs
5.50	6.95

Salad

House Salad	Ceviche Salad
3.75	6.25
Caesar Salad	Taco Salad
5.50	6.95

Splash

Pescado al Cilantro 9.95
grilled and topped with a cilantro butter sauce

Pescado a la Veracruzana 10.25
fillet steamed in foil, with capers, olives and spices

Camarones al Chipotle 13.95
shrimp sauteed in a spicy chipotle sauce covered with melted cheese

Peep Peep

Pollo en Mole Poblano 9.95
sauteed chicken in a Puebla style mole sauce

Pollo al Tamarindo 9.95
sauteed chicken in a sweet tropical tamarindo sauce

Mooo!!

Carne Asada a la Tampiquena 10.25
served with a cheese enchilada, rajas poblanas and guacamole

Medallones al Limon 11.50
medallions grilled then sauteed in a lemon sauce

Sabana Arriera 13.50
very thin filete grilled and topped with a spicy arriera sauce

Filete Chemita 14.95
filete sauteed in a chicken, butter, lemon and Lea & Perrins sauce

Oink, Oink

Arroz Cabezon 8.50
marinated pork and chicken in an achiote sauce over rice

Cochinita Pibil 9.95
pork leg marinated in a Mayan Indian sauce

Fajitas
(Mix fajitas with two orders or more)

Seafood Fajitas 12.25 per person

Vegetarian Fajitas 8.95 per person

Guadalajara Combo 13.95 per person

Del Comal
Rice and Beans

Enchiladas 6.95
two corn tortillas filled with your choice of:
Chicken   Beef   Cheese   Cancun

Flautas 5.95
two rolled flour or corn tortillas fried with your choice of:
Chicken   Beef   Cheese

Tacos 6.50
three corn tortillas topped with your choice of:
Carne Asada   Shredded Beef   Grilled Chicken   Fish

Quesadilla 6.25
flour tortilla filled with melted cheese and topped with your choice of:
Grilled Chicken   Garlic Shrimp   Pibil   Vegetarian

For additional information see page 104.

HARBOR'S EDGE

Menu Changes Seasonally

TOSS 'N' SERVE SALADS

Dessert and Vegetables not included

CLASSIC CAESAR $ 7.95
Romaine Lettuce Tossed with Our House Made Caesar Dressing,
Fresh Croutons and Parmesan Cheese

GREEK MEDITERRANEAN $ 8.95
Roasted Garlic, Warm Eggplant, Anchovies, Calamata Olives, Cucumber, Feta Cheese,
Tomato, Mushrooms and Red Pepper on Greens, Tossed in Vinaigrette

DUCK AND CHICKEN NICOISE $10.95
with Green Beans, Olives, Potatoes, Chopped Egg, Capers, Anchovies and Vinaigrette

PASTA

LINGUINI VONGOLE $10.95
with Sicilian Red or White Clam Sauce

GRILLED SALMON & PASTA $13.50
Tomato Cream Sauce, Mushrooms, Peas and Red Pepper

**SPAGHETTI WITH RED ROMA TOMATO SAUCE
AND CHICKEN** $11.50
Spaghetti, Topped with Grilled Breast of Chicken

THIN CRUST PIZZA

Dessert and Vegetables not included

PUTTANESCA STYLE: $ 7.50
with Eggplant, Anchovies, Garlic, Onion, Tomato and Capers

CLAM: $ 8.95
with Pesto and Whole Garlic

FRESH CHICKEN: $ 8.95
with Mushrooms, Red Pepper and Onion

BAKED FOODS

Complimentary Dessert From Our Bakery Included
Items that are suited for Vegetarians are marked*

BAKED FRESH SEA BASS $13.50
Boston Style, Sherry and New England Crumbs

FRESH SALMON LASAGNE $13.50
with Ricotta Cheese Sauce

NAVARIN OF LAMB PIE $13.95
with Whole Onions, Garlic, Red Wine Sauce, and Baked with Mashed Potato

*BAKED POLENTA $ 9.95
on Black Beans with Fresh Vegetables and Cheddar Cheese

*STEAMER BASKET OF FRESH VEGETABLE SPEARS $ 8.95
with Oriental Dipping Sauce and Steamed Rice. Especially for Vegans!

DUNGENESS CRAB CAKES $14.50
with Chili Remoulade

With the following Dinner Entrees Your Choice, Family Style
*Garlic Mashed Potatoes *Wild Rice Croquettes *Green Beans with Garlic Crumbs
*Steamed Fresh Vegetables *Country-Style Beans

ROTISSERIE BIRDS

Complimentary Dessert From Our Bakery Included

COUNTRY STYLE CHICKEN $11.95
Herb Crusted, Cut for Finger Eatin', with Texas Sauce

SPIT ROASTED CRISP DUCK $13.95
with Jalapeno-Mustard Almond Glaze or Double Cherry Sweet and Sour Sauce

LEG-OF-DUCK-IN-THE-POT JAMBALAYA $12.50
Braised Nightly with Spicy Creole-Style Rice

CHAR-BROILED MEATS AND SEAFOOD

Complimentary Dessert From Our Bakery Included

BROILED FLAT-IRON STEAK $15.50
Caramelized Onions and Mushrooms

BROILED FRESH SALMON FILET - With Capers and Chives **$16.50**

BROILED GIANT PRAWNS - Creole Style in Garlic Sauce   **$17.50**

GIANT SEA SCALLOPS - Chili Remoulade   **$17.50**

PEPPERCORN SIRLOIN STEAK   **$18.95**

BROILED BARON OF LAMB - Double Loin Cut   **$19.95**

For additional information see page 56.

COFFEE SHOP

BREAKFAST SERVED ALL DAY

UMMLETTES CAUSE A STIR

Spanish Omelette	5.85
Fresh Spinach Omelette with Cheese	6.00
Ortega Chili Omelette with Cheese	6.00
Guacamole, Bacon and Cheese Omelette	6.10
Chili Bean and Cheese Omelette	6.10

PANCAKES & WAFFLES — BATTER UP

Pancakes .... Stack ... 3.50 .... Short Stack ... 3.20
Your Choice of Buttermilk, Buckwheat, Whole Wheat, or Oatmeal.

Crisp Bacon or Nutty Waffle	5.00
Waffle with Frozen Yogurt and Fruit	5.50
Raisin Walnut French Toast	4.10

BELGIAN WAFFLE
with Strawberries or Blueberries and Whipped Cream
5.85

STRAWBERRY or BLUEBERRY SPECIAL
Waffle, Pancakes or French Toast with Whipped Cream
5.25

NUTTY BANANA WAFFLE
5.50

PANCAKE, WAFFLE or FRENCH TOAST SANDWICH
with Egg and Bacon or Sausage
4.90

Harry's .. CLUB&GRILL

Char-Broiled Chicken Breast Sandwich 5.00
Served with Lettuce and Tomato.
   With Dijon Honey Mustard Sauce 5.50

Sante Fe Chicken Breast Sandwich 5.55
Served with Guacamole.

Grilled White Albacore Melt on Sourdough 5.00

Harry's CHAR BROIL·BURGERS

KETCHUP
WITH
FRIENDS

Mexi Burger 5.60
Served with Guacamole, Swiss Cheese and French Fries.

Sourdough Cheeseburger 5.05
Cheeseburger served on Grilled Sourdough Bread with Grilled Onions and French Fries.

British Burger 5.25
Bacon, Cheese, Tomatoes with French Fries.

Harry's BEST DISHES FORK LORE

CHAR-BROILED HALIBUT STEAK 6.50
French Fries, Coleslaw and a Biscuit.

21 SHRIMP IN A BASKET 6.35
Served with French Fries and Coleslaw.

QUICHE OF THE DAY 5.75
Served with Fresh Fruit and Our Special Muffin.

CALIFORNIA STYLE CHILI SIZE 6.35
Choice Beef Patty topped with Chili and Grated Cheese (onions upon request).
Served with Tossed Green Salad and Crackers.

For additional information see page 28.

Hob Nob Hill

Tasty Salads

TANGY CAESAR SALAD
Croutons

FANCY TOMATO
Stuffed with Chicken or Tuna Salad

GARDEN FRESH SPINACH
Hard Boiled Eggs

FIESTA SALAD
Fresh Lettuce and Black Olives,
Topped with Cheddar Cheese and
Warm Meat Sauce

Six Forty-Five

COBB SALAD
Cured Turkey, Bacon, Tomato, Avocado,
Blue Cheese and Boiled Egg

SALADS SAMPLER
Assorted Cold Plate of Chicken, Tuna, Pasta
and Waldorf Salad, Cottage Cheese
and Fruit Garnish

CALIF. FRESH FRUIT PLATE
Apple, Orange, Pineapple, Banana and
additional Fruit in Season

Seven Forty-Five

Sandwiches
Your Choice of Chilled Gazpacho, Juice, Soup du Jour, Tossed Green, Caesar, Fiesta,
Fresh Spinach, Waldorf, Marinated Bean or Pasta Salad.

REUBEN SPECIAL, Hot Corned Beef, Swiss Cheese, Sauerkraut on Rye .... Six Ninety-Five
THREE DECKER CLUB HOUSE, Bacon, Tomato and Turkey .... Six Ninety-Five
SLICED BREAST OF TURKEY with Peach and Cranberry .... Six Ninety-Five
KING SIZE HAMBURGER, 8 oz. with French Fries .... Six Forty-Five
COLD ROAST BEEF .... Six Forty-Five
CORNED BEEF ON RYE .... Six Forty-Five
COLD or FRIED HAM .... Six Forty-Five
BROILED CHEESEBURGER .... Five Eighty-Five

From Our Broiler

FRESHLY GROUND ROUND STEAK with Mushroom Sauce .... Nine Forty-Five
CENTER CUT SMOKED PORK CHOPS ....Ten Forty-Five
CHOICE FILET DINNER STEAK ....Twelve Forty-Five

Dinners

Your Choice of Juice, Chilled Gazpacho, Soup du Jour, Tossed Green, Fiesta, Caesar, Fresh Spinach, Waldorf, Marinated Bean or Pasta Salad

ROAST PRIME RIB OF CHOICE BEEF, au Jus .... Eleven Forty-Five
CATTLEMEN CUT .... Thirteen Ninety-Five
OLD FASHIONED CHICKEN 'N DUMPLING .... Nine Forty-Five
BABY BEEF LIVER, Grilled with Onions or Bacon .... Eight Ninety-Five
FRENCH FRIED EASTERN SCALLOPS .... Nine Ninety-Five
ROAST TOM TURKEY with Sage Dressing and Giblet Sauce .... Nine Ninety-Five
CHICKEN FRIED STEAK with Country Sauce .... Nine Ninety-Five
GRILLED FISH FILLET with Tartar Sauce .... Eight Twenty-Five
TURKEY CROQUETTES .... Seven Seventy-Five
with Giblet Sauce and Cranberry Relish

SUNDAY
ROAST LEG OF LAMB
Sage Dressing and Mint Jelly
POT ROAST OF BEEF
Jardiniere, Buttered Noodles

MONDAY
CORNED BEEF 'N CABBAGE
Home Cured
ROAST LEG OF PORK
Fruit Dressing and Apple Ring

TUESDAY
BRAISED SHORT RIBS OF BEEF
1/2 COUNTRY FRIED CHICKEN
Cream Sauce

WEDNESDAY
OLD FASHIONED BEEF STEW
Dumpling
ROAST LEG OF PORK
Fruit Dressing and Apple Ring

THURSDAY
AUTHENTIC GERMAN SAUERBRATEN
Potato Pancakes, Red Cabbage
1/2 COUNTRY FRIED CHICKEN
Cream Sauce

FRIDAY
BAKED PACIFIC COD
Vera Cruz Style
GOURMET BREAST OF CHICKEN CURRY
Steamed Wild Rice

SATURDAY
BBQ SPARERIBS
1/2 COUNTRY FRIED CHICKEN
Cream Sauce

| Nine Ninety-Five |

House Specialty
Your Choice of Soup or Salad

BRAISED DOMESTIC
LAMB SHANK
Minted Jardiniere Sauce

(Available Daily, Except Sunday)

Nine Ninety-Five

Executive Favorite
A La Carte
CHOICE OF
COLD PRIME RIB OR BEEF,
CORNED BEEF OR ROAST TURKEY
OR COMBINATION
Cottage Cheese, Pasta or Potato Salad with
Tomatoes and Garnish
Seven Seventy-Five

For additional information see page 29.

SALADS AND APPETIZERS

BRUTUS SALAD (CAESAR)	3.75	PROSCIUTTO CON MELONE		5.95
WALDORF SALAD	5.95	ANTIPASTO SALAD		5.95
APPLES, CELERY, RAISINS, YOGURT DRESSING.		SALAMI, PROVOLONE, PEPPERONCINI, OLIVES AND FRESH GREENS.		
WALDORF CHICKEN SALAD	6.50	CAPRESE		5.95
THE JAIL HOUSE SALAD	4.95	TOMATOES, MOZZARELLA, OLIVE OIL, BASIL.		
LETTUCE, GARBANZOS, SALAMI, MOZZARELLA.		CHICKEN BRUTUS		6.95

ZUPPE

MINESTRONE	2.95
SHRIMP BISQUE	3.95

PIZZE

MARGHERITA	8.95	BAJA BBQ PIZZA	12.50
TOMATOES, MOZZARELLA, BASIL		CHICKEN IN A LIGHT BBQ SAUCE W/JALEPENO, CILANTRO AND GREEN ONIONS	
VEGETARIANO	10.50		
MUSHROOMS, BELL PEPPERS, OLIVES, ONIONS			

PASTA

SPAGHETTI _____ 5.95
MARINARA, MEAT, OR BOLOGNESE SAUCE.
W/ MEATBALLS _____ 6.95
W/ SAUSAGE _____ 6.95

SPAGHETTI AGLIO & OGLIO _____ 7.95
WITH FRESH GARLIC & OLIVE OIL.

**ANGEL HAIR OR SPAGHETTI
MEDITERRANEO** _____ 7.95
FRESH TOMATOES, BASIL, OLIVE OIL.

**SPAGHETTI LILY LANGTRY
(PUTTANESCA)** _____ 7.95
Lilly Langtry--another favorite of the judge!
FRESH TOMATOES, OLIVES, CAPERS AND
FRESH GARLIC.

SPAGHETTI AL PESTO _____ 8.50
FRESH BASIL, PINE NUTS, OLIVE OIL & GARLIC.

PESCI

LINGUINI VONGOLE _____ 8.95
CLAM SAUCE, RED OR WHITE.

SCAMPI FRA DIAVOLO ____ 9.95
SPICY TOMATO SAUCE WITH SIDE OF PASTA.

Fatti In Casa (Made in House)

TORTELLONI VERDI _____ 8.95
A FAVORITE DISH IN SAN DIEGO FOR
30 YEARS!
HOME MADE SPINACH PASTA, STUFFED WITH
CHEESE AND SPINACH SERVED IN THE MOST
INCREDIBLE PORCINI AND MUSHROOM SAUCE.

RAVIOLI VEGETARIANO _____ 7.95
SPINACH & CHEESE, WITH MARINARA, MEAT
OR BOLOGNESE.

TORTELLI PIACENTINA _____ 8.50
PESTO OR BOLOGNESE OR CLASSICO SAUCE.

SCAMPI GIULIO _____ 9.95
A native of Piacenza, Italy, Giulio first
came to this country in 1957. He loves
America's Great West as much as he does
great food. And just like the American
cowboy, he's made his mark on the new
frontier. The tradition lives on and this is it!
A BOUNTY OF SHRIMP, BUTTERFLIED AND
SAUTÉED WITH MUSHROOMS & GARLIC.
SERVED WITH A GENEROUS SIDE OF PASTA.

NOODLES OLD TOWN _____ 8.95
THIN EGG NOODLES, WHITE FISH, SHRIMP IN
WHITE SAUCE.

POLLAME

CHICKEN PICCATA _____ 9.50
FRESH MUSHROOMS & LEMON.
WITH SIDE OF PASTA.

CHICKEN MARSALA _____ 9.50
MARSALA WINE & FRESH MUSHROOMS.
WITH SIDE OF PASTA.

CHICKEN PARMIGIANA _____ 9.50
WITH SIDE OF PASTA.

CHICKEN CACCIATORE _____ 9.50
HEARTY HOME STYLE RECIPE.
WITH SIDE OF PASTA.

For additional information see page 85.

Kaiserhof Restaurant

Menu Changes with Daily Specials and Seasonal Entrees
(Dishes representative of our extensive menu)

Vorspeisen
(Appetizers)

Hot		Cold	
Sauteed Mushrooms	4.95	Herring In Sour Cream	4.95
Weinbergschnecken	6.75	Shrimp Cocktail	6.50
(Escargots, garlic - herb butter)		Smoked Salmon	6.95

Fish Gerichte
(Sea Food)

Rainbow Trout Muellerin _____ 14.35
   sauteed in lemon-parsley butter

Grilled Halibut Steak topped with sauteed mushrooms_____ 16.50

Sauteed Shrimp herbs, cream, Asbach Brandy_____ 17.25

Gemischte Fleischgerichts
(Mixed Entrees)

Bratwurst Swabian style, _____ (2) 13.75 (1) 10.75
   fine veal sausage, fried

Bauernwurst, smoked pork sausage_____ (2) 13.75 (1) 10.75

Zigeunerwurst, bratwurst with gypsy sauce_____ (2) 13.95 (1) 11.50

Vom Kalb * Veal

Wiener Schnitzel _____ 16.75
   breaded milk-fed veal cutlet, sauteed in butter

Schnitzel Holstein _____ 17.75
   breaded veal cutlet, fried egg, anchovies and capers

Jaeger Schnitzel _____ 18.25
   sauteed veal cutlet, mushroom cream sauce

Vom Rind * Beef

Rouladen of Beef _____ (2) 17.95 (1) 14.95
   rolled beef stuffed with bacon, onions, pickles, and carrots

Sauerbraten Bavarian Style _____ 15.25
   marinated beef braised with herbs and spices

Beef Goulash Kaiserhof _____ 14.75
   bottom round, cubed and braised with paprika

Schwaebischer Roastbraten _____ 16.25
   N.Y. steak, sauteed, fried onions, au jus

Vom Schwein * Pork

Kasseler Rippchen _____ 14.95
   smoked center-cut pork chops

Eisbein _____ 14.75
   fresh boiled pork shank

Paprika Schnitzel _____ 14.75
   sauteed pork cutlets, in paprika sour cream sauce

Prices are subject to change

For additional information see page 74.

Kansas City Barbeque

Sandwich Plates
Includes one of the following:
Slaw, Beans, Fries, Rings, Potato Salad, Corn on the Cob

Beef Rib (open face)	5.25
Pork Rib (open face)	5.25
Sliced Beef	4.75
Sliced Pork	4.75
Chicken Breast	5.25
Hot Links	4.75
Rib Tips (when available)	4.75

Dinner Plates
Includes two of the following:
Slaw, Beans, Fries, Rings, Potato Salad, Corn on the Cob

Pork Ribs	8.95
Beef Ribs	8.95
Sliced Beef	8.50
Sliced Pork	8.50
Chicken (add $1.00 for white meat only)	8.50
Hot Links	8.50
Rib Tips (when available)	8.50

Combo (choice of two meats) 9.50

Works (choice of three meats) 10.25

Sampler of four (lots of food) 38.00

Everything Else!

Corn on the Cob 1.25

Curley Fries 1.25

Onion Rings 1.25

Cole Slaw, Potato Salad, BBQ Beans
    Individual .... 1.25   Pint .... 2.50   Quart 5.00

Sandwich a la carte 3.75

Homemade Chili (when available) 2.00

Topeka Pickle (when available) 1.50

Hot Link 2.00

Beef Ribs
    One .... 2.10   1/2 Slab (4) .... 8.00   Slab (7) 14.00

Pork Ribs
    One .... 1.85   1/2 Slab (7) .... 9.00   Slab (13) 16.00

Chicken
    1/2 (4 pieces) .... 7.00   Whole (8 pieces) 12.00

Sliced Beef or Sliced Pork (pound) 7.25

Homemade Desserts

Sweet Potato Pie, Walnut Pie 1.95

Whole Pie 8.00

For additional information see page 31.

Karinya

Menu Changes Seasonally

Appetizers
———◆———

Satay   5.50
Marinated chicken, beef, or pork. Grilled and served with
a rich peanut sauce and a refreshing cucumber sauce.   Extra sauce   .75

Stuffed Chicken Wings   6.95
Boneless chicken wings, stuffed with ground pork, crystal threads, and
mushrooms dipped in batter.

Chiangmai Delight*   6.95
Hot and sour ground pork with a hint of peanuts, onions and ginger.

Firecracker Shrimp   6.95
Marinated fresh shrimp rolled in Thai rice paper, fried until golden brown,
served with our house plum sauce.

Soups
———◆———

Tom Kah*	Cup (Single)	Pot (Serves 4)
Lime-flavored coconut milk soup richly spiced with Siamese ginger, mushroom and lemongrass.		
Chicken	3.00	7.95
Vegetable	3.00	7.95
Shrimp	3.50	8.95
Po Tak*	3.50	11.95

A hot and sour seafood combination soup spiced with mint.

Salads
———◆———

Yum Nuah*   7.75
Grilled beef with green onions, tomatoes, cucumber mixed with a
special lime sauce.

Karinya Salad   7.75
Chicken, hard-boiled eggs, cucumber and crispy noodles on salad greens
covered with a creamy peanut dressing.

House Specialties
———◆———

Karinya Three-Flavor Scallops*   10.95
  Crispy fried scallops smothered with our chef's spicy three-flavored sauce.

Pad Talay*   12.95
  Sautéed mixed seafood bathed in our homemade spicy sauce.
  Our Samed Island recipe.

Volcano Chicken   8.95
  Steamed Cornish Hen quickly deep fried to seal in the juices, covered with
  peas and diced carrots in a tangy sweet butter sauce,
  wrapped in foil and served flaming.

Curries
———◆———

Gang Ped*
  Red chili paste curry in coconut milk, bamboo shoots and fresh Thai sweet basil.

Beef, chicken, pork	7.75
Shrimp or roast duck	8.95
Scallops	9.95
Vegetarian (mock) duck or chicken	7.75

Kang Kari
  Mild yellow coconut milk curry with potato and onions served
  with a refreshing cucumber sauce.

Chicken	7.75
Shrimp or roast duck	8.95
Scallops	9.95
Vegetarian (mock) duck or chicken	7.75

Entrees
———◆———

Most dishes available as follows:

Chicken, beef, or pork	7.75
Shrimp, roast duck, or calamari	8.95
Scallops	9.95
Vegetable and tofu	7.75
Vegetarian (mock) duck or chicken	7.75
Mixed seafood	12.95

Rama*
  Steamed broccoli and boiled egg slices smothered in expertly spiced peanut sauce.

Pad Ped*
  Sautéed with Thai sweet basil and fresh chili and garlic.

Rahd Prig*
  Battered and lightly fried and topped with a zesty chili sauce.

Drunken Noodles*   7.75
  Wide rice noodles pan fried with hot spices and mint.

Dishes marked with * can be ordered mild, medium, or hot.

For additional information see page 119.

Kenny's Steak House of New York

Kenny's features only the finest Prime Beef, corn-fed and dry aged for the distinctive flavor and tenderness we're famous for in New York, and now in San Diego.

Appetizers

Fresh Maryland Lump Crabmeat Cocktail 9.95

Smoked Norwegian Salmon 7.50
With Capers and Onions

Tomato and Mozarella 6.95
Fresh Buffalo Mozzarella with Sliced Tomato, Basil and Sundried Tomatoes

Scampi Mediterranean 9.95
Sautéed Jumbo Shrimp with a White Wine Garlic Sauce

Salads

Sliced Tomato and Onion 4.95
Thick Sliced Beefsteak Tomato and Red Onion

Spinach Salad 4.95
With Egg, Mushroom and a Warm Bacon Vinaigrette

Pastas

Tortellini Sofia 11.95
With a Light Cream Tomato Sauce

Linguine Seafood 15.50
Sauteed Scallops, Crab and Shrimp in a Light Tomato Sauce

Penne Antica 9.95
With Fresh Tomato and Basil

Entrees

Chicken Francaise or Marsala 13.95
  Breast of Chicken with a White Wine Lemon Sauce, or Marsala Mushroom

Cornish Game Hen 13.50
  Roasted and Served with Rice Pilaf and Orange and Raspberry Sauces

Long Island Duck A L' Orange 14.95

Veal Tarragon 14.95
  Milk Fed Veal in a Fresh Tarragon Mustard Cream Sauce

Broiled Salmon Limoné 17.50
  Broiled Salmon with a Lemon Ginger Sauce

Grilled Halibut 15.95
  With White Wine, Pistachios, Basil and Rice Pilaf

Cioppino 17.50
  Fresh Fish and Shell Fish in a Spicy Tomato Based Stew with Garlic Toast

Twin Lobster Tails .... market price

Kenny's Famous Beef

Prime Boneless Sirloin Steak 16 oz 24.95

Filet Mignon 16 oz 24.95

Broiled Milk Fed Veal Chop 24.95

Double Spring Lamb Chop 23.95

T-Bone Steak 32 oz .... market price

Corn Fed Pork Chops 15.95

Kenny's Special Mixed Grill 19.95

Filet Mignon En Brochette 17.95

Steak Diane 22.95

Roast Prime Ribs of Beef 23.95

  Kenny's Famous Beef served with choice of Baked, Stuffed, or Lyonnaise Potatoes

For additional information see page 38.

RESTAURANT

Appetizers

Aushak
Small portions of scallion-filled dumplings topped with yogurt, meat sauce and sprinkled with mint
2.95

Bulaunee
A Turnover stuffed with leek and potato, served with yogurt sauce.
2.50

Sambosa
Fried pastries stuffed with ground beef, coriander and parsley.
2.95

Hummos
A famous middle eastern appetizer of blended garbanzo beans, onion, parsley and garlic, served with Tzatziki sauce and warm pita.
2.50

Soups

Aush
Vegetable and noodle soup topped with yogurt and ground beef.
2.50

Mashawa
Five bean soup. (Vegetarian)
2.50

Salads

Greek salad
Romaine lettuce, tomato, chick-peas, parsley and olives, topped with Feta Cheese and homemade dressing.
3.50

Tabouleh
Famous Lebanese salad of diced tomato, onion, chopped parsley, mint and crushed wheat, marinated with olive oil and lemon juice, served with warm pita.
3.50

4647 Convoy St • Kearny Mesa • (619) 571-3777

Entrees

Quabili Palow
Delicately seasoned pieces of lamb under a mound of saffron-flavored rice topped with carrot strips and raisin.
13.95

Yaghout Chalow
A delicious sweet and sour rice cooked with lamb, cherries and topped with saffron.
13.95

Special Tandory Shrimp or Swordfish
Served with rice and vegetables.
Swordfish 13.50
Shrimp 14.95

Beef Shish Kabob
Pieces of beef specially marinated and charcoal broiled, served with rice and vegetables.
12.95

Shole Goshti
Special seasoned lamb with a mixture of lentils, mung beans, special rice, herbs and spices, stewed slowly for a very subtle taste.
13.95

Chalow Baunjaun
Sauteed eggplant topped with yogurt, served with white rice.
7.95

Chicken, Shrimp or Lamb Curry
Sauteed and cooked with special homemade yogurt and curry, served with vegetables and rice.
Chicken 13.95
Shrimp 15.95
Lamb 14.95

Murgh Shish Kabob
Two skewers of specially marinated boneless chicken breast, served with rice and vegetables.
13.95

Khyber Pass Specialty

Chicken Tandory
Succulent chicken (whole cornish) marinated in yogurt and special herbs, roasted to a crisp tenderness in our Tandor.
13.50

Mantu
Steamed pasta shells filled with seasoned ground beef and onion topped with a savory yogurt, garlic and meat sauce.
12.95

For additional information see page 24.

SOUTHWESTERN CUISINE

SMALL PLATES

NACHOS
Crisp blue corn tortillas with choice of:

Black beans and cheese	**4.50**	Carnitas	**5.95**
Grilled chicken or steak	**5.95**	Lobster & Shrimp	**6.95**

QUESO FUNDIDO   5.95
Mexican sausage and soft cheese baked with tomatoes and sweet corn relish. Prepared tableside

WARM CORN CREPE TACO   4.95
Filled with BBQ smoked duck, pepper sauce and orange salsa

SOUPS & SALADS

POZOLE VERDE   3.75
Chicken, large corn kernels and green chiles in broth. Served with condiments

WARM FAJITA SALAD   8.75
Steak, chicken or duck, with jicama, cucumber, roasted pepitas and cheese, tossed with a warm jalapeño vinaigrette

MESQUITE ROASTED DUCK SALAD   9.50
Warm duck served on a bed of mixed greens with dried cherry vinaigrette, grilled corn, red potatoes, cold poached green beans and yellow squash

MEXICAN SEABASS SALAD   9.95
Summer greens tossed in serrano chile-tomatillo vinaigrette with cilanto-pesto rice and fresh fruit slices

SOUTHWESTERN SPECIALTIES

SMOKED VEGETABLE PIE   9.25
Mixed vegetables and cheese baked in blue corn crust with roasted
red pepper flan and green chile pesto

NAVAJO BRAIDS   17.95
Seared braids of sizzling filet mignon and fire roasted tomatillo sauce with
orange-achiote onion rings, avocado relish and beans a la olla

SMOKED CHILE PASTA   11.45
Chicken breast with corn fettucini and grilled vegetables in a smoked jalapeno
cream sauce

SEAFOOD POZOLE VERDE   16.95
Lobster, shrimp, scallops, mussels and seabass simmered in a tomatillo and
green chile broth with large corn kernels

SEABASS TACOS   9.95
Sauteed fresh seabass on white corn tortillas with guacamole and
pico de gallo

SABANA   17.95
Filet Mignon pounded into a thin sheet, grilled with red chili adovo and
warm salsa verde

MEXICAN PLATES

CARNITAS   9.95
Tender pork steamed in banana leaves with Tucatán achiote sauce

LOBSTER & SHRIMP CORN CREPE ENCHILADAS   9.50
Tomatillo green chile sauce

TRIO OF ENCHILADAS   9.95
Beef in red chile, Chicken in chipotle and Lobster & Shrimp in tomatillo

GRILLED SEABASS CHILE RELLENO, SCALLOP & SPINACH CREPE ENCHILADA
AND LOBSTER & SHRIMP TAMALE   11.95

LOBSTER & SHRIMP BURRITO, RED CHILE CHICKEN TAMALE &
CRISPY BLUE CORN BEEF TACO   11.50

For additional information see page 117.

Les Hors D'Oeuvres

Pate Maison · Country Style Pate w/Walnuts		4.75
Rillettes de Porc · Creamy Pork Spread		4.75
Jambon de Bayonne · Thin Smoked French Ham		4.75
Saucisson a L'Ail · French Garlic Sausage		4.75
Rosette de Lyon · French Dry Salami		4.75
Mousse de Foie de Canard · Duck Liver Spread		8.75
Assiette de Charcuterie · A Little of All the Above		8.75

Leeks in Vinaigrette	3.75
Red Cabbage in Red Wine Vinegar	3.75
Carrots in Lemon Dressing	3.75
Beets in Vinaigrette	3.75
Cucumber in Sour Cream Dressing	3.75
Tomatoes in Vinaigrette	3.75
Assiette de Crudites · A Little of All the Above	7.75

Escargot de Bourgogne · 1/2 Dozen	5.75
Full Dozen	11.00
Foie Gras Truffe · Goose Liver w/Truffles	25.00
Beluga Caviar et Ses Condiments	50.00

Les Soupes

Soupe du Jour · Soup of the Day		3.25
Soupe a L'Onion Gratinee · French Onion Soup		4.50

Les Viandes & Volailles

Boeuf Bourguignon ·   13.75
   Classic Country Style Stew in Red Wine Sauce
Filet aux Deux Poivres ·   18.75
   Filet Mignon in a Green & Black Peppercorn Sauce
Carre d' Agneau des Alpilles ·   20.75
   Rack of Lamb in a Garlic & Herbs Sauce
Cote de Veau aux Chanterelles ·   19.75
   Provimi Veal chop in a Mushroom & Cream Sauce
Carnard au Poivre Vert ·   17.50
   Roast Duckling in a Green Peppercorn Sauce
Poulet a L'Estragon ·   13.75
   Breast of Chicken in a Tarragon & Mushrooms Sauce

Les Poissons & Crustaces

Truite aux Amandes ·   13.75
   Fresh Rainbow Trout in a Lemon Butter Sauce w/Almonds
Saumon Maitre d'Hotel ·   17.75
   Fresh Filet of Saumon in a Light Lemon Butter
Sole Belle Meuniere ·   21.25
   Fresh Dover Sole in a Lemon Butter & Mushrooms Sauce
Crevettes Provencale ·   17.75
   Prawns in a Garlic & Herbs Sauce
Cuisses de Grenouilles ·   15.75
   Frogs Legs in a Mushrooms, Garlic & Tomato Sauce

For additional information see page 71.

Lafonda
ROBERTO'S

Menu Changes Seasonally

ENTREMESES
APPETIZERS

CREPAS DE HUITLACOCHE
A delicious truffle-like black mushroom wrapped in a feather light crepe,
with a delicious sour cream based sauce (in season). $4.95

FONDUE CHEESE
With choice of mushrooms or chorizo, served with corn or flour tortillas. $4.95

SOPAS & ENSALADAS
SOUPS & SALADS

SOPA DE TORTILLA
Chicken based broth with cheese and tortilla strips. Delicious!!! $1.50

ENSALADA DE NOPALITOS
Tender young cactus, mild chopped onions, sliced red radishes,
cilantro and fresh cotija cheese, topped with a light vinaigrette. $3.95

ANTOJITOS MEXICANOS
MEXICAN SPECIALTIES
Served with rice & beans

SOPES SURTIDOS
Three very thick corn dough tortillas spread with beans. One with chicken,
one with beef, and one with chorizo. Garnished with lettuce, sour cream
and cheese on top. $4.95

CHILAQUILES
Bits of corn tortillas, simmered into our zesty green or red sauce, topped
with shredded chicken, sour cream, cheese and fresh onion rings. $5.95

ESPECIALIDADES E ROBERTO'S
ROBERTO'S SPECIALTIES

MOLE POBLANO (PUEBLA)
Tender chicken prepared with seven varieties of chile, chocolate-flavored and
sprinkled with roasted sesame seeds. $7.95

PEPIAN VERDE (PUEBLA)
A delicious chicken dish prepared in a sumptuous sauce of crushed
pumpkin seeds, tomatillos and serrano chilis. $7.95

COCHINITA PIBIL (YUCATAN)
From south of Mexico, juicy shredded pork deliciously seasoned with
axiote seeds, cumin and garlic. $7.95

MIXIOTE DE CARNERO (HIDALGO)
Spicy leg of lamb wrapped to preserve its own savory juices. $8.95

CHILE EN NOGADA (PUEBLA)
A large, mild, green chile stuffed with a mixture of beef, chopped fruit,
nuts and raisins, fried in a light egg batter and covered with
a creamy nut sauce. $8.95

CARNE
MEATS
*INCLUDE SOUP OR SALAD & TORTILLAS

TACO AZTECA
Juicy steak filled with tender nopalitos in sesame seed sauce, covered with
chipotle sauce & melted cheese. $8.95

FILET MIGNON
Juicy top sirloin steak, prepared with a delicious mushroom sauce
served with leonesa style potatoes. $8.95

PESCADOS Y MARISCOS
FISH AND SEAFOOD

HUARACHE AZTECA (ROBERTO'S CREATION)
Tender cactus stuffed with red snapper & finished with
a garlic & wine sauce! $8.95

CAMARONES AL GUSTO (GULF & PACIFIC)
Large shrimp, prepared with garlic, meuniere or ranchero sauce. $8.95

For additional information see page 105.

LA GRAN TAPA
CAFE & BAR

Menu Changes Seasonally

SOPAS * SOUPS

SPICY BLACK BEAN SOUP .... Cup 3.50
with Sour Cream and Salsa   Bowl 4.50

SOPA DE AJO
Rich Saffron Broth with Garlic, Poached Egg and Crouton 4.75

ICED GAZPACHO
Cold Andalusion Soup of Tomatoes and Cucumbers.................................... 4.00

ENSALADAS * SALADS

ENSALADA VASCA
Tomatoes, Cucumbers, Green Peppers, Olives, Feta Cheese 5.95

ENSALADA CABRALESE
Romaine, Tomatoes and Blue Cheese, Xeres Vinegar Dressing.................... 4.95

MARISCOS * SEA FOOD

VIERAS CON AJILLO
Scallops in Garlic and Butter 4.50   9.00

CAZON EN ADOBADO
Marinated Shark Deep-Fried with Bravas Sauce 4.00   8.00

GAMBAS A LA AJILLO
Shrimp with Garlic, Olive Oil, Chile and Paprika 9.50

PULPOS A LA PLANCHA
Octopus Marinated in Olive Oil, Salt, Garlic on the Grill............................... 7.50

MEJILLONES AL VAPOR
Black Mussels Steamed with Wine, Garlic, Butter 6.50

ALMEJAS ROMESCO
Clams Steamed in Catalan Romescu Sauce 7.75

PAELLA

WE SERVE PAELLA Every Night from 5 p.m. until 10 p.m.
Please allow 25 minutes for preparation

Traditional Paella of Saffron Rice With Chicken, Chorizo, Shrimp,
Octopus, Clams and Mussels

35.00 (for two)

PLATOS ESPECIALES * SPECIAL DISHES

JALAPENO TORTELLONI
In Creamy Tomato Sauce 8.50

PISTO MANCHEGO
Fresh Summer Vegetable Stew Baked with Cheese 4.00   8.00

FABADA ASTURIANA
Giant White Beans Cooked with Sausage, Pork, Paprika .... 4.50   ---

JAMON SERRANO
Fine Air-Cured Spanish Ham, Similar to Prosciutto 4.25   8.00

ZARZUELA
Shrimp, Mussels, Scallops, Clams, Fish, Octopus in Saffron Broth 15.50

PORK AND CLAMS
House Favorite, Spicy Pork, Chorizo, Cilantro with Clams 12.50

PINCHO MORUNO
Spicy Lamb Broquette, Grilled with Red Onion 4.75

POLLO EN AJILLO
Chicken Drumettes in Sherry, Garlic Parsley Sauce 2.75   5.50

TORTILLA ESPAÑOLA
Traditional Spanish Potato Omelet 1.75   3.50

ENSALADILLA RUSA
Potatoes, Peas, Carrots in Olive Oil Aioli Sauce 2.50   5.00

MOROS Y CHRISTIANOS
Spicy Black Beans over Basque Rice, Salsa 5.95

ENTRECOTE
Grilled 10 oz. New York Steak Brushed with Oil and Garlic 14.95

FLASH-GRILLED BEEF
Thinly Sliced Tenderloins Grilled, Volcano Sauce 13.95

HUEVOS AL FLAMENCO
Eggs Baked on Sofrillo with Chorizo, Artichokes, Asparagus 9.50

LANGOSTINOS AL AJILLO
5 Jumbo Head on Prawns, Olive Oil, Garlic Sauce 15.95

For additional information see page 117.

Menu Changes Seasonally

A Healthy Head Start

Breakfast Banana Split 3.45
Banana, strawberry yogurt, strawberries, blueberries and granola.

Dutch Apple Oatmeal 3.95
*A traditional favorite . . . laced with "Mom's" Sassy Apples® and raisins.
Served with a California Raisin Gooey Bun™ and cream cheese.*

Homespun Pancakes

Granola Cakes 4.95
Honey-laced granola and slivered almonds.

Trail Cakes 4.95
Chock-full of trail mix and riddled with "Mom's" Sassy Apples.®

Berry Crunchy Cakes 5.45
Plump blueberries, crunchy granola, sliced almonds and blueberry compote on the side.

Royal French Toast
*Vienna bread dipped in custard batter and grilled golden.
Served with a side of "Mom's" Sassy Apples® or strawberry sauce.
Choice of bacon or sausage.*
5.95

Battered Toast 4.95
A new crunchy treat! Our original toast dipped in granola and almonds.

French Toast Twist 4.75
Our imaginative cooking team introduces a new "Twist"...our original custard batter using WHITES of eggs only.

Mile-High Breakfast Crepes

Aspen Fruit Crepes... **4.65**
Tempting crepes filled with choice of bananas, strawberries, blueberries or "Mom's" Sassy Apples,® finished with whipped topping and cinnamon.

Chicken Crepes Benedict.. **5.75**
Diced chicken, fresh mushrooms, water chestnuts, broccoli and diced tomatoes rolled into our crepes and smothered with a creamy Hollandaise sauce. A gourmet's delight.

Southwestern Crepes **5.75**
Start with choice of spicy Southwestern sausage or seasoned chicken, add salsa and diced chilies, roll them into our delicate crepes. Topped with melted cheese and sour cream.

Pampered Eggs™

Green Fields Forever... **6.25**
Fresh spinach, fresh mushrooms, chicken and cream cheese share the pan with velvety scrambled eggs. A side of Hollandaise.

Bumper Crop **6.25**
Crisp broccoli, fresh mushrooms, water chestnuts scrambled with fresh eggs and cream cheese. Hollandaise on the side.

Awesome Omelettes

Tomahawk™ **Chile** **6.25**
Bursting with cheese, then smothered with our soon to be famous "Tomahawk™ chicken chile."

Seascape... **5.85**
Chunks of seafood locked in with fresh spinach, mushrooms and cream cheese, served with Hollandaise on the side.

Omni Omelette **6.75**
Diced ham, sausage, bacon, mushrooms, seasonal vegetables and blended cheese.

Panhandled Specialties

Hobo Banquet™ **4.95**
A skillet full of Peasant Potatoes,® diced onions, melted blended cheese and a lid of two basted eggs.

Desperado...Our Award Winner **6.95**
Peasant Potatoes® spiced up with chorizo sausage, green chilies, and onion. Smothered in salsa, melted cheese and topped with two basted eggs.

For additional information see page 33.

a la Carte

Appetizers

Escargots 5.95	Shrimp Cocktail 6.75
Smoked Salmon 6.25	Carpaccio 6.95

Shrimp Bordelaise (for two)   13.95

Pasta

Any of our pastas may be split for two as an appetizer or accompaniment

Fettuccine Alfredo 8.95	Cannelloni della Casa 9.95
Tortellini "Liaison" 9.00	Linguini con Vongole 9.50
Tortellini Supreme 9.50	Crab Ravioli with Lobster Sauce 13.95

Our Award Winning Prix Fixe

Stimulate your appetite with one of the following selections: a variety of our homemade patés, Raviolo stuffed with chicken and spring vegetables or our Marinated Crayfish and Bay Scallops. Sorbet follows to cleanse the palate. Dinner will be followed by a choice of freshly made desserts for an additional $5.00

13.50 Menu

Lamb Curry
Tender tips of lamb served over rice with almonds, tomatoes and a side of chutney
Chicken Jerusalem
Artichokes, mushrooms, shallots, sherry and cream

Pâtes Fraiches aux Fruits de Mer
A variety of fresh fish with calamari, shrimp, scallops,
clams and mussels (when avaliable)
in a light cream sauce with sherry wine and shallots over fresh pasta

15.50 Menu

Coquilles St. Jacques
Succulent scallops baked in a light cream sauce with mushrooms
and sherry wine with duchess potatoes

Médallions of Beef Bearnaise
Médallions of filet mignon sautéed to taste, topped with bearnaise sauce
and mushroom caps or with Roquefort sauce

Roast Duckling à l'Orange
Half a crisp duck served on the bone with orange sauce

18.50 Menu

Saumon au Beurre D'écrevisse
Salmon, shrimp and sea scallops served in a crayfish butter sauce with cognac,
mushrooms and a touch of cream

Médallions de Veau aux Champignons Sauvages
Veal tenderloin sautéed with mixed forest mushrooms in a light cream sauce with shallots

Tournedos Madeira
Centercut filet mignon, wrapped in bacon, broiled with a madeira wine sauce
with mushrooms

Specialties Liaison
(for 2) 22.50 pp

Rack of Lamb   Chateaubriand
Both presented à la Bouquetierre

All entrées served with a choice of soup or salad

For additional information see page 71.

Appetizers

Clams Posillipo.. 7.95
Clams Steamed in White Wine, Garlic and Butter

Vermicelli Manhattan... 6.95
Vermicelli in a Cream Tomato Sauce

Mezzaluna... 7.50
Half moon pasta filled with seafood, topped with a crab sauce.

Seafood Ravioli.. 6.95
Homemade Seafood Ravioli Covered with a Cream Sauce.

Salads

Manhattan Salad.. 4.95
Tossed Salad with Chopped Eggs, Croutons, Scallions, Bacon Bits and Tomatoes.
Your Choice of Dressing.

Spinach Salad...*for two*   13.95
Fresh Spinach Greens with Hot Bacon Dressing.

Pastas

Scampi Fra Diavolo Con Linguini................................... 17.95
In a Diavolo Sauce (Mild, Hot, Very Hot).

Cannelloni.. 12.50
Homemade Pasta Stuffed with Ground Veal, Spinach and Spices.

Vermicelli al Moro di Venezia....................................... 22.95
Lobster, Crabmeat, Sauteed with Shallots, Garlic, Olive Oil, Butter,
flamed with Grappa, Fresh Tomato, and Cream.

Seafood

Scampi P.J. *18.95*
A House Specialty - Jumbo Shrimp Sauteed in Garlic, Lemon and Wine.

Swordfish or Halibut Napoletano *18.95*
Sauteed or Broiled with Fresh Tomatoes.

Seafood Mediterranean .... *Market Price*
Lobster, Shrimp and Clams in a delightful Seafood Broth.

Lamb

Rack of Lamb Bouquetiere *23.95*
Roast Rack of Lamb with Parisian Potatoes and Fresh Vegetables.

Veal

We Proudly Serve Eastern Milk-Fed Veal

Veal Scaloppini Francese *17.95*
Veal Dipped in Egg then Sauteed in Lemon and Wine

Double Veal Chop .... *Market Price*
Lemon, Olive Oil, Garlic, Salt, Pepper, and Parsley. The Ultimate Veal Lover's Dish.

Beef

We Proudly Serve Aged Mid-Western Black Angus Beef

New York Steak Syracuse *24.95*
New York Charco-Broiled and Topped with Chopped Tomatoes, Black Olives,
Sweet Peppers and Fresh Oregano.

New York Pepper Steak Flambe *24.95*
New York Sauteed with Cracked Pepper and Deglazed with Cognac.

Pollo

Pollo Piccata *15.95*
Boneless Breast of Chicken Sauteed in Lemon, Capers and Wine.

Pollo Cacciatore *15.95*
Boneless Breast of Chicken Simmered in a Tomato Sauce with Bell Peppers and Onions.

For additional information see page 87.

Marius

Les Soupes

Golden Tomato Soup with Stuffed Zucchini Blossoms
Soupe de Tomates Jaunes et Fleurs de Courgettes Farcies

Shellfish Bouillon with Sauteed Langoustines and light Spinach Cream
Le Bouillon de Langoustines à la Crème d'Epinards

Les Hors-d'Oeuvres

Marinated Tuna "Charlotte" with Crisp Potatoes and Caviar
Charlotte de Thon et Croustillant de Pommes de Terre au Caviar

Wild Mushroom Raviolis with Fresh Herb Butter
Les Raviolis de Champignons Sauvages, Beurre aux Herbes

Sauteed Foie Gras with Grapes and Provençale Muscat Wine
Le Foie Gras Sauté aux Raisins de Muscat et Baume de Venise

Sauteed Pacific Shrimp and Mâche with Orange Vinaigrette
La Salade de Mâche et Crevettes Sautées, Vinaigrette à L'Orange

French Escargots on a bed of Ratatouille with Glazed Garlic Butter
Le Petit Gratin d'Escargots sur Lit de Ratatouille et Beurre à L'Ail

Medley of Baby Field Greens with Julienne of Apple and Truffle Vinaigrette
La Salade de Mesclun aux Pommes, à la Vinaigrette de Truffe

Les Poissons et Crustacés

Poached Salmon on a bed of Spinach with Courte-Nage accented with Ginger
Saumon Poché en Courte-Nage de Gingembre

Grilled Mediterranean Sea Bass with Fennel, Black Mussels and light Saffron Sauce
Le Filet de Loup Grillé, au Fenouil et Moules à la Sauce Légerement Safranée

Crisp Lobster Galettes scented with Basil and served with Julienne of Vegetables
Les Croustillants de Homard aux Pieds de Porc et au Basilic

Sauteed John Dory on a bed of Crushed Potatoes and Black Olives
with Shallot Confit
Le Saint-Pierre aux Pommes de Terre Ecrasées et aux Echalotes Confites

Les Viandes et Volailles

Roasted Tenderloin of Angus Beef served with Violet Mustard Sauce
and "Pommes Bouchon"
Le Filet de Boeuf Mariné et Rôti au Moût de Vin et Pommes Bouchon

Sauteed Young Lamb Chops with Sage Gratiné and Risotto Galette
Les Cotelettes d'Agneau gratinées à la Sauge et au Risotto

Moscovy Duck Breast Encrusted with Rosemary and Lavender Honey Sauce
Le Magret de Canard en Croute de Romarin et Miel de Lavande

Sauteed Veal Tenderloin on a bed of Creamed Spinach
with Porto Sauce and "Pommes Maxim"
Les Filets de Veau au Vieux Porto et Pommes Maxim

Les Desserts

Selection from Chef's Confectionary Creations
La Selection de Douceurs et de Patisseries

Any Three Courses $39.00	*Any Four Courses $45.00*	*Any Five Courses $50.00*
with Three Paired Wines	*with Four Paired Wines*	*with Five Paired Wines*
$54.00	*$65.00*	*$75.00*

For additional information see page 72.

225

MEXICAN VILLAGE
RESTAURANTE Y CANTINA

Menu Changes Seasonally

BOTANAS (Appetizers)

TERIYAKI CHICKEN WINGS   4.25
Generous portion of delicious wings served in a basket.

EVA'S SPECIAL QUESADILLA   5.95
Soft flour tortilla served open-faced with melted Jack cheese, bacon,
avocado slices, tomatoes and sour cream.

STUFFED JALAPENOES *   5.25
Deep-fried Jalapenoes stuffed with cheese and served with Ranch Dressing.
(*Number one appetizer in 1993)

ENSALADAS & SOPAS

BLACK BEAN SOPA   1.95
After many requests we have finally put this wonderful and traditional soup
on our menu. It's a great way to begin your meal, made fresh in our kitchen.

MEXICAN VILLAGE ROMAINE   2.75
(a house specialty for over 40 years) - Crisp romaine topped with homemade
croutons, and tossed with the World's Best bleu cheese Caesar dressing.
                                               with Chicken **5.95**

PEPE'S PLATTER (for two)

The "perfect" DINNER FOR TWO - begin your meal with a crisp
quesadilla appetizer, then enjoy a platter of Pollo Borracho,
Ground Beef Enchiladas, Stuffed Jalapenoes, Refried Beans and
Spanish Rice. Finish with a delicious Chocolate Chimi
served with two spoons.   **14.95**

MEXICAN DINNERS

All entrees served with Refried Beans and Spanish Rice

BAJA SCAMPI   **12.95**

Tender jumbo shrimp sautéed in garlic, butter and wine, served over rice, with tortillas or rolls and butter.

CARNE ASADA   **10.95**

Marinated steak strips broiled to perfection and served with guacamole and warm tortillas. (A must-order for the first-time visitor to M.V.)

POLLO BORRACHO   **8.95**

Broiled chicken marinated in a white wine sauce. A new taste sensation. (Bill Griffith, Channel 10, rates this dish ★ ★ ★ ★.)

MEXICAN VILLAGE SPECIALTIES

MEXICAN PIZZA   **6.95**

(Has been a customer favorite for 43 years and still is tops.) Crisp flour tortilla topped with refried beans, guacamole, seasoned beef, lettuce, tomatoes and melted cheddar cheese.

VILLAGE BURRITO   **6.75**

(Our very BEST burrito) A large flour tortilla filled with spicy shredded beef and topped with a savory Spanish sauce.

All specialties served with Refried Beans and Spanish Rice

FAJITAS AND CARNITAS

SHRIMP FAJITAS   **11.95**

Delicious Shrimp sautéed with peppers, onions, tomatoes and mushrooms served with condiments and warm tortillas.

CARNITAS   **9.55**

Our "Thursday Night Special" was so popular that we made it a regular menu item. Chef Pepe prepares this dish from the heart - order this dish one time and you'll be hooked forever. Start with a warm tortilla, butter lightly, top with your choice of chopped tomatoes, onions, cilantro, guacamole and a wedge of lime or use everything - finally, adding the delicious pork chunks, roll carefully - Olé!

For additional information see page 105.

Milligan's
BAR & GRILL

Appetizers

Milligan's Steak fingers 5.50
Our chicken fried steak, served with country gravy.

Shrimp Grilled on a Skewer with Salsa 7.95

Sauteed Abalone de Calamari 5.50

Soups & Salads

Milligan's Baked Onion Soup 5.50
*Onions, rich beef broth, Dry Sack Sherry, Swiss and parmesan cheeses,
with a little Milligan magic.*

Milligan's Cobb Salad 9.50
*The original with diced chicken, avacados, tomatoes, bacon, bleu cheese,
hard boiled egg, on a bed of cold, crisp romaine lettuce. Choice of our
freshly made dressings.*

Fitness with Flavor
Calories and Fat measurements are Approximate

Dijon Chicken 11.95
*Boneless, skinless chicken breast, poached in fresh orange juice with dijon
mustard and rosemary. Served with wild rice and steamed vegetables. 300
Calories, 5 Grams Fat.*

Fresh Vegetable Platter 10.50
*Fresh vegetables steamed, with a broiled tomato and baked onion.
Includes a house salad.*

Entrees

All entrees include salad tossed tableside or soup du jour, choice of real
mashed potatoes, shoestring potatoes, homemade chips, baked potato or
baked onion, plus creamed corn, vegetables medley and selections from
our fresh in-house baked breads.

Milligan's Southern Fried Chicken THE HOUSE SPECIALTY 13.50
Juicy and Crisp. Served with biscuits, honey and country gravy.

Artichoke Chicken Breast...15.95
*Baked, boneless, skinless chicken breast topped with artichoke and
parmesan cheese.*

Shrimp and Fettuccine 17.50
Tossed in fresh basil, tomatoes and cream.

Abalone de Calamari 13.95
Medallions of calamari sauteed quickly in a caper beurre blanc sauce.

Fresh Morning Market Catch of the Day .... Market Price

Spring Lamb Chops 23.95
Broiled to your liking. Served with mint jelly or garlic sauce.

Steak and Lobster 25.95
One 4 oz. tournedo and one Australian tail.

All our Beef is Aged Corn-Fed Angus Beef, The Finest Available.

Tournedos of Filet Mignon 21.00
Choice of peppercorn, garlic or bearnaise sauce.

"USDA Prime" Prime Rib of Beef Au Jus 22.00
Served with creamy horseradish sauce.

Roast Pork in a 3 Peppercorn Mustard Crust....................15.95
Served with an apple brown sauce.

Hickory Smoked Baby Back Pork Ribs .... Half rack 14.95

Smoked in our own kitchen smoker, tender baby back   Full rack 18.95
pork ribs served with a rich southwestern barbecue glaze.

Chicken Fried Steak..12.95
Pounded fresh angus beef, panfried with our specially seasoned coating.

For additional information see page 33.

MING
COURT

APPETIZERS

BARBECUED SPARE RIBS (4)	$6.95
HONEY ROASTED PORK SLICES	4.95
CHINESE CHICKEN SALAD	3.25
PAN FRIED DUMPLING (6)	4.25
SHRIMP MEDALLION (4)	6.95
SPICY FRIED CALAMARI	4.75
STUFFED CRAB CLAWS (2)	4.95
SMOKED CHICKEN W/SEAWEED	6.95
FLAMING PO-PO PLATTER	$4.50 per person (Minimum of 2 persons)

A combination of Tempura Shrimp, Barbecued Spare Ribs, Paper Wrapped Chicken, Fried Wonton, and Skewered Beef.

SOUP FOR TWO

SHARK'S FIN SOUP	$12.50
DRAGON PHOENIX SOUP	5.50
SIZZLING THREE INGREDIENT RICE SOUP	5.50

VEGETARIAN DISHES

BUDDHA'S DELIGHT	$6.25
SZECHUAN BEAN CURD	6.25
SAUTEED STRING BEANS	6.25
EGG PLANT IN YU-HSIANG SAUCE	6.25

MING COURT SPECIALTIES

MING COURT SEAFOOD PHOENIX NEST $14.45
Shrimp, scallops, crabmeat and abalone sauteed in a delicate wine sauce nestled in a crisp potato basket.

SAR CHAR SHRIMP 11.95
Lightly battered fried jumbo shrimp sauteed in spicy sar-char sauce.

FILLET OF FISH WITH CHINESE VEGETABLES 11.95
Rock cod fillets stir-fried with assorted Chinese vegetables in a special delicate white sauce.

MONGOLIAN LAMB WITH LEEKS 9.95
Sliced lamb sauteed with leeks in a rich brown sauce.

SIZZLING ODD COUPLE 12.95
Sliced beef tenderloin and scallops stir-fried with scallions and green peppers served on a hot sizzling platter.

FIVE-SPICES PORK CHOPS 9.95
Paper-thin pork chops seasoned with five condiments fried to golden perfection.

CILANTRO CHICKEN 9.95
Whole fresh chicken tenderloin sauteed in Chinese parsley, lightly battered, and thinly sliced.

MING COURT CRISPY DUCK Half 11.50
Marinated Long Island duckling fried to perfection, with petite lotus buns. Whole 22.00

YIN YANG SHRIMP 13.95
Tender shrimp prepared in two different sauces with two distinct flavors.

BEEF STEAK HONG KONG STYLE 14.95
Filet mignon marinated in chef's special sauce and pan-fried to perfection.

ABALONE WITH BLACK CHINESE MUSHROOMS 22.95
Abalone and mushrooms braised in oyster sauce.

SWEET AND PUNGENT PORK CHOPS 9.95
Thin pork chops deep fried, served in a sweet tangy sauce.

LOBSTER IN BLACK BEAN SAUCE 22.95
Lobster with shell prepared Cantonese style with imported black beans.

PEKING DUCK $25.00
Long island duckling processed in the genuine Peking manner, served with home-made crepes, scallions brushes, sliced cucumbers, hoisin sauce and carved at tableside.

Dishes marked with are served hot and spicy

For additional information see page 47.

MISTER A's RESTAURANT

Hors D'Oeuvres

Mister A's Baked Oysters	9.95	Combination Seafood Cocktail	12.95
With Wild Mushrooms, Brie & Prosciutto		Oysters on Half Shell	8.95
Baked Scallops, Shrimp	9.95	Imported Foie Gras de Strasbourg	26.50
Feta Cheese, White Wine, Garlic, Tomatoes		Smoked Salmon	10.95
Escargots à la Bourguignonne	7.95	Beluga Caviar Sur Croutes	49.00
Calamari Strips	8.95		

Salades

Butter Lettuce and Belgian Endive	6.25	Confit Duck Salad	6.50
Lemon Dressing		Raspberry Dressing	
Hot Fresh Spinach Salad, For Two	13.50	Caesar Salad, For Two	13.50

Poissons

Poached Alaskan Salmon, Dill Sauce	19.95	Whole Dover Sole, à la Meunière	20.50
Lobster Thermidor or Lobster Diablo	29.95	Calamari Steak, Sautéed Amandine	16.95
Coquilles St. Jacques, Parisiennes	18.95	Broiled Swordfish, Cilantro Lime Butter	19.95
Gamberetta All'Erba	19.95	Abalone Amandine Beurre Noir	36.95
Prawns sautéed in Virgin Olive Oil and Herbs			

Above Orders Served with Rice Pilaf or Fresh Vegetable du Jour

Grillades

Lamb Chops, Broiled à la Gastronome	26.50	*Flaming Sword Du Roi*	29.95
Rissole Potatoes, Broiled Tomato		Broiled Breast of Chicken, Filet Mignon, Lobster Tail, Tomato, Mushroom	
Entrecôte of Beef Maître d'Hotel	23.95		
New York Steak, Baked Potato, Tomato, Mushrooms		*Mister A's Broiled Veal Chop*	28.95
		Soufflé Potatoes, Asparagus, Sauvignon Sauce	

Béarnaise Sauce 2.50   Sauce Aux Cèpes 3.00
Mushroom Sauce 2.50

Mister A's Roast Tenderloin
with Duxelles of Mushrooms, à la Périgourdine Sauce
Foie Gras, Pâté Feuilletée, Vegetables à la Bouquetière
Soufflé Potatoes
28.95

Specialita della Casa

Steak Armagnac	25.95	*Saltimbocca alla Fiorentina*	24.95
New York Steak Saute, Black Cracked Pepper, Armagnac, Sauce Aux Cèpes, Dauphine Potatoes		Medallion of Veal, Prosciutto, Spinach, Mozzarella Cheese, Dauphine Potatoes	
		Escalope de Veau à l'Oscar	24.95
Tournedos Henry IV	22.50	Veal topped with Asparagus, Crab Legs, Sauce Hollandaise, Dauphine Potatoes	
Beef Tenderloin, Artichoke Béarnaise, Rissole Potatoes			

Mister A's Breast of Chicken   16.95
Roasted Breast of Chicken in Marsala Wine Sauce, Rice Pilaf

Rotisserie

Roast Prime of Beef Au Jus	19.95	*Long Island Duckling au Grand Marnier*	18.95
Creamed Horseradish, Baked Potato		Wild Rice, Basket of Mandarins	
Rack of Lamb à la Persillade de Provence, For Two	49.95	*Prime Filet of Beef Chateaubriand, For Two*	44.95
Fresh California Lamb, Jardiniere of Vegetable, Potatoes		Bouquetière of Fresh Vegetables, Sauce Béarnaise	

For additional information see page 64.

MONTANAS
AMERICAN
GRILL

Menu Changes Seasonally

DINNER MENU

STARTERS

Grilled Anaheim Chiles w/ Three Cheeses & Smoked Tomato Salsa 4.50

Smoked Pacific Steelhead & Trout w/ Horseradish Sauce 6.50

Grilled Prawns w/ Marinated Cucumbers & Spicy Remoulade 5.95

Buffalo Carpaccio w/ Arugula, Virgin Olive Oil & Aged Jack 7.95

Smoked Duck Cakes w/ Roasted Red Pepper Cream Sauce 5.95

SALADS

Mixed Greens w/ Asiago Cheese & Spicy Pecans 3.25

House Caesar Salad 4.75

Vine Ripened Tomatoes w/ Grilled Asparagus & Balsamic Vinaigrette 4.95

Mixed Greens w/ Sonoma Goat Cheese, Fresh Berries & Mint Vinaigrette 4.95

Arugula & Endive w/ Smoked Salmon, Red Onions & Capers 5.95

PASTA

Fusilli w/ Spicy Tomato Sauce, Fresh Basil & Parmesan 6.95

Fettucine w/ Four Cheeses, Cream & Roasted Garlic 7.95

Angel Hair w/ Fresh Tomatoes, Garlic & Light Tomato Sauce 7.95

Jalapeno Linguine w/ Grilled Chicken, Roasted Peppers & Cilantro 8.95

Fettucine w/ Shrimp, Sundried Tomatoes,
Fresh Basil & Tomato Cream Sauce 9.95

Penne w/ Chicken Sausage, Spinach, & Roasted Garlic 8.95

Spinach Fettucine w/ Smoked Salmon, Radicchio,
Lemon Cream & Fresh Dill 9.95

HARDWOOD SMOKED or GRILLED

Fresh Fish .... A.Q.

Smoked Sausage w/ Wild Rice & Black Beans 7.50

Grilled Chicken Breast w/ Goat Cheese, Lemon Thyme & Polenta 9.95

Pork Chops w/ Grilled Anaheim Chile & Black Beans 10.95

Smoked Chicken w/ Apple Mustard & Ovenbrown Potatoes 10.95

Skirt Steak w/ Wild Rice & Smoked Tomato Salsa 11.95

Full Slab BBQ Ribs w/ Ovenbrown Potatoes & Roasted Corn 14.95

BBQ Salmon w/ Roasted Potatoes & Grilled Vegetable 15.95

Montanas Mixed Grill (Daily Mix of Three Items) 15.95

T-Bone Steak w/ Roasted Potatoes & Grilled Portobello Mushrooms 16.95

Hamburger or Cheeseburger 5.95

New Mexican Pork Stew w/ Jalapeno Cornbread 6.95

Big Sky Chili 5.50

DESSERTS

Montanas Chocolate Torte w/ Vanilla Custard & Caramel Sauces 4.50

Hot Apple Cobbler w/ Sourmash Cream 4.50

Black & White Brownies w/ Vanilla Bean Ice Cream & Raspberry Sauce .. 3.95

Sourdough Bread Pudding w/ Fresh Berries 4.50

Vanilla Bean Ice Cream w/ Seasonal Fresh Fruit 3.95

Fresh Fruit Sorbet 3.50

For additional information see page 56.

Mykonos Greek & Seafood

MYKONOS

Menu Changes Seasonally

APPETIZERS - MEZÉDES

Melitzanosaláta   5.50
*Baked Eggplant Salad with Special Blend of Herbs and Lemon ...
Cold, with one Pita.*

Saganáki Flambé   6.95
Flaming Greek Cheese, with one Pita.

Taramás   5.50
Greek Style Red Caviar, with one Pita.

Octapódi Crasáto   8.95
Tender Octopus Baked in Wine Sauce with Vinegar and Olive Oil.

Sauteed Shrimp Flambé   9.25
Four Extra Large Shrimp prepared in Wine, Garlic and Butter Sauce.

MYKONOS Mezédes Combination   10.95
*Eggplant Salad, Tzatzíki, Taramas, Spanakopita, Fassolia, Feta Cheese,
Olives and Pita.*

SOUPS

Avgolémono   Cup **3.00**   Bowl **4.00**
*Traditional Greek Soup, made with Chicken broth, Rice, Eggs and
Fresh Lemon Juice.*

SALADS

Greek Tavérna Salad   8.95
*Tomatoes, Cucumbers, Bell Peppers, Red Onions, Greek Olives, Feta Cheese
and Anchovies. House Dressing.*

Hórta Saláta   5.25
Fresh Boiled Greens served cold with Olive Oil and fresh Lemon.

258 Harbor Dr South • Oceanside Harbor • (619) 757-8757

236

TRADITIONAL GREEK DISHES

*Entrees Served with Soup or Salad, Rice Pilaf,
Roast Potato, Vegetable of the Day and Bread.*

Moussaká - Famous Greek Specialty   12.95
*Layers of Eggplant, Potatoes and freshly ground Beef.
Baked with a Bechamel Sauce.*

Chicken Lemonáti   11.95
Half Chicken Broiled with Fresh Lemon, a hint of Garlic and Herbs.

Chicken Salónika   16.95
*Boneless Breast of Chicken - Baked with Sauteed Onions and
Spinach topped with Greek Cheeses.*

Rack of Baby Lamb   Market Price
Broiled with Greek Herbs.

Aegéan Style Leg of lamb   16.95
Roasted with Garlic and Herbs.

Gyros Platter   12.95
Generous Portion of Gyros with Tzatzíki.

SEAFOOD AEGÉAN STYLE

Island Style Shrimp   17.95
*Greek Island Style BBQ, Lemon, Olive Oil, Hint of Garlic, Herbs,
Charbroiled.*

Greek Style Bouillabaise   15.95
*Fresh simmered Fish and Vegetables with Clams, Shrimp, Scallops
and Mussels.*

Broiled Fillet of Red Snapper   13.95
Herbs and a Hint of Garlic, Garnished with Roasted Red Peppers.

Psari Plaki   17.95
Fillet of Sea Bass Baked with Onions, Tomatoes, Garlic and Herbs.

Fettuccini Ala Greka   15.95
*Prepared with White Sauce, Garlic, Herbs and Fresh Clams.
Soup or Salad only.*

For additional information see page 77.

Appetizers

Crisp Quesadilla.................. 5.00
    With rotisserie chicken, tomatillo
    salsa and queso Mexicano

Nachos 5.50
    With beans and chorizo
    (Mexican sausage)

* Ceviche 5.25
    A marinated white fish with lime
    juice, tomatoes, onion, chiles and
    served chilled with sliced avocado

Nachos 4.65
    With guacamole and sour cream

Salads

Taco Salad.......................... 4.95

* Chicken Taco Salad 5.25

Dinner Salad 2.50

Soups

Albondigas 2.95

Soup of the Day 2.20

Menudo 2.95
    Served with tortillas

Sides

* Torta 5.25
    Carne asada (beef), or chicken or
    carnitas (pork) served on a roll with
    avocado, lettuce, tomato & a side of
    beans (The Best Sandwich in Old Town)

Chicken Tamale 2.60

Chile Relleno 2.75
    Fresh chiles

3 Roll Tacos......................... 4.75
    Beef or chicken, with fideo,
    guacamole and sour cream

*Old Town Mexican Cafe Favorites

Dinners

All Dinners served with Tortillas, Soup or Salad, Beans & Rice

Carne Asada 9.25
Steak, topped with Guacamole and green chiles

Chicken Breast with Tomatillo Sauce 7.25
Oven-baked and served with sour cream and rice or beans.

Camarones 11.00
succulent Gulf Shrimp grilled in a garlic butter sauce

* Chicken Verde Enchiladas 7.75
Two chicken enchiladas with sour cream and green salsa

House Specialties

Old Town Famous Carnitas

Delicious pieces of Pork served in Mexico's traditional style, with
cilantro, onion, avocado, tomato, peppers, beans and our own tortillas.

Serves 4 Family style 25.00

Serves 2 .... 14.00

Serves 1 .... 7.25

Served Regular or Crispy Style
Our House Specials are served anytime

Mexican Style Ribs

Mexican Style Rotisserie Baby Back Pork Ribs.
Served with rice, beans and our own tortillas.

½ Rack (Seven Ribs) 7.75
Full Rack (Fourteen Ribs) Serves 2 .... 14.00

Old Town Pollo

Delicious traditional Mexican style rotisserie Chicken. Served with cilantro,
onion, tomato, peppers, rice, beans and our own hand made tortillas.

Full Chicken for Two 12.00

Serving all the specialities of Mexico with many combination plates
available and award-winning Margaritas from our full-service bar.

For additional information see page 106.

Sopas [Soups]

Sopa de Ajo	2.95	**Fabada**	3.95
Garlic Soup		*White Beans and Sausage*	

Ensalada [Salads]

Ensalada de Pollo   6.45
Grilled Chicken Breast Salad

Ensalada de Espinaca   5.50
Warm Spinach Salad with
Bacon Dressing

Ensalada Catalan   4.95
Marinated Tomato and Fresh Mozzarella Cheese

With Grilled Chicken Breast   6.95

Paellas

Paella Valenciana	*Saffron Rice with Shrimp, Seafood and Chicken*	20.95 *for two*
Paella Marinera	*Saffron Rice with Seafood and Shrimp*	19.95 *for two*
Paella Vegetariana	*Saffron Rice with Fresh Garden Vegetables*	16.95 *for two*

Tapas [Appetizers]

FRIAS [Cold]

Tortilla Española	4.50	**Chorizo Cantimpalo**	3.95
Potato and Onion Omelette		*Spicy Sausage*	
Tortilla de la Casa	4.50	**Jamón Serrano**	4.50
Potato, Bell Pepper and Zucchini Omelette		*Spanish Smoked Ham*	
Queso Manchego	3.95	**Salpicón de Mariscos**	6.50
Spanish Goat Cheese		*Marinated Octopus and Shrimp*	

CALIENTE [Hot]

Pollo al Ajillo 6.50	**Mejillones al Vino Blanco** 5.95
Chicken Sautéed in White Wine Garlic Sauce	*Mussels Sautéed in White Wine Garlic Sauce*
Croquettas de Pollo 5.95	**Empanadas de Atun** 4.50
Chicken Croquettes	*Chunk White Tuna in Pastry*
Pimientos Rellenos 5.95	**Champinones al Ajillo** 5.50
Spanish Bell Peppers Stuffed with Beef	*Mushrooms Sautéed in White Wine Garlic Sauce*
Calamares Romano 5.95	**Patatas Bravas** 3.95
Fried Calamari	*Fried Chunk Potatoes with Spicy Tomato Sauce*
Gambas al Ajillo 7.50	

Cenas [Entrees]

Pasta tres Colores   9.95
Fettuccini with Fresh Garden Vegetables in a Cream Sauce

Pasta Flamenca   10.95
Penne Pasta with Roasted Chicken and Fresh Vegetables in a Basil Broth

Pasta Mediterranea   11.95
Fettuccini with Shrimp and Seafood in a Cream Sauce

Pollo Chilindron   9.95
Paprika Chicken in Tomato Sauce

Parrillada de Mariscos   **Market Price**
Grilled Fresh Seafood

Filete de Pescado Ibiza   12.95
Fresh Fish with an Herb Cream Sauce

Pulpos en su Tinta   9.95
Octopus in Ink Sauce

Zarzuella   13.95
Fresh Seafood in a Light Saffron Tomato Broth

Solomillo con Salso de Roquefort   12.95
Tenderloin Beef Filet with Roquefort Sauce

Filete de Res Andaluz   12.95
Tenderloin Beef Filet with Tomato and Rosemary Sauce

For additional information see page 118.

PACHANGA

Antojitos

Pachanga Platter ◆ **9.75**
A tasty sampler of our appetizers, nachos, flautas, quesadilla, ceviche and
guacamole. It serves two amigos.

Queso Fundido ◆ **4.75**
Mounds of melted cheese with chorizo. Served with tortillas.

Ceviche ◆ **6.25**
Marinated scallops, fish and shrimp in citrus juices with onion, tomato, olive,
cilantro and mild chile. Served on small crispy corn tortillas.

Mexican Pizza ◆ **6.75**
A flour tortilla crust topped with our home made Veracruzana sauce and a tasty
combination of avocado, green pepper, sour cream, onion, tomato and cheese.

Fajitas Pachangueras

All served with hot corn or flour tortillas

Fajitas De La Quinta ◆ **9.75**
Tender strips of marinated steak, chicken or a combination. Grilled with spices,
bell pepper, onion, squash, mushroom and tomato. Served with guacamole,
sour cream, pico de gallo, rice and beans.

Fajitas De Vegetales ◆ **6.75**
Freshly selected zucchini, red and green bell peppers, green onion, celery,
carrots, spanish onion, mushroom and tomato, sauteed and seasoned in our
special sauce. Garnished with cilantro, and served with rice and beans.

Especialidades de Pachanga

Carnitas ◆ 8.75
Large golden brown chunks of pork specially seasoned. Served with soft hot tortillas, rice, beans, guacamole and pico de gallo. Garnished with green onion and radish.

Tamales ◆ 7.50
Two homemade chicken tamales topped with Pachanga sauce and cheese. Served with rice and beans.

Enchiladas
Served with rice and beans

Pollo Panchanchiladas ◆ 7.75
Fresh corn tortillas filled with shredded chicken, cheese and Pachanga sauce. Topped with salsa verde, cheese and sour cream.

Crab Enchiladas ◆ 9.75
Two crab filled enchiladas topped with a delicious creamy white sauce and cheese.

Mariscos

Seafood Chimichanga ◆ 10.75
Marinated scallops, shrimp, crab and fish wrapped in a large flour tortilla seasoned with onions and bell peppers. Deep fried and topped with cheese. Served with rice and black beans.

Carne Asada and Shrimp ◆ 13.75
Well seasoned top sirloin, charbroiled to your taste, and tender juicy jumbo shrimp marinated in garlic. Served with rice and beans.

Camarones Borrachos De Pachanga ◆ 12.75
Shrimp sauteed with tequila, lime and butter, seasoned with garlic and cilantro. Served with rice and beans.

Concha Del Mar ◆ 13.75
Seasoned shrimp, fish, scallops and mushrooms sauteed in a buttery creamy white sauce. Served in a large fluted tortilla shell on a bed of rice.

Camarones Jalapeños ◆ 12.75
Tender shrimp sauteed with garlic, mushrooms, red and green peppers and carrots. Topped with a delicious mild jalapeño sauce. Served with rice.

For additional information see page 106.

APPETIZERS

PHOENIX SHRIMP TOAST (4) 5.50

STEAMED DUMPLINGS (8) 5.50

PO PO PLATTER (FOR TWO) 9.50
(Chow Chow Beef, Wonton, Fish Roll, Gold Finger, Five Spice Pork Spare Ribs)

SOUP

SHARK'S FIN WITH SHREDDED CHICKEN (FOR TWO) 12.75

CHICKEN SWEET CORN (FOR TWO) 4.25

CRAB MEAT ASPARAGUS (FOR TWO) 5.25

THREE FLAVOR SIZZLING RICE (FOR TWO) 4.50

CHICKEN

SHA DEE CHICKEN* 8.25

FRESH MUSHROOM CHICKEN 8.25

LEMON CHICKEN 8.95

ORANGE FLAVOR CHICKEN* 9.50

BEEF

SZECHUAN BEEF* 7.75

BLACK MUSHROOM BEEF 8.25

BEEF WITH CHINESE VEGETABLES 7.75

PANDA COUNTRY SPECIALTIES

HOUSE SPECIAL CHICKEN* 9.75
  Chicken Deep Fried with Light Batter, Sauteed with Chef's Sweet and Pungent Sauce.

CRISPY BEEF* 9.75
  Shredded Beef, Deep Fried until Crispy, Sauteed with Garlic, Hot Spicy and Sweet and Sour Sauce.

PANDA COUNTRY DELIGHT 14.25
  Shrimp, Lobster, Chicken, Mushroom, Baby Bok Choy Sauteed in Chef's Special Light Sauce.

THREE INGREDIENT TASTES 9.50
  Shrimp, Chicken, and Beef with Vegetables Sauteed with Brown Sauce.

DUCK

PEKING DUCK 25.00

ROASTED DUCK (BONELESS) .... Half 12.50

ORANGE DUCK (BONELESS) .... Half 12.50

PORK

MOO SHU PORK 7.75

YU HSIAN PORK* 7.75

BROCCOLI WITH BARBECUED PORK 7.75

VEGETABLES

SAUTEED SNOW PEA AND WATER CHESTNUT 6.95

YU HSIAN EGGPLANT* 7.50

SEAFOOD

YU HSIAN SHRIMP* 10.25

SWEET AND SOUR WHOLE FISH 18.50

LOBSTER IN BLACK BEAN SAUCE 16.95

*HOT & SPICY

For additional information see page 47.

Phuong Trang

PHUONG TRANG

KHAI VỊ *(Appetizers)*

Chà Giò (6 cuốn an vói rau) **$3.75**
Egg Rolls (6 rolls and vegetable)

Gòi Cuốn (2 cuốn) **$2.25**
Spring Rolls (2 rolls)

Chao Tôm
(an vói rau và bánh tráng) **$6.95**
Char-grilled Ground Shrimp in Sugar-cane (with vegetable and rice paper)

Bánh Xèo **$4.25**
Vietnamese Crepe (pork, shrimp, beansprouts in fried flour)

Súp Mang Cua **$2.95**
Crab Meat and Bamboo Soup

Súp Mang Tây **$2.95**
Crab Meat and Asparagus Soup

LAU *(Hot Pot)*

	L	S
Lẩu Thập Cấm	**$11.95** -	**$15.95**

Combination Hot Pot

Lẩu Luon Chua .... **$11.95** - **$15.95**
Special Eel Hot Pot

Tà Pín Lù .... **$11.95** - **$15.95**
Combination Meat Fondue

ĐẶC BIỆT *(Specials)*

Bò Tôm Muc Nuóng Vi **$9.95**
Beef, Shrimp and Squid Marinated Hot Grilled with Vegetable and Rice Paper

Cá Nuóng .... **Seasonal**
(order in advance)
Grilled Whole Fish with vegetable and rice paper

Bò Cuốn Lá Lốp hoac Lá Nho ... **$6.50**
Ground Beef Wrapped with Grape Leaves

Cua Rang Muối .... **Seasonal**
(order in advance)
Fried Salted Crab

MÌ *(Egg Noodle Soup)*

Mì Dac Biêt Phuong Trang
(khô hoac nuóc) **$4.25**
Phuong Trang Special Egg Noodle Soup (or dry)

Mì Tôm Cua (khô hoac nuóc) **$3.95**
Shrimp & Crab with Egg Noodle Soup (or dry)

Mì Hoánh Thánh
(khô hoac nuóc) **$4.25**
Wonton with Egg Noodle Soup (or dry)

MÌ XÀO
(Fried Egg Noodle)

Mì Xáo Xà Xíu (mềm hoac dòn) $4.50
Stir-Fried Egg Noodle with Cha-Siu Pork & Vegetable (or deep fried)

**Mì Xào Tôm Cua
(mềm hoac dòn) $4.95**
Stir-Fried Egg Noodle with Shrimp, Crab & Vegetable (or deep fried)

**Mì Xào Do Biến
(mềm hoac dòn) $4.95**
Stir-Fried Egg Noodle with Seafood and Vegetable (or deep fried)

THU'C AN CHAY
(Vegetarian)

Hú tiếu Xào Chay $4.25
Stir-Fried Rice Noodle with Vegetables

Rau Cai Xào Nấm Dông Cô $5.95
Stir-Fried Vegetables with Chinese Mushroom

Com Xào Chay $4.25
Stir-Fried Vegetables with Steamed Rice

BÚN *(Vermicelli Noodle)*

Bún Thit Nuóng $3.95
Char-grilled Pork with Vermicelli Noodle

Bún Xào Tôm $4.50
Stir-Fried Shrimp with Vermicelli Noodle

Bún Cha Giò & Thit Nuóng $4.95
Eggs Rolls and Char-grilled Pork with Vermicelli Noodle

Bún Chao Tôm & Thit Nuóng $5.95
Char-grilled Ground Shrimp in Sugar Cane and Char-Grilled Pork with Vermicelli Noodle

CANH *(Soup)*

Canh Thâp Cấm $4.95
Combination and Vegetable Soup

Canh Chua Cá $4.95
Fish Sour Soup

Canh Chua Tôm $4.95
Shrimp Sour Soup

HU TIẾU XAO
(Stir-Fried Rice Noodle)

Hù Tiếu Áp Chao Tôm $4.95
Shrimp and Vegetables with Stir-Fried Rice Noodle

Hù Tiếu Áp Chao Dồ Biến $4.95
Seafood and Vegetables with Stir-Fried Rice Noodle

Hù Tiếu Áp Chao Xá Xíu $4.50
Cha-Siu Pork and Vegetables with Stir-Fried Rice Noodle

Hù Tiếu Áp Chao Tôm Cua $4.95
Shrimp, Crab and Vegetables with Stir-Fried Rice Noodle

CO'M DIA *(Rice Dishes)*

Com Tay Càm $5.50
Rice in Earthen Pot

**Com Chiên Gà Rôti hoac
Gà Quay $4.95**
Roasted Chicken or Grilled Chicken with Fried Rice

Com Gà hoac Bò Xào Xa Ot $4.50
Chicken or Beef with Lemon Grass and Hot Pepper with Steamed Rice

Com Chiên Tôm $4.95
Shrimp Fried Rice

For additional information see page 123.

Pizzeria Uno Restaurant & Bar

MENU CHANGES ANNUALLY

APPETIZERS
Sized for sharing.

PIZZA SKINS
Potato filled pizza wedges with sour cream, onion, cheddar and bacon . . . *$5.45*

TUSCANY BREAD
Garlic bread baked with nutty pesto, spinach, muenster and diced tomato . . . *$4.25*

BUFFALO WINGS
Hot & spicy chicken wings with vegetable sticks and a tasty dip . . . *$5.25*   Jumbo order add . . . *$3.00*

CHEESE STICKS
Crunchy coated mozzarella served with tomato and meat sauce . . . *$4.95*

SPINACH CON QUESO
A spicy cheese and spinach sauce served with hot tortilla chips . . . *$4.25*

SOUPS & SALADS

WINDY CITY CHILI
Beans, meats and wonderful flavor. Served with tortilla chips, chopped onion and cheddar cheese.
Bowl *$3.25*

Large salad serves 2 to 3
CHICKEN CAESAR
Caesar w/grilled chicken breast *$6.95*

SANDWICHES
All burgers & sandwiches come complete with fries & served with pickle, lettuce, onion & tomato. Soup or salad in place of fries add 95¢.
1/2 LB. Char grilled Burgers

MUSHROOM BURGER
Lots of very fresh mushrooms blended with mozzarella cheese *$5.50*

STEAK N' CHEESE
Thin slices of steak with cheese, mushrooms, onions and peppers *$5.95*

4465 Mission Blvd • Pacific Beach • (619) 483-4143

248

PLIZZETTAS
California style thin crust gourmet pizzas for one.
Large serves two or three.

LEMON-LIME CILANTRO CHICKEN
Marinated chicken breast w/garlic,
ancho chilis, green onions, fresh
lemon-lime & cilantro.
Ind .... $6.95   Large $11.95

DELUXE CHEESE
Nutty pesto, plum tomato,
basil & mozzarella.
Ind .... $4.95   Large $9.95

ARTIPEGGIO
Eggplant, artichokes, roasted red
peppers, mozzarella, feta.
Ind .... $6.95   Large $11.95

CHEESELESS
Onions, roasted red pepper, artichoke,
& mushrooms.
Ind .... $5.95   Large $10.95

PASTA
Special: House or Caesar salad
with any pasta...Only 95¢

BROCCOLI & CHICKEN FETTUCCINI
Fresh broccoli florets cooked w/
julienned chicken breast on
fettuccini noodles in a light garlic
alfredo sauce $9.95

WILD MUSHROOM RAVIOLI
Ravioli stuffed with wild mushrooms
and served in a fresh mushroom
cream sauce $7.95
With grilled chicken.. add $3.00

LASAGNA MAMIA
Tender baked pasta filled with
a blend of cheeses & topped with
meat sauce. Served with sautéed
fresh vegetables $8.95

DEEP DISH PIZZA
Individual serves one.
Regular serves two or three.

UNO
Our delicious crust filled with
outrageous quantities of cheese,
sausage, pepperoni, onions,
mushrooms and peppers.
Ind .... $6.75   Reg $12.95

CHICAGO CLASSIC
The pizza that made Uno's famous,
extra sausage, extra cheese, extra
tomato, extra crisp crust and
extra delicious.
Ind .... $6.75   Reg $12.95

CHICKEN FAJITA
Strips of marinated chicken breast on a
blend of cheeses, peppers and onions.
Picante y muy bueno!
Ind .... $6.75   Reg $12.95

SEA DELICO
A unique seafood creation highlighting
the flavors of crab, shrimp, butter
and garlic.
Ind .... $6.75   Reg $12.95

SPECIALTIES
Special: House or Caesar salad
with any specialty...Only 95¢

RIBS & WINGS
A delicious combination of hot and
spicy chicken wings with baby back
ribs and fries $8.95

CHICKEN FROMAGGI
A large boneless chicken breast baked
in a blend of cheeses and fresh tomato.
Served with sautéed
fresh vegetables $8.95

For additional information see page 111.

Menu Changes Seasonally

PANE E ZUPPA

Pane Aglio e Rosmarino
fresh garlic-rosemary bread baked in our wood-fired oven — 2.95

Bruschetta
toasted Tuscan bread; chopped tomatoes, basil,
fresh mozzarella, prosciutto — 5.50

Guazzetto di Mare
Manila clams and prawns steamed in spicy tomato broth — 7.95

ANTIPASTI

Composta di Vegetali
vine-ripe tomatoes, hearts of palm, cannellini beans,
mushrooms, beets — 5.50

Carpaccio G. Cipriani
thinly sliced raw beef, grana cheese, capers, extra virgin
olive oil, lemon — 6.95

Grigliata Saporita
grilled radicchio, endive, eggplant, portobello mushrooms,
prosciutto-wrapped goat cheese — 6.50

Insalata di Moleche
pan-fried soft shell crabs, frisee, artichoke hearts,
tomatoes, extra virgin olive oil and lemon — 7.50

INSALATE

Prego
organically grown lettuces, carrots, celery, bell peppers,
mushrooms; vinaigrette — 4.95

Soncino con Anitra
mache lettuce, cold roasted duck breast, goat cheese;
balsamic vinaigrette — 7.95

PIZZA

Dell'Adriatico
shrimp, chopped tomatoes, mozzarella, basil, garlic — 10.50

Alle Quattro Stagioni
mozzarella, prosciutto cotto, mushrooms, artichokes, fresh tomato sauce — 9.75

Profumi
zucchini, eggplant, shiitake and porcini mushrooms, tomato, mozzarella — 8.75

PASTA FATTA IN CASA (housemade)

Paglia e Fieno
thin egg and spinach pasta, grilled chicken, radicchio; prosciutto, cream, parmesan — 10.25

Fettuccine alla Crema di Scampi
ribbon pasta, shrimp, prosciutto; cream, tomato, garlic — 11.75

Fedelini alle Vongole Veraci
thin spaghetti, clams; garlic, tomato, extra virgin olive oil — 10.95

Fiorellini di Magro
flower-shaped pasta filled with spinach, ricotta; light tomato sauce — 9.95

Agnolotti d'Aragosta
half-moons filled with lobster, prosciutto, ricotta; lemon-lobster sauce — 11.95

Risotto del Giorno
creamy arborio rice, selection changes daily — A.Q.

GRIGLIA E SPIEDO

Pollo all'Aglio e Rosmarino
boneless double chicken breast; garlic, rosemary, grilled polenta — 12.50

Gamberoni alla Griglia
large freshwater prawns; extra virgin olive oil, lemon — 17.50

Salsiccia Luganega
Italian sausages; fresh spinach, polenta, roasted peppers — 10.95

Costata di Maiale
pork chops; balsamic vinegar, rosemary, grilled polenta — 13.95

Costata di Manzo al Timo
rib eye steak; Tuscan white beans, fresh thyme — 16.95

For additional information see page 90.

Rainwater's
ON · KETTNER
An Eastern-Style Chophouse

Menu Changes Periodically

DINNER MENU
SOUPS

The "Chop House" Black Bean with Rainwater Madeira
Clam Chowder — New England Style
Portugese Sopa — Spicy Beef and Vegetables
Cup 3.50   Bowl 5.00

SALADS

Caesar Salad 10.00   split 7.00
Fresh Spinach, Black Olives, Mushrooms, and Chopped Eggs in a Mustard Vinaigrette 10.00   split 7.00
California Greens with Asiago Cheese and Spiced Pecans in a Walnut Oil and Fresh Lemon Juice 10.00   split 7.00

FRESH SEAFOOD

Salmon in Parchment
Roasted in Paper with Julienne Vegetables and Fresh Herbs in a White Wine Sauce   23.00

Seabass — Baked in an Herb Crust
Served over Creamy Mashed Potatoes and Topped with Crispy Leeks   23.00

Live Maine Lobster — Broiled or Poached   Market Price

Local Halibut
Sauteed with an Avocado Cream and Gazpacho Vegetables and Rice   21.00

Broiled Escolar — with a Ginger, Black Pepper and Cabernet Butter
Served with Crispy Potatoes   21.00

Broiled Local Swordfish — with Cherry Pear Tomatoes in a Basil Vinaigrette
Served with Rice   23.00

PASTA AND POULTRY

Shelton Chicken Breast
In a Garlic Crust with Creamy Mashed Potatoes, Veal Pan Gravy and Carmelized Onions.   19.00

Fettuccine "Chop House"
Green and White Pasta, Chicken Breast, Mushrooms and Walnuts in a Cream and Butter Sauce.   17.00

Grilled Chicken Breast
with Black Beans, Rice and a Mango Salsa.   19.00

Chicken Vesuvio
Chunks of Sauteed Chicken Breast, Peas, Cayenne Pepper, Garlic, Parsley, Scallions, Tomatoes and White Wine over Penne.   18.00

Jamaican Jerk Chicken Pasta
Spicy Chicken with Scallions, Sundried Tomatoes, Garlic, Cilantro and Bowtie Pasta — Extra Virgin Olive Oil.   18.00

STEAKS

PRIME NEW YORK STRIP   24.00   Lg 29.00

PRIME NEW YORK STRIP FOR TWO
Covered with Peppercorns, Grilled and Served with our Spicy Barbeque Sauce. Rosti Potatoes.   52.00

FILET MIGNON
Bearnaise Sauce   24.00   Lg 29.00

Our Famous "PEPPER FILET"
Topped with Sauteed Mushrooms, Bacon, Onions and Black Peppercorns.   27.00

PRIME T-BONE   36.00

PRIME PORTERHOUSE FOR TWO   60.00

KANSAS CITY BONE-IN STRIP — *USDA Prime*   29.00

BLACK ANGUS RIBEYE   24.00

OTHER MEATS

Roasted Prime Rib of Beef
Creamy Horseradish Sauce and Creamed Corn   24.00   Lg 28.00

Pork Chops
Broiled. Served with Fettuccine Alfredo.   19.00

Roasted Rack of Lamb
Rosemary and Garlic Sauce with Rosti Potatoes.   29.00

Veal Medallions
with Creamy Mashed Potatoes and a Horseradish Sauce. Served with Asparagus.   28.00

Provimi Calves Liver
Thin Sliced, Pan Sauteed and Topped with Bacon, Grilled Onions and Avocado Slices.   21.00

Harvey's Three Cheese Meatloaf
Creamy Mashed Potatoes, Veal Pan Gravy and Carmelized Onions.   17.00

For additional information see page 39.

RANCHO VALENCIA
RESORT

APPETIZERS

*BAKED OYSTERS WITH BRAISED CELERY, CHERVIL
GLAZED WITH CHAMPAGNE SABAYON   8.75*

*CREAMY SCRAMBLED EGG BACK IN SHELL WITH
SCOTTISH SMOKED SALMON AND CAVIAR   8.50*

*FRESH DUCK FOIE GRAS SAUTEED WITH TURNIP CONFIT AND
STRAWBERRY VINEGAR ESSENCE   10.50*

*MARTINI COCKTAIL OF ALASKAN KING CRAB AND MEXICAN PRAWNS
IN A HORSERADISH TARTARE SAUCE   8.25*

*SCOTTISH SMOKED SALMON, CAPERS, RED ONIONS AND
HOMEMADE MELBA TOAST   9.00*

SALADS AND SOUPS

VALENCIA CAESAR SALAD WITH PARMESAN CHEESE CROUTONS   8.50

*THIN SLICES OF MANGO AND SEARED SALMON SALAD WITH
CITRUS DRESSING AND GINGER 8.75*

*WINTER SALAD WITH PEAR, ROQUEFORT CHEESE, ROASTED WALNUT AND
OLD PORT VINAIGRETTE   6.50*

VELOUTE OF FOREST MUSHROOMS, QUENELLES OF CREME FRAICHE   5.75

ENTREES

**PAN ROASTED WHITEFISH IN A CRUST OF WHOLE GRAIN MUSTARD
AND BRAISED LEEKS 19.50**

**NORWEGIAN SALMON BAKED WITH BAY SHRIMP, CRIMINI MUSHROOMS
IN VERMOUTH SABAYON 20.25**

**SAUTEED FRESH LARGE SEA SCALLOPS ON A BED OF
BRAISED BELGIAN ENDIVES AND SWEET PEPPER COULIS 24.75**

**"BLACKENED" LOCAL SWORDFISH WITH SHALLOTS AND CRACKED BLACK
PEPPER ON A KEY WEST LIME SAUCE WITH SQUASH BLOSSOMS 23.50**

**CHINO'S PALETTE OF VEGETABLES
MEDLEY OF PASTA AND VEGETABLES 18.50**

**IMPORTED FETTUCCINI WITH SAUTEED CHICKEN BREAST, LIGHT CREAM,
ROASTED SHALLOTS, SWEET PEPPERS AND BASIL 19.25**

**VEAL SWEETBREAD SAUTEED WITH OYSTER MUSHROOMS,
SPRING ASPARAGUS AND MADEIRA REDUCTION 23.25**

**OVEN ROASTED FREE RANGE CHICKEN AND NEW RED POTATOES
WITH HERBED NATURAL JUICES 18.75**

**GRILLED "PRIME" NEW YORK STEAK WITH THREE ROASTED PEPPERS,
MAUI ONIONS, GRATIN POTATO AND MARJORAM REDUCTION 26.25**

**SAUTEED VENISON CHOPS WITH BABY ARTICHOKE HEARTS AND
CELERIAC SERVED ON A SUNDRIED CRANBERRY SAUCE 23.50**

**MARINATED AND GRILLED DOUBLE LAMB CHOPS WITH A CAKE OF
VINE RIPE TOMATOES, EGGPLANT, PESTO AND ROSEMARY SAUCE 22.75**

**GRILLED "PRIME" TOURNEDOS OF BEEF WITH ROASTED BEETS,
MERLOT ESSENCE AND GAUFRETTE POTATO 26.25**

DESSERTS

**CRUNCHY HAZELNUT BAR
WITH CHOCOLATE MOUSSE AND FRESH FRUIT PUREE 5.50**

**FLOURLESS CHOCOLATE SOUFFLE
WITH ROASTED ESPRESSO SAUCE 5.50**

For additional information see page 73.

Roxanne's Boondocks

Fresh Crisp Salads
Served with garlic bread

Caesar Salad   5.95
Romaine, fresh parmesan, homemade croutons & a great Caesar dressing top this crispy delight.
With cajun spiced chicken breast add $2.00

Cajun Chicken Breast Salad   6.95
Cajun spiced chicken atop fresh garden greens, with your choice of dressing.

DINNER INCLUDES
"Boonie Zucchini"
Choice of   Choice of
Fresh Soup or Salad   Parmesan Tomatoes, Rice Pilaf,
Steamed Veggies, Baked or Ranch Fries.

From the Coop

Full Boneless Chicken Breast   11.95
Chicken Danielle; Sauteed 10 oz. Breast in a mushroom, Marsala Wine Saute, then covered with Bearnaise. Delicious!

Chicken Alexis; Sauteed in Amaretto, served amandine.

Ooodles & Noodles

Gorgonzola   10.95
White creamy sauce and imported Fettucini accent this classic dish.
With chicken breast add $2.00

Boonies Shrimp & Pasta   12.95
Large tender Pacific shrimp. Sauteed in a creamy cajun sauce, served over Fettucini noodles or rice if you like.

Under the Dock

Kettle O Lobsters Bayou Style
Kettle for One ... 13.95
Ma & Pa Kettle ... 25.95

Scallone ... 11.95
A delicious portion of Scallops & Abalone combined, served amandine.

Seafood Combo ... 17.95
Generous portions of Kettle lobsters, fish of the day & scallone.

Jumbo Shrimp ... 14.95
Your choice of Tempura; lightly battered, fried to a golden brown. Scampi; sauteed in our seasoned wine garlic butter.

Today's Catch from the Dock
Served at Market Price
Served Boonies Way -
Ask your server

Choice Iowa Beef & Pork
All cuts served _Cajun_ upon request - try it!

Prime Rib
Chef Cut ... 11.95
Boondock Cut ... 14.95
Cattleman Cut ... 17.95

Pork

BBQ Baby Back
Full Slab ... 14.95
1/2 Slab ... 10.95

Thick Center Cut Chops
Broiled ... 13.95

Steaks

Filet Mignon ... 16.95

Tournedos of Filet ... 15.95
Medallions of filet sliced & topped with Bearnaise Sauce & mushroom caps.

K.C. Peppersteak ... 15.95
New York w/ Boonies special spices broiled & topped w/ Bordelaise, fresh mushrooms, bacon & green onions.

Ground Steak
Bordelaise ... 9.95

For additional information see page 40.

Saigon Restaurant
Chinese / Vietnamese Cuisine

Menu Changes Seasonally

Khai Vi
Appetizers

CHA GIÒ (6 cuon) **3.69**
Vietnamese Egg Rolls (Served w/ Lettuce & Fish Sauce)

GOI CUÓN **2.50**
Shrimp & Pork Rolls

TOM NHÚNG BÔT CHIÊN **6.99**
Golden Brown Fried Shrimp

Bún
Vermicelli Rice Noodle

BÚN CHAO TÔM & THIT NUONG **5.95**
Char-Grilled Ground Shrimp, Pork in Sugar Cane with Vermicelli Noodle

BÚN BÌ & NEM CHUA **4.95**
Shredded Pork and Vietnamese Salami with Vermicelli Noodle

Hu Tiéu Xào
Stir-Fried Rice Noodle

HU TIÉU ÁP CHAO XÁ XIÚ **4.50**
Cha-Siu Pork and Vegetables with Stir-Fried Rice Noodle

HU TIÉU ÁP CHAO THÂP CAM **4.95**
Combination and Vegetables with Stir-Fried Rice Noodle

4455 El Cajon Blvd • East San Diego • (619) 284-4215

Món Man
Vietnamese Style Salty Dishes

GÀ XÀO XA OT **4.50**
Chicken with Lemon Grass and Hot Pepper

GÀ XÀO GÙNG **4.50**
Sauteed Chicken with Ginger

CÁ KHO **4.95**
Catfish Sauteed in Fish Sauce

CÁ CHIM CHIÊN hoặc CÁ CATFISH CHIÊN (nuoc mam gùng) ... **9.99**
Fried Whole Birdfish or Catfish w/ Ginger Fish Sauce

Dac Biêt Bò 7 Món
Vietnamese Specialties

SÀIGÒN BÒ 7 MÓN **10.99**
Saigon's Seven Course Beef: Served Flaming Hot w/ Rice Paper and Veg.

MUC, TÔM, BÒ, GÀ NUONG VI DAC BIÊT **14.99**
Hot Grill: Fresh Shrimp, Fish, Beef, Chicken, Squid
(Served w/ Rice Paper and Veg.)

LAU THÂP CAM .... **(small/large)** ...**12.99/16.99**
Combination Veg. in Hot Flavored Broth w/ Beef, Shrimp, Chicken, Pork,
Fish and Squid

LAU SA-TÉ .... **(small/large)**...**12.99/16.99**
Combination Veg. in Hot Sate (Spicy) Broth
w/Shrimp, Chicken, Beef and Pork

TA PÍN LÙ **16.99**
Flaming on Table Shrimp, Fish, Squid and Beef in Vinegar
(Served w/ Rice Paper and Veg.)

BÒ NUONG VI **16.99**
Sliced Fresh Beef Marinated in Lemon Grass on Hot Grill
(Served w/ Rice Paper and Veg.)

BÒ NHÚNG DAM **7.99**
Sliced Fresh Beef w/ Flavor Vinegar on Hot Flame
(Served w/ Rice Paper and Veg.)

CHA DÙM **6.99**
Ground Beef Mixture Steamed w/ Peas, Peanut, Bean Thread
(Served w/ Shrimp Chip.)

GOI SÚA TÔM THIT **6.99**
Shrimp and Pork w/ Jelly Fish Salad

NGHÊU XÀO hoac NGHÊU XÓI MO **6.99**
Clams in Oyster Flavored Sauce

For additional information see page 123.

APPETIZERS

Steamed Clams & Mussels Cubana
$7.00
A mildly spicy combination of mussels
& clams steamed with a touch of
cumino, chili flakes and cilantro

Open-faced Pita Sandwich
$4.50
Fresh baked pita bread
topped with tomato sauce
and braised sweet onions

Sally's Best Crab Cakes $8.00
Served with Remoulade sauce

Create Your Own...
Oysters $1.50 each
Mussels $1.00 each

Clams $0.75 each
Shrimp $1.25 each

...or Sally's Selection $18.00
6 shrimp, 4 clams, 4 mussels, 6 oysters, 2 crab legs
and half a lobster tail

VEGETARIAN MAIN COURSES

Saffron Risotto $12.00
Arborio rice, saffron and a seasonal
selection of fresh grilled vegetables

Rigatoni "Tuscany" $12.00
Rigatoni pasta prepared with fresh
sage, white beans, eggplant and tomato

PRIX FIXE MENU
Chef's nightly selection
First course, Entree and Dessert
$25.00

SEAFOOD SPECIALTIES

Bouillabaisse $17.00
This traditional Mediterranean fish soup is served with a variety of rock fish, shrimp and a lobster claw

Oven Baked Mahi-Mahi $18.00
Sauteed baby artichokes, sweet onions, basil and white wine

Flamebroiled Swordfish Steak $18.00
Cabernet Sauvignon and honey glaze, black beans, corn kernels and diced celery root

Seared Sea Scallops and Corn Pancakes $16.00
Mixed greens, corn, orange walnut vinaigrette

Steamed Halibut & Mussels $16.00
Pappardelle pasta with saffron, tomato and basil sauce

Tequila Shrimp Linguini $17.00
Sauteed shrimp, linguini pasta with a tequila, lime, cilantro and jalapeno sauce

Seafood Paella $16.00
Our own version of this Spanish dish prepared with arborio rice, saffron, mussels, clams, shrimp, & fresh fish

Seared Seabass $15.00
Served over fennel, pearl onions, black olives and tomato

Baked Salmon Filet $17.00
Topped with red chile polenta yellow tomatoes and lemon sauce

Crusted Scallops and Japanese Eggplant $18.00
Sauteed mushrooms and a light scallop onion sauce

Grilled Pacific Tuna Steak $18.00
Sauteed red and yellow bell peppers and grilled garlic mashed potatoes

Lobster Conchigliette "Au Gratin" $22.00
Lobster and pasta shells in a cognac cream sauce

Whole Live Maine Lobster $35.00
Served with twice baked potato and fresh asparagus

POULTRY AND MEATS

Lamb Couscous $16.00
Lamb shank, braised on the bone with Moroccan style couscous & vegetables

Grilled Veal Chop $23.00
with Shiitake Mushrooms
Served on a puree of celery root with a red Port sauce

New York Steak $17.00
Onion rings and cabernet sauvignon sauce

Oven Roasted Rosemary Chicken $16.00
With garlic sauce, green peas and tomato

For additional information see page 101.

◆CALIFORNIA◆
WOODFIRED PIZZA®

SALAD

Caesar's Salad
Romaine, garlic croutons, romano and Caesar's dressing............9.25

Grilled Chicken Salad
Mixed lettuce, walnuts, gorgonzola and Balsamic
basil dressing 8.95

Thai Chicken Salad
Sprouts, julienne vegetables, tomatoes, peanuts, cilantro and
chili dressing 8.95

Warm Duck Salad
Mixed greens, Mandarin oranges, sesame seeds and raspberry
vinaigrette 9.95

CALZONE

Spicy Chicken
Spicy Chicken with tropical seasonings, scallions, cilantro
and bell pepper 8.95

Vegetarian
Grilled eggplant, black olives, garlic, wild mushrooms, spinach and
goat cheese 8.95

SAMMY'S HOUSE SPECIALTIES

PASTA

Chicken Tequila Fettuccini
Bell peppers, cilantro and red onion in a jalapeno lime
cream sauce 9.50

Shrimp Angel Hair
Shrimp, artichoke hearts, wild mushrooms in a light vegetable
cream sauce 9.95

Thai Chicken or Shrimp Linguine
Scallions, carrots and bean sprouts in a peanut sesame ginger
cream sauce 9.95

Spicy Chicken Angel Hair
Olive oil, sun dried tomatoes, fresh basil and garlic 8.50

PIZZA

Sun Dried Tomato
With goat cheese, roasted pine nuts and fresh basil 8.95

Chicken Teriyaki
With bell peppers, marinated eggplant and onions 8.50

Jamaican Shrimp or Chicken
With spicy Jerk Seasoning, scallions, cilantro, carrots and
sun dried tomatoes 9.95

Garlic Chicken or Shrimp
Mushrooms, bell peppers, red onion and garlic sauce 8.95

Vegetarian
Eggplant, tomatoes, onions, mushrooms, bell peppers and
fontina cheese 8.95

LaDou's Barbecue Chicken
With cilantro, smoked gouda and red onion 8.95

For additional information see page 112.

"LAS BOTANAS"
Appetizers Hot & Cold

(6) OYSTERS ON THE HALF SHELL **$6.95**   **SHRIMP NACHOS** **$5.95**

SHRIMP "PUERTO PEÑASCO" Whole chilled shrimp, cooked in lime juice,
served with slices of cucumber, onion & serrano chiles   **$7.95**

SHRIMP "CERVECERIA" Shrimp boiled in ale, you peel and dip   **$7.95**

COLD SEAFOOD COMBO Shrimp, Octopus & Oysters   **$7.95**

QUESADILLA PABLO Crab Meat, served with guacamole & Sour Cream   **$7.95**

SEAFOOD EMPANADA Scallops, Shrimp & Fresh Fish, a Latin American Specialty **$5.95**

"TOSTADAS"

CEVICHE OF FISH Served Puerto Peñasco style   **$3.75**
CEVICHE OF SHRIMP Served Puerto Peñasco style   **$4.25**
CARNE ASADA   **$4.25**

"LAS SOPAS"

FISH SOUP "SANTA FE STYLE" All fish   **$4.25**
SHRIMP SOUP "SANTA FE STYLE" Whole unpeeled shrimp   **$6.25**
7 SEAS 7=Fresh Fish, Shrimp, Scallops, Octopus, Calamare, Clams & Crab **$12.95**

"ORDEN DE TACOS"
(2) Tacos served with rice and beans

FISH FILET Cerveza batter or grilled   **$6.25**
SHRIMP Sauteed   **$7.95**
LOBSTER Sauteed   **$9.95**
CARNE ASADA Broiled marinated filet, soft tortillas, guacamole   **$6.95**
COMBO Carne Asada & Fish   **$7.95**

"LOS BURRITOS"
Soft flour tortilla, stuffed with either seafood or meat, served with rice and beans

SHRIMP **$8.25**   **FISH** **$6.25**   **LOBSTER** **$10.95**   **SCALLOPS** **$7.95**
CARNE ASADA Broiled filet of beef, served with guacamole and salsa fresca **$6.95**

---

956 Broadway Cir • 1 American Plaza • Downtown • (619) 696-0043

"LAS ENCHILADAS"
(2) ENCHILADAS SERVED WITH RICE AND BEANS

FISH $6.95 **SHRIMP** $8.95 **CRAB** $8.95
LOBSTER $10.95 **CHICKEN** $8.75

"LAS ESPECIALIDADES"

PESCADO ENTERO WHOLE FRIED FISH, MAKE YOUR OWN TACOS
MEDIUM $15.95 **LARGE** $21.95

MARISCADA RANCHERA COMBINATION OF FISH, SHRIMP, OCTOPUS, SCALLOPS, CALAMARE & OYSTERS $10.95

LOBSTER "PUERTO NUEVO" A PLATTER OF SAUTEED OR BROILED LOBSTER SERVED BAJA STYLE, MAKE YOUR OWN TACOS (IN SEASON) $25.95

LOBSTER TAILS "PUERTO NUEVO" 8 OZ. GRILLED SLIPPER LOBSTER TAILS SERVED BAJA STYLE, MAKE YOUR OWN TACOS $15.95

SHRIMP "PUERTO NUEVO" A PLATTER OF SAUTEED SHRIMP SERVED BAJA STYLE, MAKE YOUR OWN TACOS $10.95

SEAFOOD CHILI RELLENO SCALLOPS, SHRIMP & CHEESE $8.95

"LOS PESCADOS"

FRESH FISH FILET "MOJO DE AJO" SAUTEED IN GARLIC & BUTTER $11.95
FRESH FISH FILET "MEXICANO" SAUTEED IN TOMATOES, ONIONS AND SERRANOS (HOT) $11.95
FRESH FISH FILET "PACIFICO" SERVED WITH TOMATILLO SAUCE $12.95
FRESH FISH FILET "ACAPULCO" SERVED WITH PASILLA SAUCE $12.95
FRESH FISH FILET "BRAVA CHILI DE ARBOL" SERVED WITH BRAVA SALSA (HOT) $12.95
FRESH FISH FILET "VERACRUZ" A GRILLED FILET SERVED WITH SWEET BELL PEPPER, TOMATOES, ONIONS & CAPERS $12.95

"LOS CAMARONES"
FRESH SHRIMP SERVED WITH RICE & BEANS

MOJO DE AJO SAUTEED IN GARLIC & BUTTER $13.95
MEXICANA MODERATELY HOT $13.95
DIABLA HOT! $13.95
COSTA AZUL SUPER COLOSSAL SHRIMP STUFFED WITH CRAB MEAT AND WRAPPED IN BACON $19.95

"LAS CARNES & POLLO"
BEEF & CHICKEN

CARNE ASADA "TAMPIQUEÑA" A BROILED STRIP OF JUICY BEEF SERVED WITH A CHEESE ENCHILADA, GUACAMOLE, RICE & BEANS $10.95
MARTIN'S CHICKEN "FAJITA" BROILED STRIPS OF CHICKEN SERVED WITH GUACAMOLE, RICE & BEANS $8.95

For additional information see page 108.

Särö Restaurant

Menu Changes Monthly

APPETIZERS

Toast Skagen   6.95
Grilled toast topped w/bay shrimp, onion, dill in mayonnaise mix and golden caviar

Swedish Gravlax   7.25
Genuine Swedish marinated salmon w/honey mustard sauce and toast

Smoked Salmon   9.95
Two smoked salmon slices w/horseradish creme and toast

Carpaccio   7.25
The chef's own chilled marinated beef, topped w/parmesan cheese, served with creme fraiche

SOUP/SALAD/PASTA/SANDWICH

Fish soup   cup/bowl   3.75/6.25
A clear soup du jour w/taste of saffron, garlic and tomatoes

Lobster bisque   cup/bowl   3.50/5.95
SARO's own creamy lobster bisque

Komodo chicken salad   9.25
A soy marinated breast w/mixed vegetables, mandarin oranges in a sesame vinaigrette dressing topped w/sprouts

Pasta du Jour   8.95
Vegetarian pasta combined w/fresh garden vegetables of the day in creamy white sauce

Bookmaker toast   8.25
Grilled filet Mignon w/mustard and horseradish sauce

SARO Burger   7.95
Burger topped w/green peppercorn sauce and galley fried potatoes

926 Broadway Cir • Downtown • (619) 232-7173

COMBO PLATE

Swedish specialties 13.95
Two kinds of herring, smoked salmon, egg & caviar, meatballs, skagen mix,
gravlax w/mustard sauce and cheese

ENTREES

Baked salmon 15.95
Salmon in puff pastry w/spinach served in a white wine sauce

Grilled Gravlax 14.95
Our own marinated salmon in lobster and lime sauce served w/rice

Filet of sole au gratin 16.95
Toped w/parmesan cheese and served in a white wine sauce

Mamma's Kottbullar 10.95
Swedish meatballs in creamy gravy w/lingonberries and steamed potatoes

Starboard Filet Mignon 16.95
Grilled filet stuffed w/bleu cheese, port wine sauce and galley fried potatoes

Grilled Venison Medallions 22.95
Served with Swedish morel sauce and leek potatoes

Chicken Parmesan 13.95
Chicken breast au gratin w/parmesan and mozzarella cheeses, in a
marinara sauce

Tiger chicken 12.95
Marinated chicken w/chili and oyster sauce served w/rice

DESSERTS

Hot shot parfait 4.95
Layered w/creme, galliano, kahlua and coffee

Gino 5.95
A combination of fresh fruit w/dark and white chocolate au gratin,
topped w/vanilla ice cream

Punsch Marinated Blueberries 5.25
Blueberries in a Swedish punsch topped w/ice cream

Pancakes 3.75
Swedish w/strawberry preserves and whipped cream

For additional information see page 113.

Menu Changes Seasonally

Saska's APPETIZERS

THREE STUFFED SHRIMP ... 6.95
Crab and Jack Cheese

EXTRA MESSY HOT WINGS 4.95

CALAMARI STRIPS 5.95
Deep-fried

STEAMED CLAMS Market Price

OYSTERS ON THE HALF SHELL
Market Price

RED-HOT CHILI POPPERS... 4.95
Jalapeños stuffed with cream
cheese served with Jalapeño jam

Saska's DINNER SALADS

Includes Garlic Cheese Toast and choice of homemade dressings (Ranch Style,
Honey Bleu Cheese, Creamy 1000 Island, Tangy Vinegar and Oil or Real Roquefort)

SEAFOOD SALAD **10.95**
Bay shrimp, crabmeat, scallops, whitefish, cheeses and egg

MANDARIN CHICKEN SALAD **7.95**
Broiled breast with vegetables, sliced almonds, oriental noodles and SASKA'S
own Mandarin dressing

Saska's PASTA DINNERS

Includes Garlic Cheese Toast and choice of Crab Chowder or Mixed Salad
All pasta dishes are prepared with Parmesan and Romano Cheeses

SEAFOOD FETTUCCINE **12.95**
Jumbo shrimp & scallops sauteed in cream sauce

SEAFOOD MARINARA **11.50**
Linguine topped with bay shrimp, scallops and green lip mussels
in a marinara sauce

CHICKEN BUCARELLI **11.50**
Boneless breast of chicken sauteed in garlic butter and white wine, served with
linguini and marinara sauce

Dinners include Garlic Cheese Toast & Crab Chowder or Mixed Salad. Entrees are served with Fried Zucchini and Rice Pilaf, Steamed Vegetables or French Fries (Home Fries upon request)

Saska's SEAFOOD

FRESH FISH Please ask your waitperson for tonight's selections

LOBSTER TAIL ....**Market Price**
Deep sea delight, sumptuous and flavorful

ALASKAN KING CRAB LEGS ....**Market Price**
Over a pound of these northern delicacies

SHRIMP SCAMPI **14.95**
Shrimp sauteed with garlic butter, white wine and mushrooms

Saska's TOP SIRLOIN STEAKS

THE DUKE (14–16 oz.) **15.95**
Cut for the serious steak eater

THE SASKA (10 oz.) **11.95**
Mission Beach's favorite for over 44 years

TERIYAKI **12.50**
Marinated in soy and ginger sauce, served with fresh pineapple

Saska's SPECIALTIES

NEW YORK STRIP LOIN (12 oz.) **15.95**
Mrs. Saska's favorite, succulent and flavorful

FILET MIGNON (7 oz.) **12.95**
Wrapped in Bacon, served with mushrooms

TOURNEDOS OF BEEF (7 oz.) **14.95**
Rounds of tenderloin on Bordelaise sauce, topped with mushroom caps and Bearnaise sauce

TERIYAKI CHICKEN **11.50**
Boneless chicken breasts broiled and served with fresh pineapple

For additional information see page 40.

Shien of Osaka

Menu Changes Seasonally

APPETIZERS

Yakitori (broiled chicken on skewer) *3.30*

Hiyayakko (chilled tofu) *3.30*

Beef Negima (broiled thin slices of beef wrapped around scallion) *4.25*

Nikujaga (cooked potatoes with sliced beef) *2.80*

Tuna Sashimi *8.00*

Yamakake (mountian yams with tuna) *5.15*

Oshitashi (boiled spinach) *2.90*

Tsukimi Yamaimo (mountain yams with quail eggs) *4.30*

Nameko Oroshi (nameko mushrooms with grated radish) *4.25*

COMBINATIONS

* with rice, soup & salad   ** with soup & salad

** California Roll & Chicken Teriyaki *8.95*

** California Roll & Mixed Tempura *10.45*

** California Roll & Salmon Teriyaki *12.00*

** Sushi & Tempura *14.00*

** Sushi & Beef Teriyaki *15.95*

** *Sushi & Salmon Teriyaki* *16.25*
    (sushi: tuna, shrimp, halibut, scallops & tuna roll)
    (sashimi: tuna, halibut & octopus)

* *Sashimi & Chicken Teriyaki* *11.75*

** *California Roll & Tempura & Chicken Teriyaki* *12.60*

* *Sashimi & Tempura & Beef Teriyaki* *17.95*

** *California Roll & Tempura & Chicken Teriyaki & Sashimi* *18.25*

* *Chicken Teriyaki & Mixed Tempura* *10.45*

DINNER ENTREES
** served with soup, salad & rice*

* *Shrimp Tempura* *10.65*

* *Vegetable Tempura* *7.25*

* *Chicken Teriyaki* *8.00*

* *Beef Teriyaki* *11.45*

* *Salmon Teriyaki* *11.75*

* *Japanese Style Beef Steak* *11.45*

* *Chicken Curry & Rice* *6.45*

* *Yakizakana Teisyoku (broiled fish - sanma)* *7.80*

Zaru Soba (Udon) (japanese noodle) *6.20*

Tenzaru Soba (Udon) (zaru soba & tempura) *9.90*

Tori Soba (Udon) (a large bowl of noodle topped with chicken) *6.45*

Tempura Soba (Udon) (a large bowl of noodle topped with tempura) *7.45*

Nabeyaki Udon (a special bowl of noodle topped with egg, chicken, seafood & vegetables) *7.45*

Oroshi Soba (a large bowl of noodle topped with grated radish & yams) *6.45*

* *Oyako Donburi (a large bowl of rice topped with chicken & eggs)* *6.45*

For additional information see page 99.

STAR OF INDIA

Indian Cuisine

EXOTIC APPETIZERS

CHICKEN CHAT   3.75
Tender boneless chicken pieces in spicy marinade (served cold).

LAMB SAMOSA   4.00
Two crisp patties stuffed with spiced minced lamb.

FISH PAKORA   6.75
Lightly fried, batter-dipped fish fillets.

SOUPS

MULLIGATAWNY SOUP   3.25
Delicately spiced lentil soup with chicken.

DAL SHORBA   2.75
Mildly spiced lentil soup.

TENDER LAMB CURRIES

ROGAN JOSH   13.25
Lamb cubes cooked in a sauce of tomatoes, onion and exotic spices.

SAAG GOSHT   13.75
Lamb in a creamed spinach curry.

1000 Prospect St • La Jolla • (619) 459-3355 • Call for Additional Locations

TANDOORI SPECIALTIES

The Tandoor is a tall, cylindrical clay oven. Temperature at the bottom is maintained at 800 degrees Fahrenheit with mesquite charcoal. One has to be skillful to work the Tandoor and perfect the process of baking, roasting and grilling simultaneously. All breads are cooked on the interior wall of the Tandoor oven; the meats are barbecued while hanging on skewers. This special process burns away the fat while sealing in vital ingredients.

TANDOORI CHICKEN   HALF 8.75   FULL 14.50
Chicken marinated in yogurt, garlic, ginger, vinegar, lemon and fresh herbs.

FISH TIKKA KABAB   13.75
Cubes of fish marinated in spices and herbs.

BOOTI KABAB   13.75
Cubes of boneless lamb marinated in yogurt, ginger, garlic, and fresh herbs.

TANDOORI PRAWNS   17.50
Prawns marinated in yogurt, garlic, ginger, vinegar and fresh herbs.

BARA KABAB   17.50
Lamb chops marinated in yogurt, herbs and spices.

SEAFOOD SPECIALTIES

PRAWN BHUNA   15.50
Prawns in a spicy gravy of coconut and onions.

PRAWN VINDALOO   15.75
Prawns cooked in a spicy curry with potatoes.

FISH MASALA   7.75
Fish cubes cooked in spicy sauce with coconuts

VEGETARIAN SPECIALTIES

MATTAR PANEER   8.50
Cubed farmer cheese and green peas in a gravy.

BENGAN BHARTHA   9.25
Eggplant baked in clay oven and cooked with onions, peas and tomatoes.

DAAL BAHAR   7.50
Seasonal lentils delicately spiced.

NAVRATTAN KORMA (Mixed Vegetables)   9.50
Vegetables, farmer cheese and nuts in a mild cream sauce.

For additional information see page 78.

Stefano's
CUCINA ITALIANA

Menu Changes Seasonally

ANTIPASTI

STUFFED MUSHROOMS 5.50
Mushroom caps stuffed with veal, garlic,
herbs, stuffing, red wine and fennel sauce.

ESCARGOT ITALIANO 5.50
Special fennel garlic butter with fresh roasted
garlic bulb.

CACIOCAVALLO CAUDA 4.50
Virgin olive oil, garlic, herbs, smoked Italian
cheese, balsamic vinegar, crostini toast.

COSTOLETTA E CAMPAGNA 6.50
Country Style Veal Ribs, marinated, grilled.

CARCIOFI 4.95
Fried artichoke hearts, breaded, in a
bordelaise sauce.

CALAMARI ALL'OREGANO 4.95
Squid sauteed in olive oil, garlic, white wine,
and oregano.

GNOCCHI DE SEMOLINA 3.95
Semolina with 3 cheeses, pesto marinara sauce.

SOUP

ZUPPA DI PESCE 2.95
A rich broth with lively seasonings, cream and
sherry, simmered from shellfish.

CHEESE GARLIC 2.75
An herb, garlic and egg soup topped with
croutons and melted Swiss cheese.

SALADS

HOT GOAT CHEESE SALAD 5.95
Goat cheese sauteed with sliced almonds,
served on romaine lettuce
with sun-dried tomatoes.

CAESAR SALAD 4.95
Romaine, garlic, anchovy, olive oil, lemon,
herbs and parmigiana.

CALAMARI SALAD 9.95
Italian greens sauteed in olive oil, garlic,
red pepper, fried squid, balsamic vinegar.

MARINATED LENTIL SALAD 7.95
Lentil beans marinated, herbed goat cheese,
grilled onions, basil Aioli dressing.

ADDIZIONALE

ITALIAN FLAG SPECIAL 12.95
Combination of 1/2 order each; lasagna,
cannelloni, pasta alla pesto.
Served with hot vegetable.

CANNELLONI 10.95
Crepes filled with chicken, spinach,
mushrooms, and parmesan cheese,
marinara and cheese bechamel sauces.
Served with hot vegetable.

EGGPLANT PARMIGIANA 10.95
Sliced eggplant, layered with cheese,
marinara sauce and basil.
Served with hot vegetable.

MEAT

CHICKEN CALAFIA 13.50
Double breast of chicken stuffed with Italian
sausage, garlic, and Fontina cheese, sauce of
pear tomatoes, basil, mushrooms and cream.

AGNELLO DI FILETTO 16.95
Loin of lamb stuffed with roasted garlic,
marinated, grilled, mustard sauce. Served
with hot vegetable.

RISOTTO TUSCANO 12.95
Italian sausage, breast of chicken, pear
tomatoes, red wine, garlic, herbs, Italian rice.

VEAL PICCATA 15.95
Tender escalopes of milk-fed veal sauteed in
butter and finished with capers and lemon.
Served with hot vegetable.

OSSOBUCO MILANESE 15.95
Eastern veal shanks braised in olive oil then
baked in a rich sauce of tomato, garlic, wine,
herbs and lemon. Served with Risotto Milanese.

BISTECCA ALLA FIORENTINA 17.95
Eastern Choice New York steak, 12 oz. grilled.
Basted with olive oil, garlic, rosemary. Served
with hot vegetable.

SEAFOOD

BRODETTO DI STEFANO 18.95
Fresh fish filet, shrimp, cockles and
mussels simmered in a fennel wine sauce
with fresh tomato.

SALMONE AL RIVE 15.50
Fresh filet of salmon, sauteed with olive oil,
garlic, rosemary, parsley and lemon.
Served with hot vegetable.

SCAMPI BASILICO 15.95
Large shrimp sauteed in olive oil with garlic,
pear tomatoes, sun dried tomatoes, sherry
wine, herbs and fresh basil.

PASTA

Appetizer | Ala Carte

TOASTED ALMOND SHRIMP PESTO
LINGUINI 6.95 12.00
White wine with pesto, herbs and
toasted almonds.

PAPPARDELLE AL RAGU DI
ANATRA 5.95 10.95
Duck meat stewed in a red wine sauce,
vegetables, herbs, olives and wide pasta.

QUATTRO FORMAGGI
ANGEL HAIR 5.90 10.75
A subtle blending of 4 cheeses, cream and
herbs, tossed with fresh angel hair pasta.

FETTUCCINE BUONO
VIVO 5.50 8.75
Eggless spinach pasta tossed in a sauce made
without oil, butter or meat. Pear tomatoes,
vegetable stock, herbs, red pepper and lemon.

FETTUCCINE AL
PEPERONATA 5.65 8.95
Roasted peppers simmered with onions until
lightly browned. tomato, green olives, red
wine vinegar, fettuccine pasta.

CALAMARI E CARCIOFI ... 5.95 10.95
Squid and artichoke sauteed. Olive oil, garlic,
white wine, anchovy, lemon, parsley. Spinach
angel hair pasta.

LAMB SPAGHETTINI
JARDINIERE 7.75 11.95
Lamb escalopes sauteed with mushrooms,
fresh tomato, red peppers and lamb sauce.

LASAGNA CON SPINACI .. 5.95 9.10
Layered pasta, stuffed with cheeses, plus a
cream spinach stuffing, cheese bechamel and
marinara sauce.

FETTUCCINE ALL PESTO 5.90 10.75
Sweet basil, garlic, olive oil, and romano
cheese sauce.

To include a green salad or pasta with ala carte entree, add $2.00 each.

For additional information see page 94.

275

Stella's Hideaway

PIEROGI ~ *Thin pasta shells stuffed with (A) meat, (B) sauerkraut/ mushrooms, (C) potatoes/cheese, (D) potatoes/cheddar cheese or (E) assorted; served boiled or fried. $13.95*

CABBAGE ROLLS (GOLABKI) ~ *Center is a blend of meats, topped with tomato sauce; served with potatoes & sauerkraut salad. $12.95*

POLISH SAUSAGE (KIELBASA) ~ *Authentic Polish sausage, served with fried potatoes and sauerkraut. $12.95*

COMBINATION PLATE ~ *Pierogis, cabbage roll and sausage; served with potatoes and sauerkraut. $15.95*

STELLA'S CASSEROLE (ZAPIEKANKA) ~ *Layers of macaroni, mushrooms, onions and five kinds of cheese; served with carrots. $12.95*

POTATO PANCAKES (PLACKI) ~ *Blend of potatoes, onions and seasonings, served with applesauce and sour cream. $10.95*

CHEESE BLINTZES (NALESNIKI) ~ *Thin egg pancakes filled with a blend of cheeses, topped with sour cream sauce. $9.95*

PAN FRIED LIVER (WATROBKA) ~ *Simmered in onions; served with potatoes and carrots. $11.95*

PORK CUTLET (SCHABOWY) ~ *Pork loin gourmet cut, breaded and pan fried; served with potatoes and sauerkraut.* $12.95

CHICKEN CUTLET ~ *Boneless chicken breast breaded and sauteed; served with potatoes and red cabbage.* $12.95

CUTLET DE VOLAILLE ~ *Boneless chicken breast stuffed with swiss cheese, sorrel and spices; served with potatoes and spinach.* $13.95

STELLA'S FAVORITE ~ *Polish sausage in horseradish sauce; served with potato pancakes.* $13.95

ROAST DUCK STUFFED WITH APPLES ~ *1/2 duck served with potatoes and red cabbage.* $16.95

STEAK WARSAW STYLE ~ *Marinated filet mignon, topped with mushrooms & onion; served with potato dumplings or potatoes and red cabbage.* $15.95

BEEF STROGANOFF ~ *Strips of beef/mushrooms/onions in sour cream gravy; served on french dumplings with carrots.* $12.95

FLANKEN ~ *Boiled lean beef in horseradish sauce; served with potatoes and carrots.* $11.95

HUNTER'S STEW (BIGOS) ~ *Sauerkraut, mix meat, sausage and spices; served with potatoes.* $13.95

FISH CUTLETS ~ *Minced fish filet with onion and spices; served with potatoes and sauerkraut salad.* $12.95

STELLA'S SPECIALS

MONDAY — THURSDAY
BEEF PAPRIKASH

FRIDAY — SUNDAY
CHICKEN PAPRIKASH

Served in between two potato pancakes; sauerkraut salad & topped with sour cream $12.95

Served with dumplings & carrots $13.95

SPECIALS INCLUDE: SOUP, BREAD/BUTTER, DESSERT

For additional information see page 112.

MENU CHANGES SEASONALLY

Hors d'oeuvres - Chaud et Froid

CAVIAR — Market Price Per Ounce
Beluga malossol
Sevruga malossol

ASPERGES CHAUDES — 9.00
Grilled asparagus with warm vinaigrette
of smoked bacon, shallots, garlic, olives
and tomatoes

FOIE GRAS AUX ENDIVES — 18.00
Domestic duck liver with apples, endive
and phyllo dough

SALADE DE CANARD CHAUD — 10.00
Warm duck with arugula, hearts of palm, lime
and mango dressing

RISOTTO AUX COQUILLES — 11.00
ST. JACQUES
Sautéed scallops and saffron risotto with
sweet red bell pepper vinaigrette

RAVIOLI DE CREVETTES — 12.00
Ravioli with shrimp, lemon thyme and
fried leeks

COQUILLES ST. JACQUES — 13.00
ET SAUMON FUMÉ
Smoked scallops and salmon, greens,
sweet potatoes with chive vinaigrette

HUITRES — 10.00
fresh oysters on the half shell

Soups

BLACK BEAN — 6.00
With cilantro cream

SOUPE DU JOUR — 7.00
The Chef's selection

Salads

SALADE MAISON 6.00	SALADE D'EPINARDS 8.00
Mixed baby greens, tomatoes with	*Spoon leaf spinach with raspberry vinaigrette*
tarragon vinaigrette	*topped with pinenuts and goat cheese*
SALADE CAESAR 7.00	SALADE DE TOMATE 9.00
Hearts of romaine with parmesan croutons	*Marinated tomatoes with avocado and*
and traditional caesar dressing	*goat cheese with sherry vinaigrette*

Entrees

FETTUCCINE AUX CREVETTES 25.00
ET COQUILLES ST. JACQUES
Shrimp and scallops saute with artichoke
hearts, sun dried tomatoes and basil

POULET GRILLE 25.00
Boneless, skinless chicken breast with grilled
vegetables, pesto and pasta

POULET A L'ESTRAGON 28.00
Oven roasted chicken breast with polenta,
fresh tomato and tarragon

CANARD DU CHEF 27.00
Duck dinner with roasted breast, confit leg,
fresh mulberry sauce

FILET MIGNON 28.00
Grilled tenderloin of beef, burgundy wine
sauce with smoked bacon and pearl onions

TOURNEDOS DE BOEUF 28.00
Tenderloin of beef, pan seared, green
peppercorns, cognac and cream sauce with
fettuccine pasta

BOEUF AUX CHAMPIGNONS 29.00
SAUVAGES
Certified prime sirloin, pan seared with
madeira, foie gras and wild mushrooms

COTES D'AGNEAU 29.00
Oven roasted lamb rack with roasted garlic,
rosemary sauce and herbed potato puree

ESCALOPE DE VEAU 28.00
Veal loin, pan seared with fresh tomato,
balsamic vinegar, served with basil risotto

SAUMON 27.00
Fresh salmon,
Chef's creation daily

ESPADON 27.00
Fresh swordfish,
Chef's creation daily

CHEF'S SPECIAL Market Price
OF THE DAY

For additional information see page 74.

TOP OF THE MARKET

COCKTAILS & COLD SHELLFISH

Our seafood cocktails are served on a bed of shredded lettuce and purple cabbage with cocktail sauce and lemon.

MAZATLAN PRAWNS	8.95
SASHIMI OF **FRESH** FLORIDA AHI - *With wasabi, pickled ginger, and soy sauce*	9.25
FRESH BABY BAY SCALLOP CEVICHE - *With sliced avocado, blue corn chips*	7.75
"000" BELUGA MALOSSAL CAVIAR - *Toast, egg yolks and whites, onions*	1 oz. 55.00 2 oz. 100.00

SMOKED FISH

We smoke our own fish in the mild European style, using hickory and alder woods. Served cold with marinated triple cream cheese, handmade basil pesto, sliced bermuda onions, capers and garlic croutons.

SMOKED NOVA LOX	9.25
SMOKED IDAHO RAINBOW TROUT	6.25
SMOKED CATALINA SWORDFISH	8.25

SPECIALTIES

JAPANESE EGGPLANT - *Barbequed or panko fried, served with Aioli Sauce*	5.75
FRESH CHINOOK SALMON - *Poached, served cold, mustard sauce, cucumber salad*	16.50
OUR FILO WRAPPED OYSTERS ROCKEFELLER - *With spinach, pernod, & locatelli romano cheese*	8.25
ROASTED PEPPERS AND ANCHOVIES - *Stuffed with feta cheese, sour cream and basil*	7.75
MEXICAN PRAWNS - *Sauteed with peppers, onions, tomatoes, cilantro, jalapenos*	14.95
DEAN'S PRAWNS - *Garlic, butter, white wine, basil pesto, sherry*	14.75
SAUTEED SANTA BARBARA BLACK MUSSELS - *In saffron butter and salsa*	16.45

PASTA COMBINATIONS

ALL OF OUR PASTA IS HANDMADE DAILY

FRESH ROSEMARY CAPPELLINI WITH MAINE LOBSTER, CHAMPAGNE CREAM SAUCE	18.75
FRESH ROASTED RED PEPPER PASTA, SMOKED TROUT AND MARINATED CHEESE (Spicy)	13.00
FRESH EGG CAPPELLINI , **FRESH** BABY BAY SCALLOPS AND ITALIAN PORCINI MUSHROOMS	13.25
FRESH SHELLFISH AND TAGLIARINI - *Your choice of: New Zealand Cockles or Mussels, Washington Manila Clams, or Santa Barbara Black Mussels*	16.95

All pastas come with your choice of:
Natural Sauce, Cream Sauce or Tomato Sauce

SEAFOOD ENTREES

FRESH CALIFORNIA THRESHER SHARK - *With shallot caper butter*	16.00
CAJUN STYLE MAZATLAN PRAWNS - *With scallion horseradish sauce*	20.75
FRESH CATALINA SWORDFISH - *Harpooned and caught by our own boat, the "Pilikia"*	26.50
FRESH EASTERN SEA SCALLOPS - *Wrapped in true Italian prosciutto served with a dijon sauce*	18.50

NON SEAFOOD ENTREES

FREE RANGE VEAL CHOP	23.50
RACK OF NEW ZEALAND LAMB - *Seasoned with rosemary and garlic*	26.00
FREE RANGE CHICKEN BREAST - *Marinated in olive oil, rosemary, thyme and garlic*	15.50

The above entrees are basted with virgin olive oil and
charbroiled just inches above mesquite charcoal.

SPECIALTIES

PANKO NEW ZEALAND ORANGE ROUGHY	22.00
SELECT ALASKAN KING CRAB LEGS - *Steamed*	29.75
FRESH OREGON PETRALE SOLE- *Pan fried with lemon caper sauce*	21.25
SAUTEED AUSTRALIAN LOBSTER TAIL - *With mushrooms, white wine and garlic*	31.50
SAUTEED **FRESH** EASTERN SEA SCALLOPS - *With mushrooms, white wine and garlic*	18.50
ORIENTAL STYLE STEAMED **FRESH** ALASKAN HALIBUT *With black beans, ginger & garlic*	24.00

Entrees include fresh vegetables and choice of french fries,
wild rice pilaf, rosemary potatoes, or sliced tomatoes.

For additional information see page 115.

TORREYANA *grille*

Menu Changes Monthly

APPETIZERS

Ginger Steamed Lobster $8.95
Dumplings
garlic chili drizzle

Oysters Rockefeller $8.75
spiced spinach and mornay sauce

Oysters on the Half Shell $8.75
blue point oysters and shooter sauce

Gulf Shrimp Cocktail $7.50
cocktail sauce and dijon mustard

Cajun Crab Cakes $7.95
with creole mustard

Sundried Tomato and Basil $5.75
Pesto Linguini
with black olives and roasted garlic

SOUPS

Today's Soup $3.95
a daily Torreyana creation

Lobster Chowder $4.95
with smoked bacon and sweet
cream

Double Beef Consomme $4.75
a clear rich broth

SALADS

Torreyana Salad $4.25
baby field greens with hazelnuts,
tomatoes and cucumbers

Warm Bean & Arugula Salad $5.75
alder smoked bacon and balsamic
vinaigrette

VEGETARIAN

Autumn Vegetable Torte $13.75
Herb encrusted seasonal vegetables with marinara and basil pesto

Grilled Vegetable and Black Bean Fettuccini $14.95
with ricotta cheese and marinara

Sheraton Grande Torrey Pines Hotel • 10950 N Torrey Pines Rd • La Jolla • (619) 450-4571

Each Entree is paired with a recommended wine avaliable by the glass.

SEAFOOD SPECIALTIES

Lobster Carbonara   *$19.95*
prosciutto, roasted red peppers, black olives and angel hair pasta
Raymond Chardonnay 1991, Napa Valley   *$5.25*

Torreyana Cataplana   *$18.50*
shrimp, scallops, manilla clams, pacific seafood with thyme linguini
Kendall Jackson Vintners Reserve Chardonnay, 1992   *$5.00*

Grilled Marinated Pacific Prawns   *$18.95*
oyster mushrooms, shallots and angel hair pasta
Kendall Jackson Sauvignon Blanc 1992, Lake County   *$4.50*

MEAT AND POULTRY

Sauteed Semi-Boneless Chicken Breast   *$16.95*
fontina cheese and prosciutto with mushroom glaze
Fetzer Gamay Beaujolais 1991, Mendocino   *$4.75*

Grilled Ribeye Steak and Lobster Medallions   *$25.95*
cabernet reduction with fresh herbs and sweet butter
Kendall Jackson Cabernet Sauvignon 1991, Lake County   *$6.00*

Grilled Filet Mignon   *$21.95*
au jus and white pepper pan renderings
Stags Leap Cabernet Sauvignon 1990, Napa Valley   *$6.75*

Char Grilled Lamb Chops   *$20.95*
tobacco onions, field greens, sage and tomato salsa
Clos Du Bois Merlot 1990, Sonoma   *$5.25*

GRANDE FINALE

Jack Daniels-Chocolate and Pecan Diamonds   *$4.95*
Chocolate Ganache and Vanilla Bean Cream

White Chocolate Bread Pudding   *$4.50*
English Cream and Raspberry Sauce

Passion Fruit Charlotte   *$4.95*
with Raspberry Coulis

For additional information see page 57.

TOURLAS

RESTAURANT & TERRACE

Menu Changes Seasonally

SOUP - SALAD - STARTERS

Dungeness Crab Cakes with Basil Cream and Citrus
$8.50

Wild Mushroom Streusel and Escargot in a Garlic Parsley Sauce
$7.25

Corn Fried Shrimp Tempura with Thai Peanut Sauce
and Chopstick Asparagus
$9.75

Cambridge House Smoked Salmon,
Traditional Garnish and Caviar
$13.00

Daily Soup or Vidalia Onion Soup
$5.00

Mixed Greens with Tomato, Walnuts and Goat Cheese
Tossed with Basil Vinaigrette
$4.25

Caesar Salad with Shaved Parmesan and Garlic Croutons
$6.50

Buffalo Mozzarella, Tomato & Basil with Black Pepper
Champagne Vinegar and Olive Oil
$5.25

ENTREES

Linguini Pasta Served with Fresh Clams and Shrimp
in a Champagne and Basil Ribbon Broth
$19.00

Grilled New York Steak with a Gorgonzola Crust
and Cabernet Shallot Sauce
$18.25

Filet of Halibut in Paper served with Jardiniere Vegetables
and Sauce of Scallops and Thyme
$17.50

Rack of Lamb with Paprika Crust and Merlot Glaze,
Cassoulet of White Beans
$21.50

Filet of Beef Tenderloin Grilled
and Served with Port Wine Truffle Sauce
$20.00

Sauteed Swordfish with Stoneground Mustard Sauce
$18.50

Pan Seared Salmon Filet on Wilted Baby Greens, Sauce of
Fresh Strawberries, Basil, Orange Rind and Absolut Citron
$19.25

Stuffed Breast of Chicken with Sundried Tomato,
Pinenuts and Goat Cheese Served with
Red Pepper Penne Pasta and Spicy Tomato Sauce
$15.00

Veal Chop Grilled and Served with a Ragout of
Wild Mushrooms
$27.50

For additional information see page 58.

ANTIPASTI

Muscoli Gratinati—Baked mussels with bread crumbs, ground almonds,
garlic and fresh herbs   6.95

Fiori di Zucca Ripieni—Deep fried zucchini blossoms stuffed with spinach,
goat cheese, sundried tomatoes, mushrooms and prosciutto.
Served with our spicy marinara sauce and fresh lemon   6.50

Portobello alla Griglia—Marinated and grilled portobello mushroom with
crisp fried polenta, balsamic glazed onions and smoked scamorza cheese   7.95

Melanzane al Forno—roasted baby eggplants filled with herbed goat cheese,
roasted peppers, pine nuts and a roasted tomato coulis   6.25

INSALATA

Insalata di Pollo—Warm roasted chicken and wilted spinach salad with
tomatoes, bacon, parmigiana cheese and a dijon mustard dressing   6.95

Insalata Nizzarda—Grilled tuna Provençale salad with new potatoes,
haricots verts, artichokes, tomatoes, olives and a roasted red pepper aioli   9.25

Insalata Torinese—Arugola, shaved parmigiana with roasted red peppers,
capers, red onion, lemon and extra virgin olive oil   4.75

PIZZA

Pizza di Verdure—Rustic flatbread baked with arugola, fresh tomato,
garlic, shaved parmigiana and extra virgin olive oil   7.95

Pizza dei Cinque Terre—Spicy shrimp pizza with smoked scamorza cheese,
sundried tomato pesto, red onions and fresh basil   10.95

Pizza con Funghi e Anitra—wild mushroom pizza with smoked duck,
green onions, gruyere and Teleme cheeses   9.95

PASTA

	Appetizer	Entrée

Trenette con Gamberi—Trenette pasta with grilled shrimp,
basil pesto, goat cheese and fresh tomatoes   6.95   10.95

Ravioli di Salmone Affumicato—Smoked salmon ravioli with leeks, fresh
tomatoes and a lemon-chive beurre blanc   7.50   11.50

Linguine Costa Brava—Saffron linguine with mussels, shrimp and clams
in a light fennel and tomato broth   6.95   10.95

Agnolotti di Tartufi—Wild mushroom and summer truffle agnolotti with
a marsala wine and porcini mushroom cream sauce   7.75   11.75

Tagliarini alla Siciliana—Whole wheat pasta ribbons with a Sicilian style olive,
tomato, orange zest and sweet onion sauce (no oil and no butter)   5.25   9.25

Conchiglie alla Livornese—Pasta shells with spicy shrimp, white beans,
broccoli, prosciutto and lemon zest   7.50   11.50

Linguine alla Victoria—Linguine with clams, diced red peppers, chili flakes,
garlic, fresh herbs, white wine and olive oil   7.50   11.50

Mezze Rigate alla Contadina—Pasta tubes with spicy eggplant, pancetta,
asiago cheese and a roasted tomato cream sauce   6.25   10.25

ENTREES

Pollo Arrosto con Basilico e Limone—Roasted lemon-basil chicken with
garlic mashed potatoes and tomato gratin   9.95

Agnello con Pesto de Olive—Grilled rack of lamb with a black olive and
sundried tomato pesto. Served with an eggplant timbale and rosemary
roasted new potatoes   17.95

Salmone al Pepe—Roasted peppercorn crusted salmon served over lentils
with a sherry and shallot vinaigrette   13.95

Quaglie alla Nonna—Pan roasted stuffed quail with pancetta, roasted new
potatoes, mushrooms, baby onions and rosemary   13.75

Anitra Arrosto alle Erbe—Crisp roasted duckling with a rosemary and
honey glaze served with Catalan style sauteed spinach   12.95

Bistecca Toscana—Marinated and grilled New York steak with
Chianti butter and garlic mashed potatoes   14.85

Osso Buco Triestina—Oven braised veal shank with a
vegetable-barley risotto   14.95

Paella "Acqua"—Shrimp, clams, mussels, chorizo and chicken baked with
saffron rice, peas and pimientos   16.95

For additional information see page 94.

Trattoria La Strada

ANTIPASTI

SEPPIE INZIMINO — 7.50
Baby calamari, sautéed with swiss chard, garlic, and a touch of spicy tomato sauce

SCAMPI IN GUAZZETTO — 9.25
Large shrimp in a light tomato and garlic sauce

PROSCIUTTO E MELONE — 9.95
Thinly sliced imported prosciutto with cantaloupe

CARPACCI

CARPACCIO AI CARCIOFI E FORMAGGIO — 8.95
Thin slices of filet mignon with artichokes and parmigiano

CARPACCIO AL SALMONE E MELANZANE — 10.95
Smoked salmon, grilled eggplant and toasted Tuscan bread (crostini)

CARPACCIO AL TONNO E GAMBERI — 10.95
Thin slices of fresh tuna with shrimp and arugola

INSALATE E ZUPPE

INSALATA PATRIZIA — 8.50
Arugola, avocado, hearts of palm, mozzarella and parmigiano, extra virgin olive oil

INSALATA CONTADINA — 8.50
Sundried tomatoes, olives, capers, bell peppers, goat cheese, red onions

MINESTRONE DI VERDURA — 4.50
Vegetable soup

PASTA

TORTELLI ALLA MODA DE FIRENZE   10.95
Cheese filled pockets with gorgonzola cheese and
wild mushrooms

LINGUINE ALLE VONGOLE VERACI   11.95
Flat spaghetti with fresh manila clams, garlic, parsley
and fresh spices

TORTELLI ALL'AGNELLO   11.50
Homemade cheese pockets with lamb meat sauce

PENNE ALLA PIRATA   11.95
Tube shaped pasta with baby clams, shrimp, shallots,
in a light cream sauce

GNOCCHI ALLA FIORENTINA   11.95
Potato dumpling with garlic, parsley, red pepper,
tomato and wild mushroom sauce

SECONDI

SCAMPI DE' MEDICI   15.95
Giant shrimp pan fried scampi style with champignon
flambée with brandy

POLLO TOSCANO   13.95
Tender chicken breast rolled over asparagus, prosciutto
and cheese, sauteed in a wild mushroom sauce

COTOLETTA DI AGNELLO ALLA BEATRICE   15.95
Pan fried lamb chops with bell peppers and licks

FILETTO AL CHIANTI   16.95
Filet mignon seared in Chianti, balsamic vinegar sauce

GRIGLIA

GALLETTO AL MATTONE   12.95
Cornish hen, pressed with a hot brick, with
lemon, garlic, rosemary

BISTECCHINE DI MAIALE   13.50
Grilled pork chops seasoned with fresh herbs

FILETTO ALLA GRIGLIA   16.95
Succulent filet of beef grilled to order

GRIGLIA MISTO MARE   18.95
Jumbo fresh-water shrimp, tuna and salmon filets
open-grilled with eggplants, zucchini and endive

For additional information see page 95.

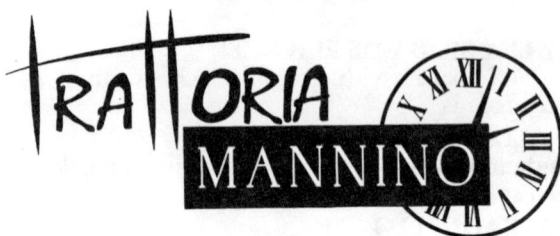

Antipasti

Carciofi Mannino	5.95
Sauteed fresh baby artichokes in garlic, basil and olive oil	
Vegetali Misti	5.95
Fresh vegetables in season, sauteed in garlic, olive oil	
Mozzarella Caprese	5.95
Fresh, warm mozzarella with Roma tomato, red onions on a bed of crisp lettuce	
Cozze Scoppiate	6.95
Fresh mussels in white wine, light tomato sauce	
Insalata di Mare	7.95
Calamari, shrimps, scallops in a lemon, herb dressing	
Carpaccio di Salmone	7.95
Thinly sliced salmon in lemon, olive oil, scallions in a bed of arugula	

Pasta

Tortelloni alla Trattoria	9.95
Veal filled pasta in a creamy tomato sauce	
Cannelloni Biondini	9.95
Fresh crepes stuffed with chicken, spinach, mozzarella, cream sauce	
Gnocchi Capricciosi	9.95
Potato pasta dumplings covered with a creamy blend of mascarpone, fontina, parmesan, prosciutto and peas	
Ravioli all'Arancio	9.95
Veal stuffed pasta with mascarpone, orange zest cream sauce	

Tortelloni all Panna Veal filled pasta with baby artichokes, gorgonzola, cream sauce	9.95
Fettuccine alla Don Peppino Shrimp, broccoli, parmesan cream sauce	10.95
Linguine & Calamari Fresh calamari rings in tomato sauce. Spicy, hot if desired	10.95
Capellini Sante Scampi Shrimp, scallops, sun-dried tomato in light seafood broth	11.95
Farfalle al Salmone Bowtie pasta with salmon, peas, laced with vodka in creamy sauce	11.95
Linguine alla Rosalia Sun-dried tomato, shrimp, pinenuts, basil, fresh tomato	12.95
Linguine di Mare Fresh shellfish & seafood in a light tomato sauce	14.95

Piatti della casa

Pollo alla Romana Chicken breast, bell peppers, spicy hot tomato sauce	11.95
Pollo alla Mannino Chicken stuffed with spinach, ricotta cheese mixture, marsala sauce	13.95
Spigola Fra' Diavolo Fresh white sea bass, spicy hot tomato sauce	13.95
Spigola Marechiaro White sea bass, mussels, clams, light tomato sauce	13.95
Vitello Nicolina Veal stuffed with salmon, spinach, provolone, champagne sauce	14.95
Vitello Valdostana Veal stuffed with prosciutto, provolone, wild mushrooms, marsala sauce	14.95
Pollo alla Roberto Chicken stuffed with shrimp, mushrooms, fontina cheese, champagne dijon sauce	14.95
Salmone alla Griglia Grilled salmon, lemon garlic sauce	14.95
Salmone Piccata Fresh salmon, lemon, butter, white wine and capers	14.95

For additional information see page 95.

Menu Subject to Change

PROMOTIONAL PRIX FIXE MENU — $16.50 Per Person

TRADITIONAL CAESAR SALAD
With Toasted Croutons and Fresh Parmesan
-or-
LOBSTER BISQUE WITH AGED COGNAC
Served with Cayenne Pepper Paillettes

❖ ❖ ❖

GRILLED HERB CRUSTED HALF CHICKEN
Marinated in Olive Oil
Served with Three Beans Ragout
-or-
SAUTEED FILET OF RED SNAPPER WITH NICOISE OLIVES
Coulis of Roasted Red Peppers
-or-
BROILED NEW YORK CUT OF SIRLOIN STEAK
Gorgonzola and Walnut Sauce

❖ ❖ ❖

COINTREAU LACED CHOCOLATE MOUSSE WITH SEASONAL BERRIES
Raspberry Coulis
-or-
CHEF'S BANANA
Served with Warm Caramel Sauce over Vanilla Ice-Cream

❖ ❖ ❖

Del Mar Hilton Hotel • 15575 Jimmy Durante Blvd • Del Mar • (619) 792-5200

A SELECTION FROM OUR
A LA CARTE MENU

APPETIZERS AND SOUPS

BUCKWHEAT CREPES filled with Sonoma Goat Cheese and Domestic
Caviar - Merlot and Shallots Sauce   5.50

CRAB & SHRIMP FILLED TIGER RAVIOLIS with Candied Ginger, Snow
Peas, Thai Peanut Sauce   6.00

LOBSTER BISQUE WITH AGED COGNAC and Cayenne
Pepper Paillettes   3.50

SALADS

FIELD GREENS WITH WALNUTS & Mustard Vinaigrette Dressing   4.00

WARM SPINACH SALAD with toasted Goat Cheese, Prosciutto Ham,
and Shitake Croutons   5.25

ENTREES

FETTUCINE with Shrimp, Scallops and New Zealand Green Shell
Mussels in a Saffron and Cream Sauce   16.50

SEARED BLACKENED AHI STEAK with Grilled Scallions and
Pistachio Butter   18.00

BROILED SWORDFISH with Sundried Tomatoes, Cilantro and
Chardonnay Sauce   17.00

GRILLED HERB CRUSTED HALF CHICKEN marinated in Olive Oil,
served with Three Bean Ragout   14.50

GRILLED FILET MIGNON with Confit of Onions, served with Three
Peppercorn Sauce   18.50

DOMESTIC LOIN OF LAMB with Roasted Garlic, Thyme and
Whole Grain Mustard   23.50

SELECTION OF DESSERTS

For additional information see page 65.

TUSCANY

the art of Italian dining

SALADS, HOT & COLD APPETIZERS

MOZZARELLA CAPRESE **6.50**
Fresh home made mozzarella, tomato, basil and virgin olive oil

TOMASO'S SALAD **4.95**
*Arugola, roasted bell peppers, Bermuda onion, shredded parmesan in a balsamic
and olive oil dressing*

ANTIPASTO ITALIANO **8.00**
*Prosciutto, caponata, mozzarella, roasted bell peppers,
olives, and mushrooms*

PASTA as WE LOVE IT in ITALY
Served With Fresh Garden Salad

TORTELLONI AL SUGO DI NOCE **11.95**
*Fresh stuffed pasta with chicken and spinach in a creamy
mushroom and walnut sauce*

RIGATONI CON POLLO AFFUMICATO **10.95**
*Rigatoni tossed with smoked grilled chicken and mushrooms in a light cream
sauce and parmesan cheese*

FARFALLE ALLA VODKA **10.95**
*Bow tie pasta tossed with fresh tomato, shallots and a touch of cream,
flambé with vodka*

SEAFOOD SPECIALTIES
Served with Fresh Garden Salad (no substitutions)

CAPPELLINI "COSA NOSTRA" **14.95**
*Angel hair pasta with arugola, wild mushrooms, shrimp
and fresh chopped tomato*

SEAFOOD PORTOFINO **16.95**
*Fresh assorted seafood and shellfish, in a light marinara sauce,
served over angel hair pasta*

CALAMARI BOCCA CALDA **12.95**
*Fresh calamari sauteed with basil, garlic, tomato and chili flakes.
Served over linguini*

SCAMPI FRADIAVOLO CON LENTICCHIE **17.95**
*Jumbo shrimp with tomato, garlic, crushed red pepper and lentils.
Served over linguini*

ITALIAN SPECIALTIES
Served with Fresh Garden Salad and vegetables of the day (no substitutions)

CHICKEN VALDOSTANA **14.95**
*Stuffed breast of chicken with cheese and prosciutto in marsala
wine sauce and mushrooms*

VEAL MARSALA OR PICCATA **16.95**
*Sauteed veal scaloppine with marsala wine sauce and mushrooms
or if preferred lemon butter and capers sauce*

TOURNEDOS OF BEEF ALLA CONTESSA **17.95**
*Grilled medallion of filet mignon finished with sauteed mushrooms
in garlic and lemon sauce*

PAILLARD OF CHICKEN **13.95**
*Grilled chicken paillard brushed with herbed olive oil and lemon,
served with string beans, potato and Bermuda onion salad*

For additional information see page 96.

tutto · mare

Menu Changes Seasonally

ANTIPASTI

CARPACCIO DI SALMONE
grappa-cured salmon; onions, capers, olive oil, lemon   6.95

CAPRICCIO MARINO
Italian crab cakes; lobster reduction and chives   7.50

POMODORO E MOZZARELLA AL PESTO
buffalo mozzarella, tomato; housemade pesto   7.75

MOSCARDINI AFFOGATI
baby Mediterranean octopus braised in red wine, tomatoes,
extra virgin olive oil   7.50

INSALATE

PRIMAVERILE
endive, radicchio, arugula, capers, pine nuts, goat cheese;
balsamic vinegar   5.95

ARAGOSTA
Maine lobster, mixed baby lettuces, hearts of palm, celery;
olive oil, lemon   10.75

PIZZE

CAPRICCIOSA
artichokes, mushrooms, salami, black olives, mozzarella,
tomato sauce   7.95

TUTTO MARE
seafood, garlic, mozzarella, tomato sauce   9.50

4365 Executive Dr • Golden Triangle • (619) 597-1188

ZUPPE E RISOTTO

CARABACCIA
vegetable soup with toasted country bread   3.95

RISOTTO AI FUNGHI PORCINI
arborio rice, porcini mushrooms, parmesan   9.75

PASTE

PAGLIA E FIENO ALLA CARDINALE
thin spinach and egg pasta, sun-dried tomatoes, chicken;
tomato-cream sauce   9.75

TRENETTE AI TRE CROSTACEI
flat pasta, crab, shrimp, lobster; spicy tomato sauce   12.25

PENNETTE RACHELE
quill pasta, duck sausage, porcini mushrooms; creamy tomato sauce   8.95

BIANCHI E NERI CON CAPESANTE
black and white tagliolini; cream, scallops, pink peppercorns   9.75

TAGLIOLINI CON GAMBERI E CARCIOFI
thin pasta, prawns, fresh baby artichokes; white wine, garlic, olive oil   10.95

LINGUINE CON ARAGOSTA
thin pasta, half Maine lobster; spicy tomato sauce   11.95

MEZZELUNE DI SALMONE AFFUMICATO
half-moon pasta filled with smoked salmon; lemon-sorrel sauce   10.50

GRIGLIA E FORNO A LEGNA

SCALOPPE DI SALMONE ALLA BORGIA
medallions of salmon sautéed with capers, green onions, white wine, fresh
tomatoes   12.95

CANESTRELLI SANTA TERESA
grilled jumbo sea scallops, fresh baby artichokes and black olives   15.95

SALSICCIA E POLENTA CON PEPERONI STUFATI
Italian sausage, polenta, stewed bell peppers and fresh herbs   9.50

LOMBATA DI VITELLO ALLA VALDOSTANA
grilled veal chop, prosciutto, fontina cheese; sage butter   17.95

TAGLIATA ALLE ERBE AROMATICHE
thinly-slice New York steak, cannellini beans, herbs; balsamic vinegar
reduction   16.50

For additional information see page 96.

The
WHALING BAR

APPETIZERS

Chilled Jumbo Shrimp or Alaskan Crab Claws with Red Sauce **7.50**

Spinach Salad with Balsamic Dressing and Pine Nuts
Appetizer **5.25**, Dinner **8.75**

Greque Salad with Feta Cheese and Sun Dried Tomato Vinaigrette **4.75**

Scottish Smoked Salmon with Capers and Red Onions **7.50**

Chef's Soup Du Jour 4.25

Escargot "Bourguignonne" Parsley,
Garlic Butter Topped with Puff Pastry **7.50**

Basil Caesar Salad with Parmesan Toasted Sour Dough **4.95**

SPECIAL SELECTIONS FROM THE GRILL

Grilled Veal Chop 11 oz with Angel Hair Pasta
and Creamy Black Olive Sauce **21.50**

Prime New York Steak 8 oz with Black Peppercorn on
Ravioli of Wild Mushroom **21.00**

Rotisserie Half Chicken with Mashed Potatoes and Thyme Juice **16.25**

1132 Prospect St • La Jolla • (619) 454-0771

Grilled Salmon Steak *9 oz on Sauteed Spinach
with Basil Citron Essence* **16.75**

Grilled Filet of Beef *8 oz with Green Peppercorn Mustard Sauce* **19.50**

Rack of Lamb *in Herb-Dijon Brioche* **22.50**

Steamed or Grilled Lobster *1 3/4 lbs with Thermidor Crust* **32.00**

Grilled Cajun Swordfish *9 oz with Saffron Rice and Salsa Papaya* **18.75**

Sea Bass *with Grilled Vegetables* **17.50**

LA VALENCIA SPECIALTIES

Roasted Prime Rib *with Buttermilk Onion Rings* **22.50**

Sauteed Sole *Toasted with Capers and Almonds* **16.50**

Angel Hair Pasta *with Rock Shrimp, Mushroom, Garlic,
Diced Tomatoes and Herb Olive Oil* **13.25**

Paella Valencia *Mussels, Scallops, Shrimp, Spicy Sausage
and Chicken with Saffron Rice* **18.50**

Carne Asada *Marinated Filet Mignon with Cheese Enchilada,
Avocado, Tomatillo Salsa, Red Beans & Rice* **17.25**

La Valencia Pizza *Changing each Week* **11.25**

BEVERAGES

Coffee 1.50 Tea 1.50 Milk 1.50 Cafe Espresso 2.00

Perrier Water 2.25 Evian 2.25

For additional information see page 36.

Menu Changes Seasonally

first

tartare of yellowfin tuna
with lemon and fresh herbs   8.

basil cured salmon with sweet mustard sauce
served with toasted brioche   8.

tchoutchouka
algerian roasted sweet pepper salad   7.

fresh fennel and arugula salad with shaved parmesan
in blood orange vinaigrette   8.

provencale grilled eggplant and roasted red pepper terrine
with balsamic vinegar and virgin olive oil   8.

grilled marinated lamb salad
over warm spinach with feta cheese   9.

tasting of three brasserie duck preparations
confit, prosciutto and smoked   9.

portabella mushroom, potato and fava bean ravioli
sauteed in brown butter with italian parsley   9.

roasted eggplant soup
with a black olive crouton and herb oil   5.

green asparagus soup
with sauteed morels and thyme   7.

entree

grilled ginger marinated salmon filet in sweet white corn ragout
with shiitake mushrooms, garlic, and scallions   19.

pan roasted eastern monkfish over a fricassee of green lentils
with curry, chives and a frisee salad   21.

fava bean, white bean and shiitake mushroom cannelloni
in buckwheat pasta with a spring vegetable nage   15.

duck confit with roasted garlic mashed red potatoes
served with a salad of fresh herbs   18.

pan roasted chicken breast with herbed zucchini ravioli
with fresh tomato coulis and a natural pan jus   18.

pan roasted veal loin in leek and morel mushroom sauce
with yukon gold potato puree and asparagus   24.

grilled lamb loin with a sweet garlic puree and black olive sauce
with sauteed spinach and oven dried tomatoes   21.

grilled angus filet mignon in caramelized shallot and red wine sauce
with a stilton and potato galette   25.

"VINTAGE FARE"

Featuring Swanson Vineyards
a three-course dinner to showcase three wines

smoked duck breast with red onion and dried cherry relish
1990 chardonnay

roasted hawaiian hebi with artichokes, fresh tomato and saffron
1990 reserve chardonnay

grilled angus sirloin with portabella mushrooms and
rosemary polenta
1988 cabernet sauvignon

29.

includes one glass of each of the wines

For additional information see page 59.

Yo España
Café and Restaurant

Menu Changes Seasonally

Appetizer

Pippirrana — $4.95
A light salad of cucumber, fresh parsley,
tomatoes and goat cheese

Ensalada De Pollo — $5.25
Grilled chicken breast with Romaine lettuce and
our homemade dressing

Tapas

Gambas al Ajillo — $9.50
Garlic shrimp, a classic tapa

Mejillones a la Marinara — $6.25
Mussels steamed in a rich seafood broth with fresh tomatoes

Rabas — $5.75
Fried calamari with aioli

Pulpo al Pil-Pil — $6.25
Classic poached octopus with lemon, butter,
red wine, garlic and capers

Queso Manchego con Frutas — $7.25
Selection of Spanish cheeses (Tetilla, Cabrales,
Manchego) with fruits

**Salmon Marinado a Las Hierbas
Con Champiñones** — $8.25
House cured Salmon

La Pasta (Pasta)

Penne Al Biablo $8.95
Lightly fried basil and garlic with
tomato sauce and hot peperoncino (Jtaliano)

Pasta Costa Brava $10.95
Fettuccine with seafood in a champagne cream sauce

Pasta Mariposa Con Salmon $11.25
Lightly fried fresh garlic with Jtalian parsley
flambéed with vodka; excellent plate to try

Cenas (Entrees)

Paella Marinera (for two) $25.00
Saffron rice with seafood, tomatoes,
green beans and artichokes

Paella Valenciana (for two) $25.50
Saffron rice with Valencia style chicken

Parillada De Mariscos (for two) $26.50
Grilled seafood

Filet De Rez Mariscos $12.95
Filet mignon Andalucian style

Cangrego a la Mallorguina $12.00
Stuffed crab in a wine base and herbs

Adouado de Pescado $11.75
Red snapper in Jtalian parsley and garlic,
served with special sauce

All dinners include vegetables and rice

Desserts

Flan $4.50   **Tiremisu** $4.50
Classic Spanish custard   Classic Jtalian espresso pudding

For additional information see page 118.

THE
ZODIAC

The Zodiac also offers a Light Style Menu that changes seasonally.

Beginnings

A Cup of Soup du Jour
2.75

NM Petite Salad
3.25
with Avocado
4.00

Beluga Caviar
with accompaniments
(available on request)
market price

Smoked Salmon
with cream cheese, dill sauce
and mini-bagels
7.75

Zodiac Express Lunch
soup of the day, green salad, choice of half
tuna-pecan, chicken salad or oven-roasted
turkey sandwich
5.85

Baked Brie
with a hazelnut crust served
with apple slices and
toasted baguettes
6.95

Fresh Fruit Salad
seasonal fresh fruits,
choice of sorbet or cottage cheese
served with nut bread
6.50

Salads and Sandwiches

Tuna-Pecan Salad Sandwich
served on sourdough bread
with tomato and sprouts
6.95

Mandarin Orange Soufflé
white meat of chicken salad
toasted almonds, fresh fruit
and nut bread
8.75

Neiman Marcus Club Sandwich
three layers of ham, turkey, bacon, cheese,
tomato and lettuce on
toasted Pullman bread
8.25

Salad Niçoise
poached fresh fish, green beans,
black olives, artichokes, cucumbers,
bell peppers, tomatoes, new potatoes
and hard-cooked eggs
with Niçoise dressing
9.00

NM Cobb Salad
chicken, avocado, bleu cheese, mushrooms,
red cabbage, spinach,
hard-cooked egg, tomatoes and
warm bacon dressing.
Topped with croutons and walnuts
8.75

---

280 Fashion Valley Rd • Fashion Valley Shopping Mall • Mission Valley • (619) 692-9100

Fresh Oven-Roasted Turkey
served on raisin-pumpernickel bread
with lettuce and tomatoes served with
cranberry-orange relish
7.25

Chicken Madras Salad
curried white meat of chicken salad
with fresh fruit and mango chutney
9.50

NM Chicken Salad Sandwich
on wheat bread with tomato,
bacon and avocado slices
6.95

Caesar Salad
romaine, anchovy and garlic
dressing topped with croutons
and Parmesan
7.50
with grilled chicken
8.75
with shrimp
10.00

Special Salad of the Day
market price

Entrees

Entrees Are Served With a Petite Salad and Monkey Bread

Chef's Creation
Today's Special Selection From Our Chef
market price

Steak and Potato Caesar
grilled tenderloin strips and oven-
browned new potatoes served hot
over chilled romaine with Parmesan
and Caesar Dressing
9.75

Souffléed Omelette
ask about our special Zodiac
omelette of the day
6.95

Chicken la Jolla
sautéed breast of chicken with artichoke
hearts, sun-dried tomatoes, black olives,
white wine and cream
8.25

The Finale

Zodiac Chocolate Raspberry Torte
Layers of Chocolate Cake, Raspberry Puree
and Raspberry Liqueur, Iced with a Thin
Layer of French Chocolate Buttercream
and Chocolate Ganache. A Chocolate
Zodiac Signature Crowns each serving.
4.00

Apple Walnut Custard Torte
Fresh Apples Folded into a Sweet Custard,
Smothered with Walnuts & Brown Sugar.
Served in an Apple Cider Flavored Crust.
4.00

Toasted Pecan Ball
Rich Vanilla Ice Cream Rolled in Toasted
Pecans and Topped with Hot Fudge or
Butterscotch Sauce and Whipped Cream.
4.00

Cappuccino Ice Cream Pie
An Exquisite Flavor Combination of Rich
Coffee Ice Cream, Kahlua and Whipped
Cream on a Chocolate Cookie Crust.
5.00

For additional information see page 36.

Index

- Cuisine
- Geographical
- Alphabetical

Index by Cuisine

Geographical Index

Geographical Index

Alphabetical Index

Alphabetical Index

Gift Order Form

THE MENU is the perfect gift for every food lover, and is available at bookstores and gift shops everywhere. If you would prefer to order copies by mail, please fill out the form below and return it to us with your payment. For gift purchases, a personalized card announcing your gift will be enclosed.

Qty

New York City & Vicinity, $12.95 x _____ = _____

Chicago & Vicinity, $12.95 x _____ = _____

Los Angeles & Vicinity, $12.95 x _____ = _____

San Francisco & Vicinity, $12.95 x _____ = _____

San Diego & Vicinity, $12.95 x _____ = _____

Subtotal = $ _____

Postage & Handling (each book) $2.90 x _____ = _____

Total Order = $ _____

I enclose payment of $_____ payable to **Menubooks, Inc.**

Name _____

Address _____

City _____ State _____ Zip _____

Phone _____

Please make check or money order payable to Menubooks, Inc.
Payment must accompany order. Please allow up to four weeks for delivery.

Menubooks, Inc.
David Thomas Publishing
733 NW Everett St., Studio 5E
Portland, Oregon 97209

(For gift orders, please fill out shipping address(es) on reverse side.)

Please Send: **The Menu,** _____
(fill in city)

Name _____ Phone _____

Address _____

City _____ State _____ Zip _____

Please Send: **The Menu,** _____
(fill in city)

Name _____ Phone _____

Address _____

City _____ State _____ Zip _____

Please Send: **The Menu,** _____
(fill in city)

Name _____ Phone _____

Address _____

City _____ State _____ Zip _____

Please Send: **The Menu,** _____
(fill in city)

Name _____ Phone _____

Address _____

City _____ State _____ Zip _____

Please Send: **The Menu,** _____
(fill in city)

Name _____ Phone _____

Address _____

City _____ State _____ Zip _____